CHICANO AUTHORS: INQUIRY BY INTERVIEW

P9-AFC-645

CHICANO AUTHORS
Inquiry by Interview

by Bruce-Novoa

UNIVERSITY OF TEXAS PRESS, AUSTIN AND LONDON

LIBRARY OF CONGRESS CATALOGING IN PUBLICATION DATA

Bruce-Novoa, Juan D   1944–
    Chicano authors.

    Bibliography: p.
    1. Mexican American authors—Interviews.
    2. American literature—Mexican American authors—History and criticism. I. Title.
PS153.M4B7   810'.9'868   79-28327
ISBN 0-292-71059-3
ISBN 0-292-71062-3 pbk.

Contents

Preface

For the student or aficionado of Chicano literature, its newness—
most of the works are recent and there are still few texts—is a
mixed blessing. One is in the enviable position of being able to
read, with relative ease, all the major Chicano works, and in some
genres (the novel for example) all the minor ones as well, though
with each passing year it becomes more difficult. However, there
is a scarcity of criticism and research materials which could guide
the reader. We have no book of criticism on our literature, though
several anthologies of critical writings are being prepared and a
few critics are writing books devoted to the subject. Recent publications have provided essential bibliographic information
(Lomelí and Urioste, *Chicano Perspectives in Literature: A Critical and Annotated Bibliography*, 1976; Tatum, "Toward a Chicano Bibliography of Literary Criticism," 1976–1977), though in
such a rapidly expanding field any such efforts will always require
updating. The bibliographies by Lomelí and Urioste and Charles
Tatum are significant, useful research tools, intended to fill a
specific need for information. This book of interviews was born
out of a similar need and aspires to be nothing more than a useful
tool for the student and an introduction to Chicano writers for
the general reading public.

The need for a book of interviews became apparent to me
when I first taught a Chicano culture course in 1970. Even then,
when there were many fewer books and known authors, students
wanted to know more about the writers, their backgrounds, opinions, and attitudes. There was little or no material to shed light
on these concerns; increased publishing has aggravated the situation. When I began to travel and lecture across the country in
1974, it became evident that students from different areas were
asking the same questions, and that non-Chicanos who were becoming interested in the literature also desired background information on the authors. In the spring of 1975, I began a project intended to respond in part to those needs.

Originally, the plan was to conduct a series of face-to-face interviews with the authors. Each interview was to be divided into two segments: (1) a twenty-four question inquiry into backgrounds and general attitudes on writing; (2) questions on the author's particular work. This format would have combined a survey with a series of individual interviews. As is often the case, however, funds were not available. Instead of abandoning the project altogether, I salvaged the survey by conducting it by mail. It is, admittedly, a less satisfactory method, but time and finances made it the only recourse. (Perhaps on the basis of this publication, funds can be found to complete the project.) I ask the reader to keep in mind, especially when the format seems too rigid, that this is a *survey*. One should not expect interviews in the sense of that genre as displayed in the recent notable examples, such as the *Paris Review* series, or Emir Rodríguez Monegal's conversations with Latin American writers, which are personal, probing, and tailored to the interviewee. Though desirable, such a procedure was not possible in this case.

The questions selected attempt to solicit the background information most generally sought by readers of the literature, i.e., age, family situation, preferred language, educational experience, the author's perception of his/her role on several levels of interaction—especially the political—whether Chicano literature is distinctive and if so why, whether it will continue to be distinctive, and which are the most important events and writers to date. In addition, it was my intention to test the validity of some of the commonly held assumptions about Chicano literature and dispel a few obvious misconceptions. For example, while meeting with the faculty of a major southwestern university, discussing my research, I was asked if it was not difficult to work with literature written by illiterate authors! For some reason it is believed that the Chicano author is a noble savage, who works in the field or walks the picket line all day, and writes after dark, without benefit of schooling. A similar view held by many Chicanos—and non-Chicanos—is that education and artistic talent are mutually exclusive, that the good writers are natural writers. Academic degrees are suspect if one is a creative writer; often the converse is also true. It is assumed also that Chicano literature shares much in common with Mexican literature, as well as the literatures of Black Americans and Mainland Puerto Ricans; a pan-hispanic or pan-ethnic commonness (the union of Black, Chicano, Native American, Latino, and Asian American writers) is expected and often imposed by observers seeking convenient categories for our literature. At the same time, though the contradiction escapes many, it is strongly affirmed that Chicano literature has a distinct world view, a particular language, that it reflects cultural values, that it is both thematically and technically revolutionary, and, in terms of United States culture and society, subversive. The political overtones ascribed to the literature lead many professionals, who have little direct knowledge of it, to relegate its use to the fields of sociology or political science. By the same token, Chicanos often dismiss works as un-Chicano if they do not meet political expectations. The questionnaire addresses these points, allowing fourteen authors to express their views.

Every author included has published at least one book, in most cases two or more; with perhaps some disagreement they are considered *leading* authors, if I can be permitted the use of this term so abhorrent to most of them. They include the three Quinto Sol Prize winners and a runner-up, the only Tonatiuh Prize winner to date, and the authors of most of the influential books in Chicano literature. Some writers who should have been included are absent, i.e., Oscar Z. Acosta, the infamous Brown Buffalo, now believed to be dead; Rodolfo "Corky" Gonzales of *I Am Joaquín*; Raúl Salinas, author of "The Trip through the Mind Jail"; and Luis Valdez of the Teatro Campesino. Each was invited to participate more than once, and one even agreed, but has not complied; their absence is regrettable, but the project cannot be delayed any longer.

Interviews with John Rechy, Ray Barrio, and Angela de Hoyos were excluded because they contained very little information not already available to the public. An extensive interview with Nash Candelaria was dropped because he more appropriately fits into a second generation of Chicano writers. The Candelaria interview will be published separately by *De Colores* magazine.

Four of the interviews—those with Arias, Delgado, Villarreal, and Hinojosa—appeared in journals in a preliminary form. The first three have been reworked to constitute new, expanded statements.

The interviews are transcribed as they were sent to me; I have been faithful to the authors' stylistic tendencies. Thus, for example, Ricardo Sánchez's use or non-use of capitalization or accentuation is his and can be taken as part of his highly individual style. Deletions (and they were very few) were made only when a statement was judged potentially libelous. Consequently, length is also a reflection of the author's choice.

Originally it was planned to publish this book in a bilingual, or what I prefer to call interlingual, form; that is, the texts were to appear in the language the author chose to use, whether Spanish, English, or a mixture. Considerations of the audience's ability to read such a text, however, forced a change in that plan. Therefore, those interviews written in Spanish have been translated; in those cases where a small amount of Spanish is interpolated into the English, the translation follows in brackets. Alurista's interview is an exception; parenthetical translations would have almost doubled the length of the longest of the interviews. It was decided to translate the Spanish, using italics to indicate where translation occurs; it is hoped that in this manner some sense of Alurista's interlingual rhythm will be conveyed.

Each interview is preceded by a brief introductory note. It was not my intention to provide plot summaries; rather, I have tried to locate the author in the context of Chicano literature and provide a sense of his/her writing. For novices I recommend the Lomelí-Urioste book, which does contain plot summaries. A chronological chart of publications, by genre, included in the Introduction, and the Selected Bibliography may serve as useful guides for the reader.

It was not my purpose here to enter into textual analysis; this is meant to be a forum for the writers and a source of primary data. Therefore, the Introduction is not an in-depth study of the literature; and, again, I do not think that plot summaries are useful introductions. Instead, I offer an overview of the main themes of the literature, citing authors and works as examples when they are pertinent. I chose not to follow a chronological treatment of the works because that approach has been taken by Cecil Robinson in his chapter on Chicano literature in *Mexico and the Hispanic Southwest in American Literatures* (Tucson: University of Arizona Press, 1977). It is my wish that the reader be informed of and led to the texts themselves. Criticism should not replace the reading.

All in all, with the reservations listed above, the inquiry should provide the reader, and the authors as well, with new insights into Chicano writers and possibly improve the comprehension of their work. My hope is that the material will be used as the basis for further research by the student and as a guide by the general reader.

Many people deserve thanks for helping to realize this project. I am grateful to Isabel Barraza, Orlando Ramírez, and Margarita Vargas for their assistance during some interviews. Prof.

Judy Salinas's help was invaluable. Gratitude also goes to Mary Ann Bruce, who patiently typed the first draft of the manuscript under the most hectic of circumstances. My special thanks are due to the National Chicano Council for Higher Education and Yale University for providing leave time from teaching to finish the book, and to the Yale Latin American Studies Program for making typists available for the final draft. To the authors we all owe the book itself; it is theirs. And finally I thank the Chicano students at Yale, without whose interest, support, and love none of this would have come to be.

Photo Credits

José Antonio Villarreal, photo courtesy of J. A. Villarreal (p. 36)
Rolando Hinojosa, photo courtesy of R. Hinojosa (p. 50)
Sergio Elizondo, photo by Elizondo (p. 66)
Miguel Méndez M., photo courtesy of M. Méndez (p. 84)
Abelardo Delgado, photo courtesy of A. Delgado (p. 94)
José Montoya, photo by Bruce-Novoa, courtesy of Cambios/Phideo
    Publications (p. 116)
Tomás Rivera, photo by Tom J. Lewis, courtesy of Books Abroad (p. 138)
Estela Portillo, photo by Bruce-Novoa, courtesy of Cambios/Phideo
    Publications (p. 162)
Rudolfo A. Anaya, photo by Klappert (p. 182)
Bernice Zamora, photo by Joel Varela (p. 204)
Ricardo Sánchez, photo by César Martínez, courtesy of Mexican American Studies, University of Texas, Austin (p. 220)
Ron Arias, photo by Joan Arias (p. 236)
Tino Villanueva, photo by V. Čáslavska (p. 254)
Alurista, photo by Rubén Sánchez (p. 266)

CHICANO AUTHORS: INQUIRY BY INTERVIEW

Introduction

Emergence

Chicano literature, as treated here, is a recent phenomenon. It is possible to trace its backgrounds and traditions as far back as 1848 and perhaps beyond,[1] as there has been a steady literary activity carried on by Mexicans living in the United States through the years; nevertheless, when we speak of Chicano literature we still normally refer to works published since 1965, with significant direct precursors appearing in the genre of the novel as early as 1959. The Chronological Chart of Publications, providing an overview of the genres, demonstrates the high concentration of that literature in the 1970's.

Admittedly, this literature, or at least its publication, was a by-product of the Chicano Movement, the socio-political civil rights struggle begun in the mid-1960's by and on behalf of people of Mexican descent living in the United States. Lacking a manifesto that could accommodate all the regional and ideological differences, the Chicano Movement is difficult to define to everyone's satisfaction. In fact, the term *Chicano* itself has been a source of controversy from the beginning and still is not accepted by large portions of the ethnic group it is intended to signify. Its etymology has been debated, with explanations from the ludicrous to the plausible vying for predominance.[2] The most accepted version traces it back to *Mexicano*, with the *x* pronounced *sh*, as it was at the time of the Spanish conquest. Whatever its origin, more significant is the fact that in the mid-1960's the term was adopted by those who experienced an awakening pride in their Mexican ethnicity, yet recognized that residency in the United States distinguished them from Mexican citizens living in Mexico. The Chicano political spectrum includes nearly every conceivable ideology, especially if one takes the position that the term covers all U.S. residents of Mexican heritage, regardless of what they prefer to call themselves. From militant nationalists to

Chronological Chart of Publications

Year	Fiction	Poetry
1959	*Pocho* (José Antonio Villarreal)	
1963	*City of Night* (John Rechy)	
1965		
1966		
1967	*Tattoo the Wicked Cross* (Floyd Salas) *Numbers* (John Rechy)	*I Am Joaquín* (Rodolfo Gonzales)
1968		
1969	*The Plum Plum Pickers* (Raymond Barrio) *This Day's Death* (John Rechy)	*Chicano: 25 Pieces of a Chicano Mind* (Abelardo Delgado)
1970	*Chicano* (Richard Vásquez)	*Crazy Gypsy* (Luis Omar Salinas) *Free, Free at Last* (Raymundo Pérez)
1971	*. . . y no se lo tragó la tierra* (Tomás Rivera) *The Vampires* (John Rechy) *Barrio Boy* (Ernesto Galarza)	*Floricanto en Aztlán* (Alurista) *Canto y grito mi liberación* (Ricardo Sánchez) *Vida de ilusiones* (Heriberto Terán) *Phases* (Raymundo Pérez)
1972	*The Autobiography of a Brown Buffalo* (Oscar Z. Acosta) *Bless Me, Ultima* (Rudolfo A. Anaya) *The Fourth Angel* (John Rechy)	*Nationchild Plumaroja* (Alurista) *Perros y antiperros* (Sergio Elizondo) *El sol y los de abajo* (José Montoya) *Hay otra voz Poems* (Tino Villanueva) *The Secret Meaning of Death* (Raymundo Pérez)

Theatre	Anthologies	Year
		1959
		1963
Foundation of Teatro Campesino: *Las dos caras del patroncito*		1965
Quinta temporada (TC)		1966
Los vendidos (TC)	*El Grito* (journal)	1967
La conquista de México (TC)		1968
No saco nada de la escuela (TC)	*El Espejo/The Mirror*, 1st ed. (Romano and Ríos, eds.)	1969
Vietnam campesino (TC)		1970
Actos: The Teatro Campesino (a compilation of actos written between 1965 and 1971) (Luis Valdez) *The Day of the Swallows* (Estela Portillo)	*The Chicanos* (Ludwig and Santibáñez, eds.)	1971
La carpa de los rasguachis (TC)	*Literatura chicana* (Shular, Ybarra-Frausto, and Sommers, eds.) *Aztlán* (Valdez and Steiner, eds.)	1972

Year	Fiction	Poetry
1973	*The Revolt of the Cockroach People* (Oscar Z. Acosta) *Estampas del Valle* (Rolando Hinojosa) *Macho* (Edmundo Villaseñor) *Blue Day on Main Street* (short stories) (J. L. Navarro)	*Bajo el sol de Aztlán: 25 soles de Abelardo* (Abelardo Delgado) *Viaje/Trip* (Raúl Salinas) *Selected Poetry* (Ricardo García)
1974	*Peregrinos de Aztlán* (Miguel Méndez) *The Fifth Horseman* (José Antonio Villarreal)	*5th and Grande Vista* (Juan Gómez-Quiñones) *It's Cold: 52 Cold Thought-Poems of Abelardo* (Abelardo Delgado) *Rebozos of Love* (Juan Felipe Herrera) *Happy Songs, Bleeding Hearts* (Lin Romero)
1975	*The Road to Tamazunchale* (Ron Arias) *Caras viejas y vino nuevo* (Alejandro Morales) *Rain of Scorpions* (short stories) (Estela Portillo)	*Noches despertando inconsciencias* (Margarita Cota Cárdenas) *Arise, Chicano* and *Chicano Poems for the Barrio* (Angela de Hoyos) *La mujer es la tierra: La tierra de vida* (Dorinda Moreno) *Los criaderos humanos (épica de los desamparados) y Sahuaros* (Miguel Méndez) *Tlacuilos* (Heriberto Terán)
1976	*Klail City y sus alrededores* (Rolando Hinojosa) *Heart of Aztlán* (Rudolfo A. Anaya) *Nambé—Year One* (Orlando Romero) *El diablo en Texas* (Aristeo Brito) *Victuum* (Isabella Ríos)	*Restless Serpents* (Bernice Zamora) *HechizoSpells* (Ricardo Sánchez) *Timespace Huracán* (Alurista) *Trece Aliens* (Heriberto Terán) *Selecciones* (Angela de Hoyos)

Theatre	Anthologies	Year
El Teatro de la Esperanza (Jorge Huerta, ed.)	*We Are Chicanos* (Philip D. Ortego, ed.)	1973
El jardín (Carlos Morton) *Guadalupe* (Teatro de la Esperanza)	*Voices of Aztlán* (Harth and Baldwin, eds.)	1974
Contemporary Chicano Theatre (Roberto J. Garza, ed.) *El fin del mundo* (TC)		1975
La víctima (Teatro de la Esperanza)	*El quetzal emplumece* (Montalvo, Anguiano, and García-Camarillo, eds.) *Festival de Flor y Canto* (Alurista, ed.)	1976

8   *Introduction*

Year	Fiction	Poetry
1977	*Memories of the Alhambra* (Nash Candelaria) *Mi abuela fumaba puros* (Sabine Ulibarrí) *The Sexual Outlaw* (John Rechy)	*Libro para batos y chavalas chicanas* (Sergio Elizondo) *El hacedor de juegos/The Maker of Games* (Rafael Jesús González) *Blood Root* (Alma Villanueva) *The Elements of San Joaquín* (Gary Soto) *Con razón corazón* (Inés Tovar) *Inocencia perversa/Perverse Innocence* (Bruce-Novoa)
1978	*The Giant Killer* (Richard Vásquez) *Lay My Body on the Line* (Floyd Salas)	*Korean Love Songs* (Rolando Hinojosa) *Sobra* (Marina Rivera) *The Tale of Sunlight* (Gary Soto) *Milhuas Blues and Gritos Norteños* (Ricardo Sánchez)
1979	*Tortuga* (Rudolfo A. Anaya) *Rushes* (John Rechy)	*Speedway* (Orlando Ramírez) *I Go Dreaming Serenades* (Luis Omar Salinas)

militant Marxist-Leninists, from self-made capitalists to Christian Socialists, from the traditional political participants—Democrats and Republicans—to the disenfranchised, one finds all kinds. The same could be said for the degree of Mexicanness or the use of the Spanish language. With regard to socioeconomic class, although one could say that the spectrum is all-inclusive, the majority of Chicanos would come under the category of working class.

Generalities aside, the Chicano Movement is most often identified with the ongoing efforts to win civil and human rights, and with the affirmation of cultural pride. Early heroes in the struggle include such personages as César Chávez, founder of the United Farm Workers (UFW) (California); Reies López Tijerina, founder of the Alianza [Alliance] (New Mexico) for the reestablishment of the property rights guaranteed by the Treaty of Guadalupe Hidalgo in 1848; Rodolfo "Corky" Gonzales, founder of the nationalistic Crusade for Justice (Colorado); and José Angel

Theatre	Anthologies	Year
Zoot Suit (Luis Valdez)		1977
	Canto al Pueblo (Leonardo Carrillo et al.) *Mestizo* (José Armas, ed.)	1978
Sun Images (Estela Portillo) *Nuevos pasos* (Huerta and Kanellos, eds.)	*Flor i canto II* (Arnold Vento et al., eds.)	1979

Gutiérrez, founder of the Chicano political party La Raza Unida [United Race] (Texas). Gonzales and Gutiérrez have published poetry, and Chicano *teatro* as we know it originated in the UFW. However, one group more than the others gave cohesion to the Movement: the students. In the late 1960's, at both high school and university levels, Chicano student activists led protests aimed at reforming curricula to include Chicano studies and at forcing universities to recruit large numbers of Chicanos and to extend to them the financial aid already available to Blacks. Though recent apathy and the conservative swing in the nation's mood also have affected Chicanos, the Movement did produce a surge of cultural interest, and perhaps its most lasting contribution will be in the arts.

That the early Chicano literary production was closely intertwined with the socio-political Movement is clear. Luis Valdez founded the Teatro Campesino in 1965 as a propaganda arm of the UFW. Chicano academicians at the Berkeley campus of the University of California founded Quinto Sol Publications and began publishing *El Grito*, the first journal of Chicano writing, in 1967. This journal, often named by the writers as extremely influential, initially favored sociological essays, but soon creative works began to appear. In 1969 Quinto Sol published the first anthology of Chicano literature, *El Espejo/The Mirror. I Am Joaquín*, the narrative poem which seemed to express so adequately the first stage of Chicano nationalism, was actually a versified statement of the Crusade for Justice's ideology. Much of the early literature, especially poetry, appeared in underground or student newspapers; most of it was political sloganism—a lot of bad songs, José Montoya remarks—justifiably forgotten. Yet, as Montoya also points out, amid the facile, ephemeral writing, there appeared serious pieces, in every genre. These quality items were often equally committed in political terms, but had literary significance as well. It is this writing that now comprises what we read as Chicano literature.

(This is not the place for a thorough analysis of Chicano literature; what follows is simply an introduction to its main characteristics, a brief *description* rather than a critical analysis. It is organized by genres rather than by authors. The introductory notes to the interviews treat the writers individually.)

Poetry

Early Chicano poetry is characterized by a sense of protest, obviously, but within the general category of protest literature it strikes certain chords: lament and anger over the Chicanos' virtues and talents being ignored, wasted, or deliberately suppressed by the majority society; the recalling of Mexican history, mythology, and popular lore; emphasis on the family, with roots in the land or the barrio; the Pachuco[3] as a precursor to Chicano cultural awareness; the opposition of Chicano oral history—"truth"—to United States written history—"lies"; the opposition of the Chicanos' humanism and harmony with nature to the technological, ahumanistic, unecological United States society; the opposition of Chicano (*mestizo*) ethnic, cultural, and racial openness to the Anglo Americans' resistance and hostility to outsiders. Viewed temporally, there is a nostalgia for a prior unity, either lost, forgotten, or in the process of disappearing; a lamenting of alienating oppression in the present, a situation which must be corrected lest Chicano culture disappear; and a hope for a future regrouping in a homeland (Aztlán) reclaimed from the United States, and around cultural/historical traditions—a recuperation of the lost unity. This temporal perspective lends the poetry a diasporic tone. The fear that Chicano culture has reached a crisis point in the present infuses a sense of urgency: having forgotten the past, Chicanos may be about to lose their identity and dissolve in the melting pot of assimilation. The literature assumes the task of instructing the Chicanos, especially the younger generations, about their heritage—thus the didactic tone of the greater part of the poetry. Some examples of these characteristic topics follow.

One of the most succinct examples of Chicano protest poetry is Abelardo Delgado's "Stupid America." Textual analysis establishes many of the characteristics of Chicano poetry.

> stupid america, see that chicano
> with a big knife
> in his steady hand
> he doesn't want to knife you
> he wants to sit on a bench
> and carve christfigures
> but you won't let him.
> stupid america, hear that chicano
> shouting curses on the street
> he is a poet
> without paper and pencil
> and since he cannot write
> he will explode.
> stupid america, remember that chicanito
> flunking math and english
> he is the picasso
> of your western states
> but he will die
> with one thousand masterpieces
> hanging only from his mind.[4]

The poem violently laments the wasting of aesthetic talents through ignorance on the part of the United States. Time is telescoped to encompass the past and future, while centering on the present. The Christ-carving sculptor evokes the image of the *santero*, the traditional carver of religious statues in Spanish Colonial provinces occupying the present Southwest of the United States. Abelardo recalls a centuries-old art form unfamiliar to the majority of Americans, Anglo-Americans and Chicanos alike. The reference is a synecdoche for the Hispanic society of the Southwest, unified through religious belief and cultural tradition. By extension, Abelardo challenges the misconception of the Atlantic coast origins of U.S. culture perpetuated in biased textbooks and popularized by "How the West Was Won" type propaganda. The future is evoked through Picasso, the epitome of the modern artist and, of course, a Spaniard of universal influence. The reference projects the santero's cultural tradition into a futuristic time zone from the perspective of the stereotypical image of the backward Chicano. The apparently gratuitous image of Picasso is adroitly pertinent—it challenges the U.S. claim to leadership in modernity, for this country has no artist to rival Picasso. Picasso revamped art, first by defining modern multiperspectivism—Cubism—then by reviewing and renewing traditional art forms through a series of actualizing parodies. Moreover, the santero and Picasso share what is the essence of Chicanismo, the art of synthesis. The santero adopted European aesthetics to the rather primitive, limited conditions of the peripheral colonies, creating a distinctive art through practical synthesis. The fact that that synthesis also involved indigenous influences is significant. Picasso, in his parodies, synthesized traditional and modern trends to create a forward-moving art at a time of general cultural crisis. Abelardo subtly, implicitly proclaims the Hispanic capacity for progress through regeneration, without the chaotic rejection of the past so associated with U.S. culture. Thus Abelardo offers the United States a possibility of salvation.

Between the sculptor and the painter, in the center, and by implication at the present moment, stands the poet, referenceless except as the author's persona. The poet desires to transform his "oral" expression into written form, but America obstructs him by refusing to provide materials—an image of economic/racial oppression. America wastes the significant contribution that the Chicano could make. The reference to "flunking math and english" underscores a constant leitmotif in Chicano literature: the school system as the hostile agent of socialization, intolerant of alternative forms of American culture.

The poem rises above commonplace protest doggerel through its imagery, which concentrates, in each section of the poem, on the hand as a creative or destructive instrument. The outcome is left in the balance, to be decided in the future—will the hand be allowed to constructively contribute to America or be forced to destroy it? The poem didactically instructs the majority culture to look beyond appearances, to overcome its racist paranoia, to cease being stupid, and to open itself to the positive contribution of Chicano culture. At the same time, it implicitly instructs the Chicanos to redirect their aggression into constructive pursuits, ones which are not alien, but traditionally Hispanic. (In passing, it should be noted that the poem alludes to the contrast of U.S. culture as technological ["math"] and Chicano culture as artistic or aesthetic. This appeal to the aesthetic order is found also in the works of Rodolfo Gonzales, José Montoya, Tino Villanueva, Ricardo Sánchez, and Alurista.)

By centering the frustration and the poetic space in the poet's dilemma, Abelardo creates a truly Chicano image. At the heart of the matter he places a divided self caught between apparently opposite poles—here, methods of expression: oral or written—which in truth are two aspects of the self: the mouth and the hand. At the same time, the division is between the Mexican—oral tradition—and the American—written tradition. Yet the Chicano has a right to both. Chicanos must learn from the images offered by the poem and synthesize a new unity of oral and written expressions, the curse and art, the mouth (spirit) and the hand (body). Otherwise they will remain divided and, in turn, undermine the society in which they live; from the perspective of U.S. society, if the Mexican culture is not allowed its legitimate place, the divided society will self-destruct. Chicanismo is the positive answer.

Finally, in a manner characteristic of the most significant Chicano works, this poem responds to itself by the fact of its own existence. The poem states the Chicano's frustration at not being permitted expression in U.S. society. The poem, however, is the author's realization of expression within the written medium denied his poetic persona; it is the sign and proof of his recuperated unity. It should be noted that the written poem maintains the shouted curses of the oral expression—"stupid america!" Abelardo shouts in violent lament when he recites the poem. Moreover, the realization of the goal of writing does not cancel out the original situation; America ignores santeros and the Hispanism of Picasso, and it will ignore Abelardo's poem. Yet the poem transcends the stupid rigidity of U.S. culture by claiming a space for itself in the U.S. written tradition—the fact that it is in English is not coincidental—while remaining faithful to Chicano concerns and its oral origins. The poem is thus revolutionary in its challenge of unyielding "stupidity" and its seizure of the space denied the Chicano artist. This synthesis of apparent oppositions without abandoning one's ethnic heritage is the most Chicano note of all. Abelardo synthesizes cultures apparently hopelessly at odds. Not that he falsifies reality—no, the poem faithfully reflects the conflict and even ends on a pessimistic note. But the fact of the poem's existence is already a step toward transcending the impasse. By applying the method he evokes—aesthetic and cultural synthesis—Abelardo achieves his poem, a lesson in Chicanismo.

There are many poems recalling the Pachuco and the barrio, the most famous being "El Louie" by José Montoya and "The Trip through the Mind Jail" by Raúl Salinas.[5] Each of these poems rescues its central figure from disappearance, establishes it as an image in the poem, and displays its history for the reader to observe and learn from. They begin, respectively:

> Hoy enterraron al Louie,[6]
> [Today they buried Louie,]

and

> LA LOMA
> Neighborhood of my youth
> demolished, erased forever from
>   the universe.[7]

The central figure in each case represents the signifying center of the poet's peer group.

> times of the forties
> and the early fifties
> lost un vato de atolle [a great dude]
>
> . . . .
> But we had Louie

and

> i needed you then . . . identity . . . a sense of belonging.

Disappearance threatens the potential disintegration of identity. The poems retrieve the images—in the ambiguity of their positive/negative, creative/self-destructive dualities—and restore them to visibility, now transmuted to the verbal written order. The poems satisfy the personal need of the author to recuperate significance, and at the same time they provide for Chicanos who did not know those times a source for learning about their heritage.

The Pachuco and barrio motifs are joined to another important Chicano theme, the pinto [convict] experience, by Ricardo Sánchez. In his two collections of writings, *Canto y grito mi liberación* and *HechizoSpells*, Sánchez creates the aesthetic response of a Pachuco/Pinto to Anglo-America's threat of extermination. From the depths of isolation—solitary confinement—Sánchez emerges, tempered like steel and ready to hone his weapons. He attacks American society on every moral front, as metaphorically symbolized by the dates and geographical locations which preface his poems. His America is devoid of humanism, familial spirit, love, sensual pleasure, dignity, or transcendent values. Yet to be a Chicano is not enough to merit salvation; one must consciously activate one's humanity. Despite the typical assumption that Chicanos have the advantage of not being as decadent as the Anglo-Americans, survival still demands resistance to assimilation. Sánchez depicts the Pachucos as early resisters; yet he also admits the futility of their efforts to achieve transcendence by writing on the barrio walls (an act that Chicano poets often utilize as a sign of embryonic art prefiguring the Chicano murals of the present day). "Pachucos, sensing the loss and hurt of their humble yet rebellious lives, striving to impress their names and histories on crumbling tenement walls, hoping against hope that somehow these same walls would last and become the eighth wonder of a society falling apart at the seams all around them."[8] The material world is ephemeral, and, as Sánchez demonstrates in one of his best poems, "Homing" (*HechizoSpells*, pp. 144–148), even the barrios are being razed. Yet the Pachuco's instincts were correct; only the materials were wrong; and Sánchez turns to writing literature. In "Homing," a Chicano publishing house becomes the center of political activism, and, in the light of the complete destruction of the poet's home, the publishing house becomes the new home in the sense of spiritual signifying center—writing, family, love, cosmic significance merge with politics, as Sánchez insists they must.

Sánchez is not an escapist, and, like Abelardo in "Stupid America," he ends "Homing" ambiguously: the poet departs to write another parole report. Writing itself becomes the disputed action to be defined in struggle with the oppressor; shall it be liberty or imprisonment? The poem responds as an act of liberty, but the characteristic synthesis incorporates the threat into the statement, because Sánchez insists that to be a Chicano—to be human—is a continuous struggle.

While Sánchez's works give the impression of a chaotic outpouring of spontaneous emotion, lacking any ordering element except the author himself, other Chicano poets—Alurista, Sergio Elizondo, Rodolfo Gonzales, and Miguel Méndez—have produced carefully planned books, developed on an ideological substructure, all of which combine the diasporic and didactic tones and the most common Chicano motifs. All four writers portray the Chicano as the victim of the United States, which is given the role of a callous conqueror, a highly technological, dehumanized, unecological, and sterile, though powerful, society. The Chicano, by contrast, is the faithful child of nature and rightful owner of the Southwest, or Aztlán. The four, though Méndez less explicitly than the others, propose a return to the Mexican heritage of family, culture, and communion with nature—the land—and advocate resistance to further Anglo-American encroachment. Of course, while treating essentially the same reality, each develops a particular vision. (In passing, note that they come from and live in different areas: Gonzales was born and resides in Colorado; Elizondo, born in Sinaloa, Mexico, now lives in New Mexico; Alurista, from Mexico City, is now in California; Méndez was born and still lives in Arizona.)

Gonzales's *I Am Joaquín*, still the best-known Chicano poem, begins with Joaquín lost in the chaos of the Anglo-American industrial society, from which he retreats to his people to contemplate his history—mostly Mexican—before deciding his future. He discovers that, in spite of a tradition of bravery, sacrifice, and greatness, he is considered inferior by those who stole his land. The response is two-sided: (1) to return to the Mexican roots, with emphasis on teaching the younger generations about the past before they completely "disappear behind the shroud of mediocrity never to look back to remember me" (p. 82); (2) to unite and reclaim the land. Joaquín, the Chicano Everyman, instructs his children through the poem itself, and it becomes a rallying call for revolution.

Miguel Méndez eschews the historically factual events in favor of poetic allegory in creating his tale of capitalist oppression of the poor, *Los criaderos humanos*. The narrator discovers a strange land, a human stockyard whose inhabitants' blood is forcibly extracted and turned into riches for the privileged classes. The experience teaches the narrator his complicity in the human condition and reveals to him the poet's role of socially committed interpreter of Chicano tradition (encompassing myth, history, and literature). The diasporic tone manifests itself in the wandering, lost narrator, who searches for his origins, as well as in the desperate yearning of the oppressed to become plants, symbolizing a return to a mythical paradise of peace and harmony. The didactic tone appears, first, as an autodidactic consciousness awakening in the narrator, and, second, although actually simultaneously, as the introduction of the reader into the narrator's voyage.[9]

Elizondo and Alurista resemble Gonzales and Méndez in their view of the Chicanos as a colonized, exploited people in need of relearning their history in order to regroup around a Mexican and/or proletarian identity. Both add, moreover, the systematic debunking of the Anglo-American oppressor. In *Perros y antiperros* [Dogs and Antidogs] Elizondo begins from a sour-grapes fixation on the despised Anglo-American. The title shows that the Chicanos' identity as a reaction to Gringo inhumanity (*perros*) serves to center that inhumanity in themselves, leaving the Chicanos as mere *anti(perro)s*. He ends with a scathing satire of the American way of life. Between the two points, he rescues Chicano history, focusing on the U.S. Southwest and northern Mexico. While he topples the Gringo from a moon landing, complete with a "dead flag," to a pathetically subhuman life on earth, he raises the Chicano from a perhaps jealous onlooker to a proud child of the sun, who plants a living banner—the UFW flag—firmly in the human reality of the earth. The dogs become less than dogs in their plastic inorganicness, while the antidogs learn of their humanity and redirect their lives according to traditions of family, love, and dignified labor.

Alurista purposes to liberate Chicanos from the fear of the capitalist oppressor; having forgotten their past, Chicanos passively wait for illusory future rewards. By slowly evoking the past, but always within an expanding sense of the present, Alurista strengthens the Chicanos so that they can activate their spirit in the present and define the future in the Raza's own terms. The oppressor is revealed, again, as inorganic, unecological, dehumanized—a suicidal monster run amuck.

but his massacres must stop
we must bind his paws
and file his fangs
he may not kill
not us
not himself.[10]

The Chicano is "organic," in harmony with nature, humane, capable of caging the monster and returning him to his lost humanity.

Alurista evokes the Nahuatl spiritual tradition, not as a closed nationalism, but rather as a basis for a Chicano synthesis of all humane traditions, from Greek mythology to Mexican Revolutionary ideology, from European symphonic music to Black jazz to Bob Dylan or the Doors or the Beatles, or to Mexican music of all kinds. He seeks to transform humanity into the Cosmic Race, but only from the starting point of racial equality. First Chicanos must assert their own identity by overcoming their fear of living in the present; then they can rescue society from the abyss. The human race, led by Chicanos, will become like a multicolored sarape, each group with its own hue, but all of them in harmony and order creating a lovely, bright unit. *Floricanto en Aztlán* and *Nationchild Plumaroja* are manuals for the realization of Alurista's goal, didactic survival manuals for exodus from the diaspora. They offer the wandering tribe an ideology (the Nahuatl concept of Floricanto)[11] and a purpose (the recuperation of the mythical homeland of Aztlán).

The personal tone is not lacking in Chicano poetry, although even then, in the most notable examples, there is a sometimes explicit, sometimes implicit affirmation of social commitment. Tino Villanueva's *Hay otra voz Poems* is an *ars poetica* in which the poet's persona moves from the aesthetic, personal rendering of existentialistic themes of universal concern—existence as self-affirmation in the present, in the face of menacing death—to the decision to dedicate his skills to his people's cause. What distinguishes Villanueva from the majority of the aforementioned poets and their followers is his studied use of traditional European versification and imagery, the founding of the poem in the metaphor, his refusal to resort to the facile cliché, and the definite lyrical quality of his verse instead of the usual narrative mode. Bernice Zamora shares Villanueva's poetic attitude and takes the exploration of mainstream literary techniques even further. Zamora constructs refined, personal epiphanies of reality by

focusing on the world's surface and intensifying the elements until a new dimension is revealed—a dimension that cannot be spoken but only alluded to. In spite of the direct naming of objects
and a firm grip on material reality, something escapes and remains in the mystery just beyond the logic of expository writing
so common in many Chicano poets. At the heart of Zamora's poetry lies the conflict between life impulses—eros—and any and
all limitations—death—even the self-imposed ones of seductive
security. Yet, through intertextual links to poets of social protest,
such as Robinson Jeffers, Zamora establishes a social perspective.
She allows other writers to echo in her work, broadening and liberating Chicano literature through universal concerns, while, at
the same time, Chicano-izing those concerns through parody.

Villanueva and Zamora avoid blatantly didactic statements,
though valuable lessons can be drawn from their work, especially
by would-be poets with respect to poetic language. Both do manifest the diasporic tone, Villanueva in his creation of a voice for
his disenfranchised Raza, and Zamora in a certain yearning for a
past in which the old traditions, though oppressive for women,
rendered the world meaningful. Villanueva incarnates that voice
and establishes it firmly within the realm of written literature so
long closed to the Chicano. Zamora transforms the snakelike image of Penitente rituals ("clacking prayer wheels jolt/the hissing
spine to uncoil wailing tongues"),[12] the signifying center of traditional New Mexico–Colorado culture, into the insatiable "restless serpents" soothed by lyrics, the driving force of her poetic vocation. Both poets are essentially Chicano, especially in their
ability to synthesize cultures and literary influences into their
own art.

Most recent Chicano poetry seems to be either mired in the
clichés of social protest or following the personal line of Villanueva and Zamora. The facile, superficially Chicano poem elicits
less reaction from an audience which has heard it all before. Not
that social conditions have improved greatly—they have not; but
the themes, and particularly the phrases, wear thin. Among the
serious poets less emphasis is being given to narrative poetry and
more to the lyrical;[13] technique and craft are no longer considered
agringado concerns. Names like Gary Soto, Lorna Dee Cervantes,
and Orlando Ramírez head the list of younger poets who construct tight poems of clean, sparse verse based on imagery more
than anecdote. Most promising is the quantity and quality of
women poets beginning to publish, most notable among them
Zamora, Cervantes, Alma Villanueva, and Marina Rivera. As with

Tino Villanueva and Zamora, the didactic purpose seems less important in the works of the newer poets; in addition, the diasporic tone is fading. These poets appear to be more secure of their identity and less dependent on historical reference. Literature creates its own tradition, and perhaps the recuperation of origins carried out by the first wave of poets is taken, if not for granted, as a now established fact, freeing new poets to write less panoramically and more personally.

Drama

Chicano theatre is a dynamic, rapidly developing phenomenon;[14] long past are the days when El Teatro Campesino of Luis Valdez was the only group creating works worthy of study. Since 1965, Chicano theatre has expanded its scope from extemporaneous agit-prop skits to sophisticated drama of social protest, and even to the "legitimate" stage. Today, in every part of the country where Chicanos are found, there are Teatro groups, and several of the best attract international attention. Luis Valdez, always a trend-setter, broke all attendance records in Los Angeles in 1978 with his play *Zoot Suit*, and in the spring of 1979 premiered it on Broadway.

The Teatro Campesino originated in 1965, when Valdez offered to organize dramatized skits to support César Chávez's fledgling union in California. Soon a group of amateur actors formed and developed a genre called *acto*: a short, dramatic sketch, focused on one specific social reality, following the outline of a situation but open to improvisation. The roles are *archetypes*, or *stereotypes*, depending on one's perspective—caricatures of readily identifiable characters: the Grower, the Worker, the Student, etc. The acto is very brief, the longest lasting approximately half an hour. It satirizes the enemy or Chicano vices, with a simplistic Manichean vision only justifiable if one considers the drastic situation which produced the genre. In 1970 the Campesino introduced a second genre, the *mito* [myth], to allow them to sustain a plot line, impossible to do in the limited acto. The mito plot, according to Valdez, is "a parable that unravels like a flower Indio fashion to reveal the total significance of a certain event. And that vision of totality is what truly defines mito. In other words, the CONTENT of a mito is the Indio vision of the universe. And that vision is religious, as well as political, cultural, social, personal, etc. It is total."[15] The mito attempts not only to represent universal harmony, but also to act as a ritual capable of effecting that harmony—a religious sacrament. *Zoot Suit* is yet another genre: commercial drama synthesizing influences well known to followers of the Campesino—influences such as Brecht, pantomime, documentary theatre, and the techniques perfected in the acto and mito. Continually expanding Chicano theatre beyond its frontiers, forcing constant evolution and re-evaluation, Valdez remains its most influential figure, and only he knows where he will take it next.

The common experience for other Chicano Teatros has been to begin by imitating the Campesino's acto, and most of them remain within its limits. A growing number, however, have remained together long enough to develop their own style. El Teatro de la Esperanza is second only to the Campesino, and one of its plays, *Guadalupe*, rivals anything the Valdez group did up to *Zoot Suit*. Esperanza perfected the documentary play, taking a civil rights issue, studying and documenting it thoroughly, and then collectively creating scenes to portray the case. Yet it is not the facts that convince the audience, despite what even the actors themselves might wish, but the skillful use of theatrical techniques and the polished performance. Esperanza's success proves the rewards of discipline, study, and a knowledge of the dynamics of dramatic performance. Lack of attention to these concerns has undermined many a socio-politically committed, well-intentioned Teatro.

The latest trend among Teatros is a growing acceptance of professionalism, including a departure from collective creation. More plays are being written by individual dramatists. (To date, Estela Portillo's plays, *The Day of the Swallows* and *Sun Images*, are the most outstanding, and almost the only, examples of traditional plays written by a Chicano author.) Also, Chicanos are beginning to graduate from universities with degrees in drama. These trends are bound to change Chicano theatre.

Whatever the future holds for those groups that, like the Campesino, seem to be moving toward professional, commercial theatre, the vast majority of Chicano Teatros will probably continue to be amateur groups of community or student activists who use drama as a political tool. These less skilled, often cliché-ridden presentations offer little of literary value per se, but it should be remembered that they are the grass-roots training ground for the professional troupes and they create a demand for better theatre by educating a public not accustomed to theatrical performances. And finally, it should be kept in mind that the

Broadway play *Zoot Suit* began as an acto somewhere in the fields of the San Joaquín Valley.

Novel

There is less ideological or technical cohesion among the prose writers than among the poets, and no one figure dominates the genre as Valdez does the theatre, so general statements are more difficult. I will only offer an overview of some commonly shared points.

The novel is less didactic than either the poetry or the theatre, and the sense of diaspora is less explicit. Certainly one finds in most of the novels a portrayal of the Chicano as an outsider in U.S. society, but, except in Miguel Méndez's *Peregrinos de Aztlán*, the topic is not elevated into an explicit political statement. Regarding historical perspective, the novel's frame of reference is the twentieth century, with only one exception, José Antonio Villarreal's *The Fifth Horseman*, which explores the origins of the 1910 Mexican Revolution. Most of the other novels take that same revolution as a distant degree zero, making at least a reference to some member of the family who came from Mexico fleeing the war. *Bless Me, Ultima*, by Rudolfo Anaya, set in New Mexico, is another exception of sorts, evoking centuries-earlier migrations, one sometime during the Spanish colonial era (sixteenth to nineteenth centuries) and another during the brief Mexican period (1821–1846). The present moment for the events depicted in most of the novels is reduced to the last thirty years. Thus, the novels differ from the poetry in historical reference; whereas the poets often utilize the distant past, particularly Mexican pre-Columbian mythology, or images from the Mexican Revolution, the novelists prefer the present or recent past in the United States. The difference in orientation dissipates both the didactic and the diasporic tones.

As in the poetry, there is a preoccupation with the possible disappearance of the oral tradition. Miguel Méndez claims that no one listens any longer to the old people, so the past is slowly, and literally, dying away; Rolando Hinojosa seems to share the opinion. Both of them distrust official written records. Méndez calls written history a "puta que no otorga favores si no pulsa el oro de la paga" [whore who does not grant favors without being paid in gold]; [16] while Hinojosa illustrates journalism's callous reduction and falsification of human suffering in his "Por esas cosas que pasan" ["One of Those Things"] (in *Estampas del Valle y otras obras,* pp. 91–102; translation, pp. 103–114). Both authors respond by writing of themes and people that in the past would have been preserved in the oral tradition, claiming for them an area within the mistrusted written tradition; as in the poetry, the written media are being invaded as a response to the loss or falsification of self-imagery. In Tomás Rivera's . . . *y no se lo tragó la tierra* and Anaya's *Ultima,* the narrator must rescue the people or person who stabilized his childhood. Moreover, both novels are essentially stories about learning how to "read"; . . . *tierra* in a very literal sense of schooling and learning words, which then are the secret to controlling fear; *Ultima* in that Antonio learns from the old curandera how to *read* the world as a unified, harmonious text. The narrators' need to write what they have learned is at the heart of both novels. Yet, in both of them, what is about to disappear is a facet of Chicano culture that normally would have been preserved through oral tradition.

Since writing is a major concern, one might expect the novels to treat the apprenticeship of the writer, and several can be read in this way: Villarreal's *Pocho,* Rivera's . . . *tierra,* Anaya's *Ultima,* Oscar Z. Acosta's *The Autobiography of a Brown Buffalo* and its continuation, *The Revolt of the Cockroach People,* John Rechy's *City of Night,* and even Alejandro Morales's *Caras viejas y vino nuevo. Pocho* is the most blatant, with the protagonist stating several times that he intends to be a writer. In Acosta's grotesque autobiography, the bad-faith decision to become a lawyer instead of a writer condemns him to continue in a schizophrenic chaos which he might otherwise have escaped. These novels also share the autobiographic form, as do Nash Candelaria's *Memories of the Alhambra* and Rechy's *Numbers, This Day's Death,* and *The Sexual Outlaw.* (Rechy has said that all of his novels are autobiographical, but not all of them are written in that manner; his next book is titled *Autobiography: A Novel.*)

The case of Ron Arias's *The Road to Tamazunchale* is a bit different, but related. The dying protagonist, a book salesman and avid reader, revolts against passively waiting for death and embarks on an active demise. Since he no longer can carry out an adventurous excursion, he invents escapades, writing his death, so to speak. He draws from both his literary and his everyday memory, mixing intertextual parodies of literature (*Don Quijote, Faust,* a short story by Gabriel García Márquez), and films (Marlon Brando's *Burn,* Bunuel's *Trip on a Mexican Bus,* the Hope and Crosby *Road to . . .* series) with specific East Los Angeles references. The result is a humorous, sophisticated fantasy and the best Chicano novel to date.

The novels also spotlight the family, but depict it as being subjected to fragmentary social pressures. The Rubio family in *Pocho* disintegrates when the parents' Mexican social and sexual mores prove unadaptable to their changing sex life; the lack of communication inherent in machismo and the woman's anti-erotic upbringing underlie the eventual irreconcilable split. The young protagonist rejects marriage, along with all other traditional social values—Mexican or American—in favor of the asocial freedom he believes necessary to be an artist.

In most of the other novels the results are less drastic, but the pressure is constant. The family in *Ultima* is a marriage of traditional opposites: farmers and wandering *llaneros* [people of the open range]; the father dreams of escaping his sedentary existence by running away to California. Rivera subtly portrays the family as superstitious, limiting, unresponsive, and even cruel, though in the end the protagonist returns home to begin the creation of his aesthetic world. Hinojosa's extended families are racked with interfamilial conflicts, and death is always present. Acosta satirizes his father's imposition of the *Seabee's Manual* as the standard of comportment, and Oscar's life savings are stolen by his own brother. Rechy's narrator in *City of Night* speaks of his father's violent rage and his mother's suffocating love; the portrait of the love-hate struggle between mother and son in *This Day's Death* is one of the best studies of the fatherless family in Chicano literature. Candelaria relates how in the 1930's a young Chicana had to force her husband to leave New Mexico to escape the dictates of the extended family; once in Los Angeles she insists on the Americanization of her child. The main plot follows her husband in his futile flight to Spain in search of an identity or nationality he somehow lost, in no small measure because of the split in the family.

Miguel Méndez and Alejandro Morales are extreme in their portrayals. Méndez's families are degraded and shattered by social conditions and capitalistic exploitation. The victimized poor, forced to migrate, lose communal roots and often die in the process. One of Méndez's favorite motifs is that of the young woman forced into prostitution, a situation which inevitably leads to the anguish and death of a male relative or friend. Morales brutally distorts everything through his anally fixated, surrealistic lens, creating scenes reminiscent of Bunuel's *Los olvidados* or Valle Inclan's *esperpentos* [grotesquely exaggerated characters]. Members of one family literally try to kill each other. Ironically, the narrator, whose family seems normal and secure, envies his friends' violently disintegrating home life.

The pressures on and within the family are reflections of social unrest. In the background, like a stage set behind the main action, society is unsettled; it is often implied that the Chicano is being pulled out of a securely structured society and into another which is in crisis. Anaya, Méndez, Acosta, Hinojosa, and Villarreal all evoke war as a disruptive factor. Hinojosa, in *Korean Love Songs*, a versified installment of his multivolumed novel, and Villarreal, in *The Fifth Horseman*, take the reader directly into battle. Anaya kills off one character driven mad by his war experience and refers to the development of the atom bomb as yet another unsettling product of progress. Law enforcement agencies and the judicial system are less than admirable in these works. The police beat a group of teenagers one of whom is Chicano, in *Pocho*, as they do a farmworker in Méndez's *Peregrinos*. A young Chicano is murdered in his jail cell in Acosta's *Cockroach People*, and earlier in the same book the police bludgeon and mace into submission an ethnically mixed group of demonstrators in a church. In Arias's *Tamazunchale* and Candelaria's *Alhambra*, the police illegally incarcerate U.S. citizens because they are "Mexican," and in Rechy's novels the police constantly harass street people and refuse to protect them from attack. The courts are no better. An Anglo receives no punishment for murdering a Chicano child in Rivera's *. . . tierra*, while what we know to be "justifiable homicide" wins a Chicano fifteen years' imprisonment in Hinojosa's *Estampas del Valle*. In *Peregrinos*, the judge, after compassionately releasing a young Anglo woman who has killed her baby, sentences a Chicano to four years in prison for stealing four bottles of wine. Acosta encounters a corrupt kangaroo court in Mexico and a blatantly prejudiced one in the United States. The most scathing exposé of judicial prejudice is Rechy's *This Day's Death*, in which a judge finds the protagonist guilty in spite of proof that the prosecution's witness perjured himself.

With society unsettled, one might well expect Chicanos to seek refuge in their traditional religious beliefs, but the novels seriously challenge that supposed faith. *Pocho*'s Richard Rubio is first introduced to us just after making his first confession, during which the priest has introduced him to sexual taboos. This later sets off a conflict with his mother. Religion will intermittently produce attacks of guilt in Richard. Finally, he challenges the priest's authority in the confessional and rejects the Holy Eucharist; yet he knows he will never entirely escape his religious training. Antonio, in *Ultima*, expects the sacraments to infuse him with cosmic understanding; when they fail, he turns away from the church. His disappointment is augmented when the clergy prove incapable of helping the faithul on two separate occasions, while Ultima knows exactly what to do. In Anaya's *Heart of Aztlán* the parish priest is in league with the exploiters of society and refuses to support the workers' strike. In the . . . *tierra* episode "First Communion," a young boy on his way to his first confession happens across a couple having sex. Confused and stunned, he does not confess the incident; the fact that he thinks it may be a sin reflects on his confusion as well as on the puritanism of a Catholic upbringing. After his First Holy Communion, he is racked with guilt. Rivera creates a poignant image of a religion based on fear and taboo. In the title episode, the boy forsakes his parents' beliefs and curses god; when the earth does not swallow him, a feeling of freedom sweeps over him.

On occasion the criticism is humorous. Hinojosa tells of a priest who kills a parishioner by refusing to help him out of a pit because the man has insulted him. The victim dies of heart failure, while the priest, unaware of the attack, ironically recites a prayer for the dead ("Al pozo con Bruno Cano," in *Estampas*, pp. 36–37). The anecdote is hilarious, especially in language, but the seriousness of the satire should not be overlooked. Oscar Zeta Acosta also satirizes the church by depicting the Catholic Archbishop of Los Angeles as a luxury-loving, right-wing bigot. Acosta does, however, include liberal clergymen, and women, among the ranks of cockroach revolutionaries.

For Rechy religion is like the justice system, a moral code that restrains through imprisonment but refuses to help those in need. From the depths of despair, the protagonist of *City of Night* phones Catholic churches for help. Most of the priests refuse to speak to him; the one who finally does can offer only a sympathetic but impotent "I know." In *The Fourth Angel* the young rebels visit a church to play a cruel game of confession in which the ugliness and arbitrariness of the human condition are exposed. The chapter ends with the protagonist saying that if he could condemn anyone it would be God. Religion offers him no logical explanation for his mother's death. In *The Sexual Outlaw*

Rechy attacks the hypocrisy of using the Bible to justify oppressing homosexuals, while ignoring its prohibition of war and killing. As for many Chicano writers, religion is for Rechy another of society's controlling agents for the perpetuation of mainstream mores; it can offer little in the line of an alternative to the society it serves.

Despite the various pressures, however, the culture survives, and, as Hinojosa and Rivera state in their interviews, this is the topic of Chicano literature. There may be doubts, even pessimism, but in the end what triumphs is a will to survive in the face of all odds. The writing itself constitutes that affirmation.[17]

Language

Much attention has been given to what is usually termed bilingualism in Chicano writing, the use of Spanish and English in the same work, of which more will be said below; but the language of Chicano literature is much more than a simple mixing of languages. First, it should not be overlooked that many writers use standard English and/or standard Spanish without mixing them. For example, Bernice Zamora parodies Shakespeare's Sonnet CXVI, "Let me not to the marriage of true minds," with a purposefully archaic English.

> Do not ask, sir, why this weary woman
> Wears well the compass of gay boys and men.
> Masculinity is not manhood's realm
> Which falters when ground passions overwhelm.[18]

Tino Villanueva utilizes an English reminiscent of Dylan Thomas in "My Certain Burn toward Pale Ashes," yet later offers another tribute to Thomas, this time in a Spanish which manages to echo the Welsh master: "Un eco vago vibra del pasado/y aviso da que el tiempo con presteza/al fin te vence, fuga, y no regresa" [A faint echo vibrates from the past/giving notice that time, in its haste,/finally overcomes you, flees, and does not return].[19]

John Rechy is a master at approximating urban street language, especially in *City of Night*. His disrespect for grammar and spelling give his language the throbbing pulse and excitement of the rock-and-roll music that (one knows) blares in the background of his scenes. Alurista has continued the use of rock music and street language, though his context is much more interlingual, as will be seen. Rolando Hinojosa is equally skilled with regional Mexican Spanish and its particular humor of the *albur* or phonetic word play. In "Al pozo con Bruno Cano," Cano y Melitón Burnias search for buried treasure in a cemetery at night; Burnias claims to know magic prayers for just such occasions. When Bruno, down in the pit, strikes something metallic, the following exchange takes place with the slightly deaf Melitón.

> Te digo que vamos cerca. [Bruno]
> Ah, sí, pues entonces, ¿qué rezo yo?
> ¿Qué?
> ¿Que qué rezo yo?
> ¿Cómo que qué resolló?
> ¿Qué resolló algo?
> ¿Que resolló algo dices?
> ¿Qué resolló? ¡ay, Diosito mío!
> Diciendo esto, Burnias voló, abandonó la pala y a su socio.[20]

The play of words is typically Mexican and very difficult to translate, since it stems from Spanish phonetics.[21] What is significant is that the language is more than just standard—it is steeped in Hispanic flavor. Passages could also be cited from Tomás Rivera or Miguel Méndez or Sergio Elizondo in which standard Spanish appears. Yes, each one uses regional speech, but no more so than Argentines, Mexicans, or Spaniards. How much more regional can writing become than that of the Mexico City group known as La Onda? Regionalism is not a vice, nor does it detract from the authenticity of language—usually quite the contrary. We also have the case of Alejandro Morales, who writes in Spanish, but with an almost totally English syntax. The creative power of his violent, often cumbersome mixture is recognized by José Agustín, a leading Mexican writer,[22] but many Chicanos are still unconvinced, seeing it as merely bad Spanish. From the Chicano perspective one feels that he could achieve a more natural language by using English when and where the Spanish seems forced, producing the feeling of someone limiting himself to only one facet of his being.

Between the poles of standard usage we find some authors, like Alurista, who mix the languages. "Mis ojos hinchados/ flooded with lágrimas/de bronze/melting on the cheek bones/of my concern";[23] "must be the season of the witch/la bruja/la llorona/she lost her children/and she cries/en las barrancas de industry."[24] Nick C. Vaca, one of the best writers from the early days of *El Grito*, does the same thing in prose: "y mis manos están heladas, con el frío y la fog of the morning. Chingado animal, even in the cold morning you don't leave me alone. Vete, antes que me mate, then you will have no home at all."[25]

This type of mixture, what linguists call code switching, was defined as a "binary phenomenon" by Philip Ortego; ". . . linguistic symbols of two languages are mixed in utterances using either language's syntactic structure."[26] Tino Villanueva takes this explanation further by attributing to the Chicano a *bisensitivity*, the feeling of experiencing something "from two points of reference: on one side from the dimension that the object can suggest within the Chicano context; and on the other side, from the dimension that the same reality suggests within an Anglosaxon context."[27] He goes on to give examples of experiences, such as playing marbles, that have two separate cultural contexts, implying that the particular context will determine the usage, producing the choice of code.

As convincing as these explanations seem, I disagree; they are misleading in their binary bound system. Chicanos do not function as constantly choice-making speakers; their language is a blend, a synthesis of the two into a third. Thus they are interlingual, not bilingual. The codes are not separate, but intrinsically fused. Taking, for instance, Villanueva's marbles example, the two contexts form a binary phenomenon only in a subjectless objectivity. As soon as the subject, the Chicano, appears, the two cease to be separate poles, blending together within the speaker. For the Chicano, within the *marble* there lurks the *canica* and vice versa. The feeling that one is saying more than the word means in either language, although the context can be entirely one or the other, is a common Chicano experience. A bilingual takes the meaning of a word such as *actual, ignore,* or *realize*[28] from the context of the language being spoken; the Chicano feels both, even though one may predominate, not simply because one language is being spoken, but because the entire semantic context is relevant. The bilingual will resist the "error"; the interlingual senses no "error." Chicano speech expands both the connotative and the denotative range of words in both languages, creating not a binary phenomenon, but a new phenomenon unfamiliar to the bilingual.

José Saldívar has demonstrated the interlingual phenomenon at work in Anaya's *Bless Me, Ultima*, explaining how the interlingual reader will sense in the word *moon* the word *luna*; they are one. So when, in a dream, the moon becomes Antonio's mother, a Luna by birth, the transformation is merely the adjustment of the surface representation, the word.[29] The possibility was there all along.

The expert in this linguistic synthesis is José Montoya. His poetry flows naturally, with no sensation of "code switching." He writes one language, his own, in which Spanish and English are no longer independent codes, but a single hybrid. Decoding his language in all its riches will be possible only for the interlingual reader, though the bilingual can come to "understand" his poems; the monolingual, of course, will be lost.

As long as we are bound by a linguistic science that insists on forcing all languages into binary structures, Chicano speech will be misinterpreted. Yet finding another, more suitable approach is no easy task, as George Steiner clearly demonstrates in *After Babel*, while arguing convincingly for the need to rethink the nature of the bilingual and polyglot speaker as one who "undercuts lines of division between languages by reaching inward, to the symbiotic core."[30] He could be talking about the Chicano.

Conclusion

Chicano literature has firmly established its presence in American letters in the years since 1965. It counts an increasing number of serious practitioners; among the best are the fourteen writers who participated in this project. These fourteen represent what we can call, perhaps, the first generation or, as Tino Villanueva suggests, the generation of Chicano renaissance writing, although the accuracy of that term is now disputed. Whatever the eventual nomenclature may be, these writers and their peers are bound by the fact of synchronic publication—not by their age. To their credit they have the breaking down of many barriers and the praiseworthy attempt to open some doors that, nevertheless, remain closed. Their writing has opened a literary space, however, with identifiable themes, characteristics, and standards—in short, they have created and defined contemporary Chicano literature. If changes occur, and they certainly seem imminent, the dimensions of that space will alter, but that is only natural and healthy; it will not cancel the significance of the pioneering efforts of these first writers, even though their works may be superseded. The student of Chicano literature will look back at this group and this first period as the foundation of whatever is to come, even if only as the generation against whom those to come rebel. The best of the best will survive—but then survival is an old Chicano tradition.

Notes to the Introduction

1. See Anselmo Arrellano, ed., *Los pobladores nuevo mexicanos y su poesía, 1899–1959* (Albuquerque: Pajarito Publications, 1976); Luis Leal, "Mexican American Literature: A Historical Perspective," *Revista Chicano-Riqueña* 1, no. 1 (1973): 32–44; Clara Lomas, "Resistencia cultural o apropiación ideológica: Visión de los años 20 en los cuadros costumbristas de Jorge Ulica," *Revista Chicano-Riqueña* 6, no. 4 (1978): 44–49; Doris L. Meyer, "Anonymous Poetry in Spanish Language New Mexico Newspapers (1800–1900)," *Bilingual Review* 2 (1975): 259–275; Alejandro Morales, "Visión panorámica de la literatura méxico-americana hasta el boom de 1966," dissertation, Rutgers University, 1975; Philip Ortego, "Backgrounds of Mexican American Literatures," dissertation, University of New Mexico, 1971; Juan Rodríguez, "El florecimiento de la literatura chicana," in *La otra cara de México: Los chicanos,* ed. David Maciel (Mexico City: Ediciones El Caballito, 1977), 348–369.

2. The best review of the etymological possibilities is Tino Villanueva, "Sobre el término 'Chicano,'" *Cuadernos Hispanoamericanos* (Madrid), no. 336 (June 1978): 387–410.

3. Pachucos were young Chicanos who adopted the extravagant style of dress known as the zoot suit in the late 1930's and 1940's. They came to national prominence when U.S. military men attacked them on the streets of Los Angeles in 1943 in what are now known as the Zoot Suit Wars. Chicano literature has created out of the Pachuco a model of early resistance to assimilation into U.S. society—a model which also represents a proud declaration of difference from traditional Mexican customs; the Pachuco was a synthesis of cultures, a Chicano.

4. Abelardo Delgado, "Stupid America," in *Chicano: 25 Pieces of a Chicano Mind* (Denver: Barrio Publications, 1969), p. 32.

5. Both poems are analyzed in Bruce-Novoa, "Literatura chicana: La respuesta al caos," *Revista de la Universidad de México* 29, no. 12 (August 1974): 20–24.

6. José Montoya, "El Louie," in *Aztlán: An Anthology of Mexican American Literature,* ed. Louis Valdez and Stan Steiner (New York: Random House, Vintage Books, 1972), pp. 333–334.

7. Raúl Salinas, "A Trip through the Mind Jail," in ibid., pp. 339–344.

8. Ricardo Sánchez, *Canto y grito mi liberación* (El Paso: Mictla Publications, 1971), p. 103.

9. See Bruce-Novoa, "Righting the Oral Tradition," paper read at the MLA convention, New York, 1978.

10. Alurista, "Hombre ciego," in *Floricanto en Aztlán,* poem 6, n.p. Published by the Chicano Studies Research Center, University of California, Los Angeles. Copyright 1971 by the Regents of the University of California.

11. Alurista uses the term to mean the combination of the ephemeral, *flor* [flower], and the lasting, *canto* [song], which represents the Nahuatl concept of poetry as a means to humanize, teach, and make joyful the total being of all peoples in natural harmony (Alurista, "La estética indígena a través del floricanto de Nezahualcoyotl," *Revista Chicano-Riqueña* 5, no. 2 [1977]: 48–62). For a more accurate explanation of the term as the Nahuas themselves used it, see Miguel León-Portilla, "Flores y cantos: Lo único verdadero en la tierra," in *La filosofía nahuatl estudiada en sus fuentes* (Mexico City: Universidad Nacional Autónoma de México, 1966), pp. 142–147.

12. Bernice Zamora, "Penitents," in *Restless Serpents* (Menlo Park, Calif.: Diseños Literarios, 1976), p. 8.

13. Rolando Hinojosa's *Korean Love Songs* (Berkeley: Editorial Justa, 1978) is a recent notable exception in its narrative technique.

14. For articles on Chicano theatre, see Bruce-Novoa, "El Teatro Campesino de Luis Valdez," *Texto Crítico* 10 (May–August 1978): 65–75; Bruce-Novoa and David Valentín, "Revolutionizing the Popular Image: Essay on Chicano Theatre," *Latin American Literary Review* 5, no. 10 (Spring–Summer 1977): 43–50; Jorge A. Huerta, "Del templo al pueblo: El teatro chicano de hoy," in *La otra cara de México*, ed. Maciel, pp. 316–347; Francisco Jiménez, "Dramatic Principles of the Teatro Campesino," *Bilingual Review* 2 (1975).

15. Luis Valdez, "Notes on Chicano Theatre," *Chicano Theatre* 1 (Spring 1973): 7.

16. Miguel Méndez M., *Peregrinos de Aztlán* (Tucson: Editorial Peregrinos, 1974), p. 177.

17. For how Chicano literature's common deep structure—its paradigm—is a response to the menace of chaotic dissolution, see Bruce-Novoa, "Literatura chicana: La respuesta al caos."

18. Bernice Zamora, "Sonnet, Freely Adapted," in *Restless Serpents*, p. 47.

19. Tino Villanueva, "Camino y capricho eterno," in *Hay otra voz Poems* (Staten Island: Editorial Mensaje, 1972), p. 15.

20. Rolando R. Hinojosa-S., "Al pozo con Bruno Cano," in *Estampas del Valle y otras obras* (Berkeley: Quinto Sol, 1973), p. 36.

21. In Spanish, "¿qué rezo yo?" [what prayer should I say?] and "¿qué resolló?" [what was that noisy breathing?] sound alike. The translator of *Estampas del Valle* has tried to approximate the effect by translating *rezar* as "chant" and *resollar* as "pant":
    " 'I said we're gettin' close.'
    " 'Okay, what should I chant?'
    " 'What?'
    " 'What do I chant?'
    " 'What do you mean, what do I chant?'
    " 'You heard something pant?'
    " 'Pant, you say?'

"'What panted? Omigod!'

"'Saying this, Burnias fled, abandoning his shovel and his companion." (*Estampas del Valle*, p. 75)

22. José Agustín, personal communication, spring 1978.

23. Alurista, "Mis ojos hinchados," in *Floricanto en Aztlán*, poem 40, n.p. Published by the Chicano Studies Research Center, University of California, Los Angeles. Copyright 1971 by the Regents of the University of California.

24. Alurista, "Must be the season of the witch," in ibid., poem 26, n.p. Published by the Chicano Studies Research Center, University of California, Los Angeles. Copyright 1971 by the Regents of the University of California.

25. N. C. Vaca, "The Week of the Life of Manuel Hernández," in *El Espejo/The Mirror*, ed. Octavio Romano (Berkeley: Quinto Sol, 1969), p. 137.

26. Philip Ortego, "The Chicano Renaissance," *Social Caseworker* 52 (May 1971): 306.

27. Tino Villanueva, "Apuntes sobre la poesía chicana," *Papeles de Son Armadans* 271–273 (October–December 1978): 51. Translation by Bruce-Novoa.

28. *Actual* means "of the present time" in Spanish; *ignorar* means "not to know"; *realizar* means "to achieve," as in English "to realize an action."

29. José Saldívar, "Faulkner, Borges and Anaya," senior essay, Yale University, 1978.

30. George Steiner, *After Babel: Aspects of Language and Translation* (London: Oxford University Press, 1975), p. 119.

INTERVIEWS

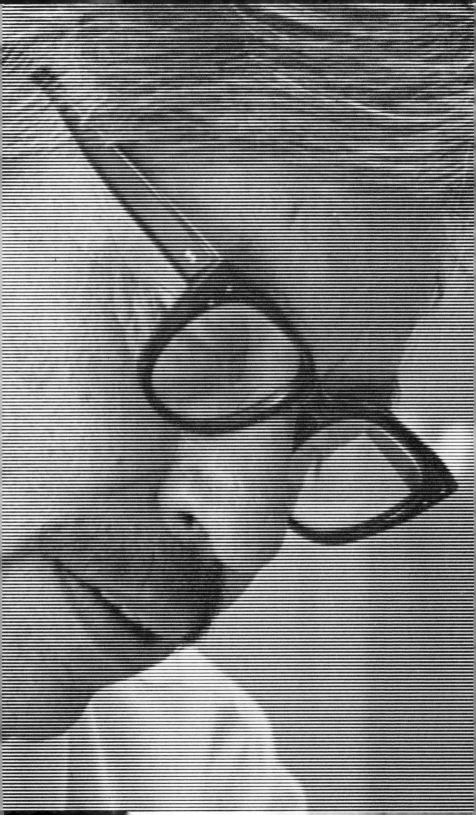

José Antonio Villarreal

Within contemporary Chicano literature, the position occupied by José Villarreal is highly significant on several counts. Though it predated the Chicano Movement by some years, his first novel, *Pocho* (1959), clearly prefigured the major works in the genre that were to appear ten to fifteen years later. Its category of *Bildungsroman*, its pattern of veiled autobiography, and the treatment of such themes as immigration, Mexican and Chicano sexual and religious taboos, father-son parallelism, mother-son antagonism, and the pressures of assimilation on the family are repeated in novels that follow. Moreover, *Pocho*, having been modeled on Joyce's *Portrait of the Artist as a Young Man*, narrates a writer's apprenticeship, a theme that lies at the heart of such Chicano landmarks as *Bless Me, Ultima*, . . . *y no se lo tragó la tierra*, *The Autobiography of a Brown Buffalo*, *The Revolt of the Cockroach People*, and even Miguel Méndez's narrative poem *Los criaderos humanos*. *Pocho*'s historical frame of reference, a period beginning with the Mexican Revolution and extending to the contemporary period, is also that of the first dozen or so Chicano novels. The Mexican Revolution became the zero degree for early Chicano prose; no author attempted, at least in the novel, to probe the historical period prior to that point. In these elements, *Pocho* is obviously the first Chicano novel.

The Fifth Horseman (1974), Villarreal's second novel, broke the temporal frame established by *Pocho* by focusing on Mexico just prior to the 1910 Revolution. The novel creates the mythological, heroic ancestor of the modern Chicano. It is highly significant that, at the end of the novel, its protagonist, an authentic hero of the Revolution, must choose between betraying the revolutionary ideals or becoming an outlaw in the eyes of the victors; he must choose, that is, to remain in the army and reap the benefits plundered from the people, or to remain on the side of the Mexican people and break with the military. He is true to the ideals of the people's revolution, and so must flee Mexico, becoming one of the thousands of refugees who sought temporary asylum in the United States, and who eventually stayed on to become the grandparents of the Chicanos of today. This positive portrayal of the refugee directly responds to the negative image common in Mexico, and thus constitutes a Chicano redefinition of a Mexican stereotype, not just an Anglo-American one. And Villarreal accomplishes it by writing a novel that can only be categorized within the subgenre of novel recognized as the most typically Mexican: the novel of the Revolution. With respect to the Chicano novel, *The Fifth Horseman* effectively expands its time-space, while exploring the Chicano's Mexican roots. As *Pocho* had done previously, Villarreal's second novel opened new possibilities in Chicano fiction.

As important as he is to Chicano literature, Villarreal is still a controversial figure. He openly questions the validity of the term "Chicano literature" itself. Having suffered at the hands of nonliterary critics, he is rightfully skeptical of criticism based on social, political, or racial criteria. He would prefer that his work be judged solely on its merit as literature, and recently *Pocho* has begun to be studied in that light. Yet whatever his opinion about the validity of the term Chicano, and in spite of his refusal to call himself Chicano, it would be difficult to understand Chicano literature without taking into account the work of José Antonio Villarreal.

A first draft of Villarreal's responses to the questionnaire appeared in *Revista Chicano-Riqueña* 4, no. 2 (Spring 1976). The final, revised interview was completed in writing in August 1979.

When and where were you born?

July 30, 1924, in Los Angeles, California. Although I was born in the United States, I am now a Mexican citizen.

Describe your family background and your present situation.

My father, José Heladio Villarreal, was born in the state of Zacatecas, Mexico, in 1882. My mother, Felícitaz Ramírez, was born on the same hacienda as my father. My father was a Villista for seven years. They came to this country in 1921 after the Revolution, bringing three children, one of whom died in Texas shortly after their arrival. They came to California in 1922. The early years through the 1920's were spent in migrating throughout the state, following the seasonal crops. They settled in Santa Clara in 1930, the year that I started school. This is a very important milestone in my life. The fact that my parents decided on Santa Clara to end their odyssey was an important factor in my development as a human being; in short, my posture with respect to Chicano politics, which is important here when talking of the literature, was established during my formative years growing up in the San Francisco Bay region, which was at that time perhaps the most democratic portion of America. It also had to do with my idea of literature—art, because San Francisco was and is a cultural center, and it was difficult to not be aware of this. For that reason, I suppose, I have never and it seems I cannot become excited about Chicano writing as literature. I cannot, as the great majority of Chicano "critics" do, assess this work in a literary sense based on socio-political or socio-economic terms. Quite simply, the work is not that good.

My father and mother had seventeen children, three boys and fourteen girls. Twelve of us survived. My early life was spent strictly within the Mexican peasant culture, speaking Spanish, living in enclaves with our own people. However, after 1930, the situation changed and my life style became one where both Mexican and American cultures were present. My mother died in 1955. My father now lives in Mexico after having spent forty-two years in the United States.

At present I am a resident of Mexico, having been repatriated six years ago. When we did the first interview, in 1975, I was in residence and lecturing in the English Department at the University of Santa Clara. Since then, I have taught at the University of the Americas here in Mexico and at UNAM [Universidad Nacional Autónoma de México]. I have taught English literature and creative writing at the University of Colorado, Boulder, and at the University of Texas at El Paso. I currently teach at the Preparatoria Americana of the American School Foundation in Mexico City. My wife and three children live here in Mexico, where my children attend school.

When did you first begin to write?

I began to write short tales and some poems at about age eight when my vocabulary in English built up to a point where I felt I could communicate.

What kind of books did you read in your formative years?

I read everything that I had access to. It was very difficult in
those years to find reading material until I began using the town
library. I had no direction whatsoever and the only specific direction my reading took was fiction. To this day nonfiction interests me very little.

I read simplified stories from Greek and Roman mythology,
fairy tales, adventure stories such as *Tom Sawyer* and *Huckle-
berry Finn*, *The Bobbsey Twins*, *The Rover Boys*, and such series. I also stumbled on and read such things as *Candide,
Gulliver's Travels, Tom Jones*, and later, through the town library, I read a great deal of historical fiction, Western novels and
Civil War stories. My favorite book in those days was *Toby
Tyler, or Ten Weeks with the Circus*, and I'm ashamed I can't
remember the name of the author, since I must have read the
book at least ten times. At about age eight I discovered that I
could read in Spanish, but we had few books. Until then my
mother had read to us every night or older Mexican people
would tell stories about their tierra [homeland]—the oral tradition has always been very strong in me. But now I began to read
La Opinión, a Mexican newspaper from Los Angeles, to my parents in the evenings. On Sunday, which we received on Monday,
the paper ran cuentos [short stories] and features which kept me
quite busy.

What is the extent of your studies?

My formal education consists of a B.A. in English literature at
the University of California at Berkeley. In addition I have done
graduate work both at UCLA and at Berkeley. Informally, of
course, I have gained an immeasurable amount of education
through self study, that is, reading.

Has formal education helped or hindered you as a writer?

Formal education has, of course, aided me a great deal because it
gave me some direction and through the acquired knowledge of
critical analysis, I was able to take a more objective view of my
own work. Without my formal education I doubt that I would
have been able to write what I have written. For one thing, my

work is full of historical reference. For another, I have been influenced very strongly by those authors I have studied.

Which was the predominant language in your home as a child? Which do you speak more fluently now?

As I stated earlier, during the early years we spoke nothing but Spanish. I did not really learn English until I was in school for at least a year. For a long time after that we still spoke Spanish at home because my parents insisted upon it. Gradually, however, although my mother and father did not know English and would not attempt to learn, we did begin to speak both languages in the house.

Although Spanish can be considered my native idiom, English is my language. I have had my entire education in English and I have been, of course, influenced very much by the English and American writers. Although I have read extensively in Spanish, to this day I find myself much more comfortable reading in English. This holds true also in conversation.

Does Chicano literature have a particular language or idiom?

Here, I think I must qualify my answer, the reason being that to this day I have not seen accepted criteria for what Chicano literature is. I must add also that the term "Chicano" itself is somewhat nebulous in my mind. As for the question, "Has this literature we call Chicano literature a particular language or idiom?" the answer must be *yes*, if only because of the cultural overtones within the narrative or the dialogue and in some cases, of course, the use of Spanish words as well as Mexican philosophy. Pochismos and caló* lend a very specific flavor to the idiom in terms of the culture, but certainly not in any artistic sense. There is nothing new about the use of dialect. It is traditional in letters.

How do you perceive your role as a writer vis-à-vis: (a) the Chicano community or Movement; (b) U.S. society; (c) literature itself?

---

* Pochismos are the words and grammatical changes present in Spanish when English has exercised a strong influence. Caló is slang in Spanish. The frontier between the two usages is not clear among Chicanos.

I believe that as a writer I have contributed much more toward the Chicano community and the Chicano Movement than I would have as a political activist.

As an American writer I find that my role within the American society is a very important one. This is not to indicate that I specifically write for America as I certainly do not write for the Chicano community. What I mean is, my idea, my intent, goes far beyond barriers or limits imposed upon a writer by any social or political movement, or by any chauvinistic design. Yet, although I do not call myself a Chicano writer and I do not think of myself as one, mainly because the name alone implicitly brings out restrictions and inhibitions detrimental to my achieving the aesthetic level I seek, I am not disturbed by being classified as such. This is because I write of my pueblo [people], I share an experience with Chicano writers, and I make every effort to re-create it.

As for literature itself, I think that this is closest to what my role in the artistic community is. Again however, I must say that it is not in the nature of art for art's sake with complete and total disregard for social-economic conditions in the world about us but again more in a universal sense.

What is the place of Chicano literature within U.S. literature?

As I stated above, I think there is a great need for guidelines with respect to what constitutes Chicano literature. Nevertheless, whether Chicano literature is based on the Platonic concept which calls for political and social significance in literature, or whether it is based on the fact that we have Spanish names, or on the fact that we write about Americans or a particular ethnic heritage, it still will remain a part of American literature, or U.S. literature as you call it. It is, as I mentioned, a part of American literature, as the southern writers, as the western writers, and as any regional writers are a part of American literature. In short, I do not believe that there ever will be a Chicano literature that can be separate from American literature; and that makes it directly traceable to English literature. I say this because we write in English for the most part, and when we do not, we translate it into English. We have been educated in English, the major part of our reading history is in English, and despite the fact that we do experiment to a slight degree in bilingual writing, experimentation with language is not new. It has been done. And we are by style, form, and technique extremely traditional and adhere very strongly to the tradition of American letters.

What is the relationship of Chicano literature to Mexican literature?

The relationship here is, of course, much stronger than would be indicated in the answer to the last question. Certainly many of us do read in Spanish or are familiar with Mexican works as well as Latin American works in translation. Because that culture is really so close to ours, we identify and sympathize and retain, which is most important, some facets of that literature. However, Mexican literature is not that different from American literature, excepting for the idiom, because in the development of literature in the western world, Spain contributed to the development of the English novel. Therefore, we cannot deny that Mexican literature is a strong influence on what we create.

Do you perceive yourself and your work as political?

My work is extremely revolutionary in the strictest interpretation of the term. In a sense it is political because it can be used for political purposes, but intrinsically it is not political mainly because the intent is not political. Actually I perceive myself as an artist who does not deny the fact that the artist can be political. Certainly a great many of the Mexican writers are and also, of course, Latin American writers. I make every effort, however, to remove the political side of me from my creative side.

Does the Chicano author have anything in common with the majority group writers? Differences?

I think I answered that already. Chicano writers have everything in common with the majority group writers in America in terms of craft, style, and, as I said, literary tradition. They also have protest or revolutionary tendencies in common. Outside of ethnicity, I find nothing singular to Chicano writing. Certainly it has been thought that because this literature is a literature of protest it makes it unique, and certainly we have a great tradition in America of protest literature.

The only real difference seems to be the difference in ethnic background, the difference in life styles, the difference in the mores of particular groups of people.

***Does Chicano literature share common ground with Black literature?
Differences?***

Here I believe that the most obvious common characteristic
would be that they are both literature of minorities. They both,
of course, are protest literature also. Nevertheless we must understand that some of Steinbeck's work was protest literature,
that some of James T. Farrell's work was protest literature, and
certainly Howard Fast spoke of the same problems in universal
terms.

The main difference as I see it is that Black literature has
had many, many more years to develop and certainly for a long
time Black writers have been classified as American writers.
Langston Hughes, for example, was assessed and looked upon as
an American writer and his work was in keeping with the writers of today's Black literature.

***Is there any relationship with the literature of other Spanish-speaking
groups?***

If we are speaking of Puerto Rican writers, I am sorry I cannot
answer this because I do not know their literature. Nevertheless,
it seems logical that the problems and the goals would be the
same regardless of geographical location and the difference in
situations, that is, the ghetto as against agrarian-type living (although we also have Mexican ghettos).

***Does Chicano literature have a distinctive perspective on life? What
effect does it have on the literature?***

Despite the fact that Chicano activists insist that this is true, I
have seen no evidence of it. There is, of course, the perspective
on life that comes from cultural patterns that have survived
through the transition of life in Mexico to life in America, such
as, for example, the Mexican idea of death or the matriarchal
versus the patriarchal family unit. The difference does not have
any effect on the literature other than subject matter, and the
universality of literature allows for such differences.

***Does Chicano literature improve communication between Chicanos
and Anglo-Americans?***

During the early years of the Movement, when Chicano literature emerged almost as a political necessity, it did nothing to
improve communication between Chicanos and Anglo-Americans—in fact it was detrimental to such improvement. In this,
what I call the first phase of what can well be a subgenre in
America, it was obvious that the intent was not only to create
an awareness of inequities, an awareness of our Mexican
heritage, and motivate our young people to stand up and be
heard, but also to generate hatred and incite racism, a combination that very quickly discouraged the Anglo-American community from reading through our work, much less sympathizing.
We have, by my way of thinking, now entered a second phase of
the "artistic" effort of the Movement with such works as Rudolfo Anaya's *Bless Me, Ultima*, some poetry, and even going
back to Galarza's *Barrio Boy*, assimilationistic as it may be, and
that is not entirely bad. The literature is taking on a degree of
respect and credibility. Indications are that political rhetoric and
harangue, used to great advantage in the early years, is no longer
necessary and out of fashion, and I see the day when our young
people will develop and create a literature with universal overtones. A case in point is Ron Arias and his novel *The Road to
Tamazunchale*, a little jewel of a novel about Mexicans—a fantasy, and again in the tradition of American letters. The book, in
Mr. Arias's words, deals with "an old Mexican bookseller who is
dying and bravely assaults death in a humorous way." That, by
the way, is the only thing Mexican in it. It is a work that can
very well appeal to English-language readers regardless of where
they might be. This to me is very encouraging, since I have been
waiting many years for us to begin to make a real contribution
to literature, expressly because we are capable of creating art. Dr.
Ralph Guzmán said to me once that we could not afford the luxury of attempting to create art and to this I say it is not a luxury,
it is an obligation, and more importantly, a responsibility for our
raza.

In short, these latter works (and I will include *Pocho*) can
improve communication and understanding between the Mexican-American community and other ethnic groups, including
the dominant portion of American society. Intelligent readers
will much more easily empathize through the acquisition of information and education with respect to our pueblo through intelligent and artistic presentation of who and what we are. The
insulting, blatant, cursi [bad-taste] propaganda which is unfortunately expounded in most of our writings, be it poetry or

prose, will largely remain unread except by our people, who already know about our situation.

Does Chicano literature reevaluate, attack, or subvert the value system of the majority society? Is it a revolutionary literature? Thematically? Technically?

Chicano literature thus far has attacked the value system of the majority society. To a certain extent it has reevaluated it, but in no way has it subverted it.

Yes, it is revolutionary; in every sense of the word it is revolutionary, but only thematically. Technically there is nothing new with the slight exceptions I mentioned above.

What problems have you encountered in publishing? Were they racially founded?

I have encountered every problem a beginning writer faces during my early years. Even today, with two novels in print and with a number of credits in national magazines, I am not sure that I will be published. I have recently finished a novel which is beginning to make the rounds of the publishing houses and at this point I can only hope for the best.

As to whether these problems are racially founded I must answer absolutely not. We must understand that publishing is a business—there are no ideals involved, and to a publisher the writer, regardless of race or creed, is a producer of, hopefully, a saleable product. Publishers operate on the law of supply and demand and if they can make money it does not matter to them what your color is, what you believe in or do not believe in.

Are Chicanos at a disadvantage in trying to practice the art of writing?

Only if they do not have a commitment to the art. All writers are at a certain disadvantage, and the greatest disadvantage is an economic one. The only disadvantage that a Chicano writer would have outside of the economic one mentioned is one that *any* writer would have—perhaps not enough talent. The problems of the writer are really the same no matter what his ethnic background is. Writing is a lonely life, and through modern history, a writer before he achieves success is by definition outside of his society—at odds with his society simply because he wants to be a writer. Therefore, unless he makes a lot of money, for success is measured by that yardstick in our day, he is considered weird.

What are the most outstanding qualities of Chicano literature? Weaknesses?

There is really only one outstanding quality of Chicano literature and that is that it is informing the vast majority of Americans that there are Americans who look different, live differently, and who have been lost to the rest of America, except the great agrarian corporations. Other than that there is very little outstanding. Much of our prose is little better than mediocre. Much of our poetry is even worse, and the only area where the output is first rate, because there is so little of it, is drama. We are very new and have a long way to go, and I think it disastrous if we do not admit this.

One of the greatest weaknesses comes from the fact that until now we have had no real criticism. Until now the word "literature" has been abused and for that reason I do not use it, preferring the term "Chicano writing." This comes from the fact mentioned earlier that the quality of a work has been assessed almost strictly for political expediency. I am not saying that this was not necessary at one time but merely that if we are to have a literature the time has come for a redefining of Chicano literature as literature, and, as literature, still important in enhancing the political arm of the Movement.

What are the milestones so far in Chicano literature?

The moment of awareness that we write about ourselves must be a milestone, because it was not the beginning. The only other milestone is today when we are on the threshold, both in literature and in criticism, of transcending the commonplace and going on to more honest creativity.

What is the future of Chicano literature: distinctiveness, or the de-emphasis of the distinctive characteristics?

It should or, rather, must be understood that a literature is not created overnight, and that is what we contend we did. Anything written by a Spanish-surnamed person is considered literature no matter how incompetent the writer or how bad the work. I know of no "Chicano critic" who has undertaken a comprehensive study of this genre and repudiated a major portion of it as pure nonsense. This is partly due to the familia [family] concept, but also because if it should turn out that there is no such thing as Chicano Literature, many people would be out of employment; university departments in Chicano Studies and degrees up to the doctoral in this literature would not exist. And we all know how many of us find a soft billet and a particular amount of income from this—we have many reasons for propagating this activity. This is not to say that a number of good works have not come of it, yet the literature is no different from the rest of American literature in that we seem to be in an extremely low phase in American literature. I see nothing in American prose that I consider great since Faulkner. Of course, time, the ultimate measure, will tell. To answer your question, I do not see one piece of Chicano work that will be read fifty years from now except in college courses. Its philosophy, socioeconomic, makes it a temporal phenomenon. Its cultural subject matter will make it valuable to historians and sociologists. I see it falling into the category of folklore, costumbrismo, if you will, very much like Western Americana. My wish and hope is that Chicano writers, and the probability here lies with the young people, will one day transcend the idea of writing about the plight of the Chicano in purely explicit terms and encompass humanity. Then our talent, our artistic potential—which no one can deny our people have—will blossom to allow us to stand among the great writers, regardless of language.

Who are the leaders among Chicano writers, and why?

Writers have no leaders. As I said earlier, writing is a very intimate and a very lonely thing and a writer, if he is a writer and retains his integrity, does not think in those terms.

Rolando Hinojosa

In 1972 Rolando Hinojosa was awarded the Quinto Sol Prize, the most prestigious literary prize in the field of Chicano letters at that time, for his book of short prose pieces *Estampas del Valle y otras obras*. Before that, he had published under the pseudonym P. Galindo, his "Mexican American Devil's Dictionary" (*El Grito* 6, no.3 [Spring 1973]: 41–53), an excellent example of his satirical wit. However, it was *Estampas* that converted him into one of the most important writers among Chicano authors, and his eloquence made him one of the most sought-after speakers. A few years after *Estampas* was published, portions of a new work in progress began to appear in different literary journals. At first glance they seemed to be continuations of *Estampas* both in form and in content, but no one expected that the next book would bring even higher honors to Hinojosa. Then, in 1976, La Casa de las Américas, the Cuban publishing house, announced the awarding of its prestigious prize for the best novel of the year to Rolando Hinojosa for *Klail City y sus alredededores*, focusing international attention on the author and on Chicano literature in general.

His style—precise, clean, with not a word of excess; his ironic and subtle humor, so well within the Hispanic tradition; his undeniably popular and regional themes, incarnating universal verities while portraying faithfully his South Texas neighbors; and a persistent, welcome understatement—all blend to make Hinojosa's work unmistakable, and a joy to read. Not so clear as yet to many readers is that through the brief episodes, the short stories, and even the poetry into which his works are structured, he is slowly and unconventionally creating a novel on a grand scale. The pieces obviously interrelate, in the manner of a mosaic; eventually they will reveal the vast pattern of a tightly interlocked whole.

Hinojosa the man is the reflection of his work: eloquent, lucid, intelligent, sure of his origins and goals, ironic, sometimes

sharp and critical, but with the constant good humor of a man who knows human nature and loves people without idealizing them. His labors on various national committees for higher education prove the esteem of his peers. At this time he is the chairman of Chicano Studies at Minnesota University. In 1978 *Korean Love Songs*, the versified third installment of the novel, appeared, and he is now working on the fourth.

Rolando Hinojosa completed his questionnaire in the spring of 1975. It was published in *Latin American Literary Review* 5, no. 10 (Spring–Summer 1977) and appears here with only minor revisions. It should be noted that while the interviews have been reproduced as the authors presented them, allowing each one to choose his/her form of expression, as I explained in the introduction, Hinojosa's case is special. He is the only writer to send me two versions of the interview, one in Spanish and one in English.

When and where were you born?

January 21, 1929, in Mercedes, Texas.

Describe your family background and your present situation.

My father's family came to the Valley with the Escandón colonists in the 1740's. The family settled in Ciudad Mier, Tamaulipas, which is in the upper part of the Lower Río Grande Valley. Many Hinojosas still live there and many of us within a 200–300 mile radius of it on both sides of the Río Grande.

My mother was of Illinois-Mississippi stock. She came to the Valley as an infant and therefore was completely bilingual, as was my father. My Anglo grandfather fought for the South in the Civil War; he died in 1927 and so I never got to know him.

My father—like so many other Chicanos—was in the Mexican Revolution. He started out by selling horses, moved on to munitions, and, through friendships, became a lieutenant colonel in the Finance Corps. He was in and out of Mexico for a long time while my mother kept home and family together on the American side. My father was quite liberal personally and yet he backed Almazán against Avila Camacho in 1940—figure that one out.

My mother had been a teacher as had her mother before her; of the five children in our family, four of us went into teaching and we're still in the profession.

At present I'm teaching Chicano literature; I hold an appointment as professor of Chicano Studies and American Studies.

When did you first begin to write?

I think I started writing in high school; at least there is some evidence of it in the Mercedes High School library. The pieces form part of a collection called *Creative Bits* which were selected annually by the English teachers. They were written in English, of course. Most of what followed was also in English and all of it bad, sloppy, and stilted.

What kind of books did you read in your formative years?

My first schooling was in a neighborhood school paid for by subscription and run by a Mexican national. We were all there, some 50–60 of us reciting aloud, working on penmanship, arithmetic, and, somehow, reading. I can still remember the cover of the third year reader: *Poco a poco* [Little by Little]; it shows a young boy in short pants on his way to school.

I read everything that came my way and, being a sickly child for some 2–3 years there, I could read all day if I wanted to and I did.

Formative years? The very first things I read were pulps in Spanish, usually translations of American and French novels and short stories. Reading was something that everyone did in our family and, according to my family, I taught myself to read. That's probably true.

In junior and senior high school I read what I could, usually at home. Nothing systematic in my reading or in the selection, although my leaning was toward nineteenth- and twentieth-century English and American authors. I have no advice to offer on the matter of reading, but I don't see how one can expect to write if one hasn't read anything. The Army was a good place for reading and every post library was well stocked. At the University of Texas it was the same thing: I worked in the reserve room and this was like choosing a rabbit to guard the lettuce patch. The reserve reading room was full of books on history, biographies, the classics in translation, and M.A. and Ph.D. theses, horrendous stuff that. But, as I said, nothing systematic. I'd stick with an author until I either tired of him or ran through the entire work. I didn't read the Russians, the Germans, or the Scandinavians until later. This may have been a good thing; I was ready for them then.

At Texas I read Mexican and Hispanic-American literature and nineteenth-century Peninsular for my major. I waltzed out with a baccalaureate degree and with some 47 advanced hours and never heard of Borges; that should give you some idea of the age and direction of the faculty at the time. I did read Roberto Arlt at Texas and, years later, when I mentioned him to some Argentine colleagues, they laughed. Arlt's stuff is being published again— he died in 1942—and this should feed and clothe some literary critics and their families . . . So, in short, a lot of reading and of a varied nature. During this time there was a need to write, but nothing came of it. I can't recall talking to anyone *about* literature; that came later in graduate school. I still can't *talk* about it . . . I prefer to read and write.

What is the extent of your studies?

I do have a Ph.D., but my doctor tells me that with proper rest and care I should live to a ripe old adage. We'll put that down as the proverbial pun.

Has formal education helped or hindered you as a writer?

Formal education, in my case, has been an advantage: I tend to be wary of excesses in language or direction. Literature has so many good examples to draw from and so many bad ones to avoid that it is just a matter of following one and avoiding the other. Didacticism, totalitarian themes, boxed-in theses, and set propositions are intolerable and inexcusable for the serious writer of fiction and nonfiction, or of criticism for that matter. If my formal education hindered me, it must have been unconsciously . . . once you hit that trail you're on uncharted ground. No hay vueltas. [There is no turning back.]

Which was the predominant language in your home as a child? Which do you speak more fluently now?

At first, when I was growing up, we spoke Spanish. I was the youngest in my family and as my brothers and sisters grew up, it became English and Spanish. In my neighborhood, el pueblo mexicano [Mexican town], and in the others, el rincón del diablo [the devil's corner], el rebaje [the pit], la colonia Garza [Garza district], it was Spanish. Strictly. The movie house, the news-paper, the radio, and, of course, the school I mentioned earlier. I must have been eleven or twelve when I first spoke to an Anglo boy or girl, but there must be over a million Chicanos in Texas who can say the same thing, so one shouldn't stress this as a telling point in a Chicano's life—not in mine anyway. My early life, indeed up to seventeen when I enlisted, my daily life was really lived, for the most part, in Spanish. This comes out in my writing and it's no state secret. I speak both languages with equal fluency. But you're asking more fluently, so it's a tie, al-though I prefer to write fiction in Spanish and have for the most part.

Does Chicano literature have a particular language or idiom?

Chicano literature is written in Spanish, in English, in Spanish and English, in some of the Pachuco caló, and usually colored by the regionalism which may be due to the author's background. To date, the essay is about the only genre where English pre-dominates over Spanish. This is due to the essayists' training in higher education. Poetry and drama are written in one language or the other or in both; it may be that the use of both languages is what the Chicano language or idiom is all about. Vaya usted a saber. [Who can say?] The novel and the short story are written in one or the other, but not in both, to date. I am committed to writing in Spanish, although if something comes out in English, then I must write it in that language. I really have no control on the choice of language; I have enough trouble trying to write without worrying about which language. But, as you know, I pre-fer Spanish.

Examples of the contemporary Chicano novel and short fic-tion reveal a diversity of language: Rivera's . . . *y no se lo tragó la tierra* in Spanish; Anaya's *Bless Me, Ultima*, English with a few Spanish locutions; Vásquez and Villarreal, English; Méndez's *Peregrinos de Aztlán*, Spanish and Chicano passages which are a tour de force. The short stories are probably divided between En-glish and Spanish, but if they come from outside of Texas, say New Mexico, Colorado, or California, it's a safe bet they'll be in English. Philip Ortego calls Chicano literature a binary phenom-enon with reference to the use of English and Spanish, but I'm sure he'll get an argument on that point from many quarters. He'll get no argument from me; I don't object to his use of it.

How do you perceive your role as a writer vis-à-vis: (a) the Chicano community or Movement; (b) U.S. society; (c) literature itself?

My role as a writer . . . I've not given much thought to this one so I'll probably ramble. My role—if that is what it is—is to write. There are some eternal verities and anyone who writes wants to state them for himself and for his time. In my home state there is something called the Texas Academy of Arts and Letters—I may not have the title right, but it's that type of thing, and some of the people in it are Larry King, Larry McMurtry, Bill Moyers, and so on. Now, I don't believe that they as Texans have read Chicano literature, and so their view of Texas is lacking in one big respect. That aside, they, as Texans, are writing about other verities in Texas and they certainly know what they are writing about. I write about Belken County [a fictional county in South Texas] and its people . . . who knows them as well as I do? No one; my role is to write and then to try to get the stuff published; in the meantime, I keep writing. I'm not setting myself as an example; I see myself as a writer, and, as I have just said, I try to get published.

What is the place of Chicano literature within U.S. literature?

I don't know what the place is—or that there's *one* place. Some universities use my *Estampas* (the English version by Gustavo Valadez) in English departments; others in the Department of Spanish and Portuguese or Modern Languages or Ethnic Studies. Some use the writing as just an extension of Spanish American literature. This is what's happening to Chicano literature; it's being read in the universities for the most part. It is read outside, of course, but at this stage, Chicano literature is being discussed in universities through symposia, colloquia, seminars, etc. This, I suspect, is due to the dual language aspect. Maybe the succeeding Chicano generation of writers will write in English and thus take a place in U.S. literature, if that's what the author wants. It could probably stand alone, again because of the language.

What is the relationship of Chicano literature to Mexican literature?

Chicano literature's relationship to Mexican literature would have to depend on the Chicano author. The first consideration is the language, but Chicano literature does not restrict itself to Spanish, as you know, so it depends on the author and his roots. These may be superficial in some cases and deep in others, but the Chicano author will usually write about the Chicano's life in his native land, the United States. Mexico would probably never be the main locale of a novel—unless a Chicano sets it there and writes about a Chicano's life in Mexico—the point is that Chicano literature is not Mexican literature . . . Mexican literature may serve as an educational background, but not, necessarily, as the base. It is merely one of the many elements of the present Chicano writers.

Do you perceive yourself and your work as political?

Some of my work may be perceived as political; I perceive it as my work and let others perceive it as they wish. Some say it isn't political—maybe they mean not political enough . . . who knows? I can't stop to worry over this aspect of my work. I do know one thing—it isn't didactic; my experience in reading political literature is that it tends to be didactic and, hence, intramural. The last thing that literature should find itself is between walls—no matter who builds them.

Does the Chicano author have anything in common with the majority group writers? Differences?

I guess that by majority group writers you mean non-Chicanos . . . I can't say Anglo because where does that put Roth or Bellow, who write in most instances of the Jewish experience in the United States? Or where does this put Salinger or Heller, whose characters may or may not be Jewish? So I say non-Chicano because I certainly couldn't include Richard Wright or Hughes or Baldwin as Anglos . . . Is the last one a majority writer? And let's see . . . there's Robert Penn Warren, John Hershey, certainly; Capote . . . Katherine Ann Porter . . . now they are Anglo, but I don't see them as Anglos or as anything else . . . they're writers. It would be ridiculous for me to write as if I were an American Jew . . . or as if I were a Kentuckian or a Tennessean . . . I could write about sports, I guess, since that has little to do with the reality of daily living . . . But to write of Mississippi? The Philadelphia Main Line? I wouldn't know where to begin. That's better left to people who know what they are writing about. You seldom see a serious writer writing out of his element; that's for television and for popular magazines. Do I sound snobbish? Petulant? I'm neither . . . it is a matter of established fact that a writer had damn well better know what he's writing about or it won't be good writing. The writer should know or sense or suspect when he's fooling around or when he's on shaky ground. It may be that someone may think this is medieval in that it begs for the shoemaker to stick to his last . . . well, how many novels did O'Neill write? How many plays did Faulkner produce? I guess that Cervantes has got to be the best example of a writer who tried drama and poetry for years before he found himself in his novel. Don't forget the Byzantine type he came up with in the *Persiles* was written by the same right hand that wrote both parts of the *Quijote*.

Now . . . the Chicano writer who decries his lack of popularity or of recognition had better decide to do something else with his life. This is not a Spanish-speaking country for the most part; if he wants recognition then he better sell his wares to Mexico, Central and South America, and Spain. If he does and if he does it well, good for him, but will he still be a Chicano? Perhaps . . . who's to know?

Does Chicano literature share common ground with Black literature? Differences?

Black writers, majority group writers? I think I've said it all or as much as I could. I think I understand and appreciate their writing, but then I also think I understand and appreciate *Dead Souls* by Gogol and *Vidas secas* by Graciliano Ramos, the Northeast Brazilian. Writers are writers. Look, I've never been to Germany and yet when Böll speaks of "the Beast" in *Billiards at Half Past Nine*, I understand . . . I'll say I do . . . It's loud and clear as a bell. When a Black says he suffers, I see and understand. When a Black critic tells me I don't *feel*, then I must tell that critic, Black or not, that if I don't *feel* then *that* is the writer's fault. Pure and simple.

Is there any relationship with the literature of other Spanish-speaking groups?

I don't mean to be either picky or cute here, but do you mean an affinity for and with other Spanish-speaking groups? In the U.S.? I'm very interested in the Chicano urban experience in Los Angeles and elsewhere . . . the urban Chicano . . . When the Chicanos from Chicago, Gary, Hammond, Detroit, or the 75,000 in Iowa, or the Chicanos in El Paso, Phoenix, Denver, Kansas City, Wichita, come out with their work then I'll begin to see what Chicano literature is like there—in those places. The Puerto Ricans? Those who have never been to the Island? That's a coming thing. And how about the young Cubans who came here with their parents in 1959 and after? It will be interesting to see what acculturation or assimilation takes place . . . At present there is a Chicano-Boricua* publication—the *Revista Chicano-Riqueña*—out of Indiana University put out by Luis Davila, a Chicano, and Nicolás Kanellos, a Boricua. The relationships are new, and, once again, on an individual basis. I'm in touch with Manuel Ramos Otero, a Boricua who lives and works in New York, and he in turn will put me in contact with others and I will let them know of others and so on.

I have read of the Brazilian interest in Chicano literature. I've seen some general critical reviews of Chicano literature in Mexico . . . not much. The relationships are just beginning, that is, the formal relationships. The blood has been there for years.

Does Chicano literature have a distinctive perspective on life? What effect does it have on the literature?

I would say that Chicano literature has its own perspectives on life, but then so does any other literature. The uninformed say that the themes and perspectives of Chicano literature are restricted to agricultural settings. Well now, that type of assertion is naïve, self-revealing, and parochial . . . Chicano literature is like varietal wine . . . The effect of variety is that it tends to present many shades and hues of the central theme: our life here, in our native land.

Does Chicano literature improve communication between Chicanos and Anglo Americans?

---

* Boricua is an emic term for Puerto Ricans, derived from Borinque, the Taíno name for the island.

It may, but I've seen little evidence of literature teaching anybody anything other than the way people live. I don't believe that one should write with the idea of communicating . . . It probably boils down to this: communication is a personal thing . . . it is based on personal relationships not on government edict. I was in my teens when World War II was grinding down and I still recall reading about Eisenhower's non-fraternization rule . . . he was a cynical old man . . . through his knowledge of history he knew full well that it was unenforceable and yet he made a big show of it to the so-called "folks back home." The first GI, and who knows what color he was, and his fraulein were already communicating before Ike's prattle . . . I don't know if literature improves communication and as for teaching . . . well, it doesn't appear as if we have learned to employ all that we know.

Does Chicano literature reevaluate, attack, or subvert the value system of the majority society? Is it a revolutionary literature? Thematically? Technically?

All serious literature—and some funny literature is serious stuff, right?—anyway, all serious literature usually assesses our present life. The author tells his tale, but there is an assessment, an evaluation, yes, perhaps a reevaluation of society. It may also attack or subvert certain elements of that society or bring them to light, and this depends on style and manner—satire, wit, sarcasm—or the chosen genre—prose, poetry, the essay, and so on. Revolutionary? Yes and even totalitarian as is some criticism by Chicano critics. However, when someone offers a writer a chance to publish and stipulates that the writing must be socially and politically relevant, then the writer isn't given much of a chance to be creative, is he? But let me switch here . . . I think that Chicano literature is as technically revolutionary as the Chicano writer is able—or dares—or cares—or knows . . . In *Estampas*, I wrote a novel—in four parts . . . each part has a different title and three of the parts are different in structure from each other. Are you familiar with it? *Estampas* is different from *Cosas* and both are different from *Rafa*. *Vidas* resembles *Estampas*, but that's all, a resemblance. I still hold to the word *novel* in the original intent of *novella, algo nuevo* [something new], something dynamic, ever changing . . . And yet I hear *Estampas* referred to as *cuentos* or *vignettes* or short pieces or as a *new* genre, for crying out loud. Oh, it's true all right . . . some teachers debated about it in a conference in New Orleans . . . what a waste of time. *Estampas* is a novel and that's it. There's a bit of fooling around with time and space, but the plots are there—there's no novelistic statute that says I have to end a novel in one tome or two . . . I have just finished another novel—you have the manuscript [*Klail City y sus alredededores*]—and I'm starting another one—I use epistles, dialogues, monologues, a prologue here and there at the beginning of each division and anything that can help me tell my story—and that is it—anything that can help you to tell your story is one of the keys to writing. If my multiple use of forms helps other writers, fine, but they had better come up with a plot for the characters or it won't go anywhere . . . It comes to that, as always; one must have something to say irrespective of the form.

What problems have you encountered in publishing? Were they racially founded?

My problem is that of any Chicano writer: the dearth of independent Chicano publishing houses . . . and since I prefer to write in Spanish I must rely on translations.

    Racial problems in publishing? Who knows? And how is one to prove that? Anglo publishing houses would probably publish if money could be made by publishing a Chicano novel . . . in English. Money . . . Lionel Trilling, I think it was, said that money made for more fluid society . . . I think he called it the great leveler . . . I think of it as a lever . . . una palanca . . . I'm firm in this, if money were to be made, Chicano literature in English would be published . . . mine? In Spanish? I've not tried to sell it as yet . . .

Are Chicanos at a disadvantage in trying to practice the art of writing?

Only if they have nothing to say. A writer—even when he's not writing it down—is thinking and that's working at writing. It isn't writing, but it's working at it. If one's eight-to-five job is so demanding that one can't even think about writing, that's a tragedy, not a disadvantage. The main disadvantage certainly is finding no Chicano publishing outlets . . . but if by disadvantage you mean economic disadvantage then the answer is yes . . . Es una desgracia. [It's a disgrace.]

What are the most outstanding qualities of Chicano literature? Weaknesses?

The weaknesses of Chicano literature must always lie with the authors. If the author is not able to appreciate or to be aware of the universality of the Chicano's life, then what can one expect? Pearl Buck's *Good Earth* was set in China, certainly, but it went beyond the Great Wall . . . Chicano literature should be treated by Chicano writers in that light . . . beyond our own walls, whatever they may be. Some well-meaning people fret that Anglos may not receive a good impression of us—their own words—in some of the episodes of *Estampas*. They do not recognize that their reservations are weaknesses. That's taking your hat off and going to see the boss to say, "See what I have here? I'm being a good boy." If the Chicano writer tries to please that part of the Chicano public, he's in trouble. He's also in trouble if he tries to please any one special sector of the Chicano population. The writer should write the best he can; if he has weaknesses in his writing they'll show up soon enough. Chicano literature in all its phases and through all its genres may be a reflection of the Chicano and his life; however, what weaknesses there are must be leveled toward the authors who couldn't—or wouldn't—present the verities (as they honestly saw them) of all Chicanos: rural, urban, young, old, good, bad, sick, well, at home, at work, in love . . .

Outstanding qualities? The presence of the Chicano and his endurance—write about that and, at the risk of being intramural, you will have captured, through literature, the most outstanding qualities of the Chicano's life. In passing, one of the weaknesses is the lack of a truly first-rate work of Chicano literary critique by Chicanos.

What are the milestones so far in Chicano literature?

Number one? Quinto Sol's First Annual Literary Award to Tomás Rivera . . . No question about it. The revised edition of *El Espejo*, a first-rate job that . . . you'll find Rivera, Anaya, Elizondo, Alurista, Montoya, Portillo, Romano, Padilla, todos [all of them] . . . Yes, that *Espejo* was a good one . . . The Aztlán series out of UCLA . . . Anaya's *Ultima*, for many reasons . . . many issues of *El Grito* . . . Méndez's *Peregrinos* may be a language milestone. More to the point, what the original group at Quinto Sol did and what the subsequent publications did to foment and to bring Chicano literature to our schools and universities . . . those are the milestones . . . The next and future milestone is for us to publish in Mexico and in the rest of Hispanic America . . . no te parece [don't you agree]?

What is the future of Chicano literature: distinctiveness, or the de-emphasis of the distinctive characteristics?

The future depends on a number of points: the Chicano writers and their productivity; Chicano publishing houses and distributors; the Chicano reading public; and—to another large degree—its continued dissemination and analysis by our academic colleagues. Like it or not, these points, and others, are wedded and welded to each other.

Another point certainly worth mentioning is the future of Chicano literature written in Spanish here in the United States. It just may be—and I've touched on this a couple of times during our conversation—that we who write in Spanish may just have to submit our work to Mexican publishers. Their distribution may work out just fine in Mexico, but it would be largely restricted in this country to college and university bookstores . . . for the most part anyway . . . At any rate, that's our problem and we have to solve it from within.

On the matter of distinctiveness or de-emphasis of the distinctive characteristics . . . that does sound pedantic, doesn't it? . . . well, I can't see any change in either direction, since worthy literature usually touches and affects so-called universal themes; Chicano literature, like any other, deals with man and his existence . . . If you mean setting, the agricultural motif, I don't think that's worth serious debate . . . Rivera treats it in one way and Raymond Barrio in another . . . some of my characters are rural, that's for sure, but not strictly agricultural . . . what I'm trying to say here is that the land is a characteristic, but not the only one . . . just as one cannot—should not—look upon cold weather in Russia as a distinctive characteristic of Russian literature . . . it's what happens to people in the crop fields or in the cold or wherever that matters. The Chicano lives and works in the agricultural fields, in an Inland Steel factory, on the Ford Motor Company assembly lines, out in the Coachella Valley *surcos* [furrows], and so on . . . the Chicano is everywhere . . . a matter of change . . . the Chicano is an American citizen—*para comenzar* [to begin with]—and as such we're not all migratory workers either. One main thing on this, the migrant experience is still going on for some of us and still could be into the twenty-first century. Although this particular Chicano experience has been told adequately and expertly, it isn't over yet.

There are many other avenues to explore, and Chicano writers will get to them as time goes on. And, as time goes on, the writing will most certainly be in English . . . this is true in the urban areas already. This may not be the case in poetry, where both languages are mingled quite successfully in the case of Alurista and Montoya and others such as Ricardo Sánchez and Abelardo.

The distinctive characteristic is our presence in our own native land as people who continue to maintain an identity that will not disappear any time soon. That this presence will continue to produce Chicano writers is something no one knows. I suspect it will; it has up to now and I see nothing that will cause it to completely change or to completely disappear.

For a' that and a' that, our continued presence and the daily pressure of the majority population will probably also cause Chicano literature to be recognized as such by Chicanos and non-Chicanos alike . . . ni modo [there's nothing you can do about it]!

Who are the leaders among Chicano writers, and why?

Leaders? I would probably embarrass them if I called them that . . . At any rate, there would have to be a division because of direction and genre . . . I'll get to language later. In the essays field there's Arturo Madrid, Raymond Padilla, Salvador Alvarez, Romano, of course, Juan Gómez-Q., and—somewhere, since he writes fiction, criticism, and essays, Philip Ortego. There are many more, but what is important here is that all of them write about Chicanos from a Chicano perspective.

When it comes to poetry it's an entirely different matter— Sergio Elizondo's *Perros y antiperros* is a standard, but then so are Abelardo's and Ricardo Sánchez's works. Tino V. Villanueva and Flaco Maldonado certainly deserve the highest of recognition, and what could I possibly add to credit Alurista's long list of fine, sensitive work? Now, I'm not convinced that Chicano poetry is better than Chicano prose, but Chicano poetry—like any other poetry—gets to the heart of the matter quicker than any other writing . . . a matter of what Emerson called "the force of few words." I imagine that this will hold as long as we're fortunate to have poets and poetry.

As for prose fiction, I guess that could be divided by language. Although I don't know if one should make that separation or distinction, anyway. José Antonio Villarreal's *Pocho*, in English, was the first Chicano novel I ever read. As you know, he has since followed that with *The Fifth Horseman*. Anaya's *Ultima*, also in English, is in its third printing, so that means that someone is buying it out there. He also has a second novel out, *Heart of Aztlán*, but I haven't heard from Rudy lately so I don't know how that's coming along. I don't know how successful Oscar Zeta Acosta's *Autobiography of a Brown Buffalo* and his *The Revolt of the Cockroach People* have been, but I keep running across them in university bookstores wherever I go. There's Ricardo Vásquez, who wrote *Chicano*; it's now in paperback, too, by the way . . . he has received mixed reviews on that work. Ron Arias has just completed a manuscript which Tomás Rivera read and deemed it as a solid piece of work. I'm name-dropping here, of course, and I guess the reason is that it's embarrassing for all concerned to single somebody out as the leader or whatever. That being the case, I mention those writers and their works which set a varied standard for Chicano prose fiction in English. As for those who stand out as long prose fiction writers in Spanish, there's Tomás Rivera, who is now rewriting his second novel, *La casa grande*, and Miguel Méndez M., who published *Peregrinos de Aztlán*. There are also any number of Chicanos who write and publish short fiction in Spanish and English; Rivera and Méndez must be included in the short fiction group as well. The list is a long one, but it should be longer.

Drama is a big part of the Chicano scene and among those who write it are Carlos Morton, Luis Valdez, Estela Portillo, and, lately, Alurista. What is exciting here are the touring companies; I've seen them in Oregon, Iowa, California, and here, in Minnesota. A lot of it is intramural, but it's good . . . Solid. It's funny as hell, sometimes . . . total theater, really; music, dance, blackouts, and, often, fast-moving . . . there's also a lot of motion on stage. And, as usual with small, intimate companies, audience participation.

I haven't mentioned literary criticism here, and maybe I should. Juan Rodríguez is highly trained and he's training a number of the new generation in La Jolla. Roberto Cantú of *Mester* and *Escolios* is also a serious critic. There's Herminio Ríos, Brito, and Francisco Jiménez from Santa Clara; Francisco also publishes short prose pieces.

I guess you could call them leaders . . . I was in Chicago recently and someone called me a precursor, for crying out loud. He meant well, but it does give one pause . . .

Sergio Elizondo

In *Perros y antiperros* (1972) and *Libro para batos y chavalas chicanas* (1977) Sergio Elizondo combines traditional meters, popular language, social criticism, and a well-defined dualistic vision of the world into a positive vs. negative struggle. There is no ambiguity in his world view: the battle line is the image of the railroad tracks, and no quarter will be given to the inhabitants on the other side. The poet in *Perros* disclaims proprietary rights to the poetry, declaring himself simply the singer of tales related to him by Chicanos, a true *trovador* who wanders the geographic, historical, and spiritual realm of Aztlán, listening to the people and spreading the news of the common struggle, with an openly didactic purpose, as the author admits in his interview. The later book displays a shift to a more personal tone, especially in the superb love poetry, though a goodly portion of that collection too is dedicated to social protest.

Technically, Elizondo's poetry reveals his keen ear for sounds and rhythm, a narrative tendency, and an at times ambiguous imagery. The latter can only be understood in the context of a system of evolving motifs within the complete text. However, his clear "ideology" is successfully transposed into popular terms through his knowledge and manipulation of traditional poetics. The result is poetry meant to be read aloud, that aspires to be popular, but in reality is highly stylized, in the best sense of the word. The process is not new in hispanic letters, by any means, two examples being *Martín Fierro* and *Pedro Páramo*; there are even some who would say that *El Cid* itself would be another. The cultured poet garners the cries of the people, distills an essential sentiment, synthesizes a common language, and creates for the *pueblo* its song. The key is, as always, in doing it well; Elizondo is an expert.

Elizondo wrote the answers to the questionnaire in October 1978.

When and where were you born?

April 24, 1930, in El Fuerte, Sinaloa.

Describe your family background and your present situation.

My father was the superintendent of public schools in El Fuerte
and Ahome in Sinaloa, and also in the states of Sonora and Baja
California, between 1911 and 1942; apparently he was employed
as a professor of education in Monterrey, Nuevo León, Mexico.
My parents had seven children; six are still living. I am the second youngest. My mother died in 1935, my father in 1942. I suspect that my father was one of the initiators of the Mexican
Revolution. He served during the whole Revolution, reaching
the grade of colonel in one of Francisco Villa's factions com-
manded by General Juan Banderas in Sinaloa, where, after their
defeat, he decided to stay.

I arrived in this country in a strange way, as a wetback. It
seems that at the start of the Revolution, my father, professor
Cristino Santiago Elizondo, brought his mother and three sisters
to El Paso, Texas, away from the violence in Monterrey, Nuevo
León, where they lived. They never saw him again. In 1950,
when I was studying in the Sinaloa Normal School, one of my
aunts placed an ad with a Tampico radio station—she was looking for Don Cristino. His *compadre*, Ernesto Felix, of Ahome,
heard the ad and wrote to Macaria Elizondo, my aunt, who was
living in Harlingen, Texas, and at the same time he sent her my
name and address. She wrote me and I responded. They sent me
fifty dollars for the fare to Brownsville, Texas. I tried to get a
thirty-day pass from the U.S. Consulate in Mazatlán, but they
refused. I still remember the Consul's name—Mr. Metcalf, god
bless him. Anyway, he advised me to go to Matamoros, Tamaulipas, telling me that maybe once I was closer to Brownsville
they might let me cross over. Well, those S.O.B's wouldn't let
me pass. I waited 45 days in Matamoros, waiting, waiting, also
dead from hunger. One day Macaria's granddaughter, Evangelina
Martínez, took me to the border, and when the car stopped at
the crossing, the guard just passed us through. Incredible! I
didn't want to enter illegally and I returned to Matamoros. Eva
left me twenty dollars with which I ate a few days. I was down
to ten dollars, and one day, after giving it a lot of thought, I de-

cided to cross. I paid a *patero*, a character with a small boat who made his living transporting Raza to the Gringo side. But the day I wanted to go, the boat was in for repairs, so we crossed the river (it had water in those days) with the help of a tree trunk, because I couldn't swim. Puse la ropa encima del palo y llegue bien al otro lado. [I put my clothes on the end of a stick and made it to the other side.] No problem. The rest is a long story. Finally, immigration caught me. Actually, several times they came to the hospital kitchen where I was working, but they never asked me if I was wetback. For a while I lived in Ohio under an assumed name, an unnecessary precaution because I never saw the immigration people again until I turned myself in, in 1953. I consider myself an authentic wetback.

Now I live in Las Cruces, New Mexico. I have two sons, Sean Santiago, who is in Italy, and Mark, in Redlands, California. I have traveled in North Africa, Europe, Canada, Mexico, Colombia, South America, and I know the U.S. well. I have taught at the University of Texas at Austin, San Bernardino State College in California, was dean of a small college connected with Western Washington State College, and arrived in Las Cruces in 1972. I am a professor of Spanish and Chicano literature at New Mexico State.

When did you first begin to write?

My first attempt with the pen was at Findlay College in the spring of 1954, having returned legally from Mexico. I decided to write a narrative, in short story form, about a strange event that had happened to me in Mexico City while I was arranging my visa to return to the U.S. I made friends with an old soldier, who was conspiring, with some character I never got to meet, to start an armed revolt. They wanted me to buy the weapons in this country. After returning to Ohio, I never knew what became of that. It was one of those naïve things one does. I published it in the small review published by the students of Findlay College, *The Scribbler*.

I continued to write a sort of biography, for the benefit of my sons, in English; that story had also been in English. Until more or less 1969 I tried to write in English. I think it was a failure. I wrote in English because I believed that it would be useless to do so in Spanish; where would I publish in Spanish? At least I didn't know of any Spanish-language magazines or newspapers, until 1964, when I found a newspaper, *La Fuerza*, in Austin, while I was working at UT. A story in Spanish appeared in the magazine published by the Spanish students of UT; it was a modest one developed humorously. The magazine only lasted for one or two issues. Although I had published that story, I continued to write poetry in English; I consider it all a failure because it never satisfied me. Really, it seems I was determined to prove I could write in English. Finally, when I was in San Bernardino, I started writing in Spanish and I liked it. When I read the first issues of *El Grito* in 1968, I was inspired to write more seriously; but those first attempts in English are still around here somewhere. From one of those poems written in English about 1965–66, I liked an image, and I developed it into "El Lugar" ["The Place," a story], which appeared in the *Latin American Literary Review* (vol. 5).

Look, I've always wanted to write. Or, at least, as a child and adolescent I wanted to be a classical dancer and actor. Ha, ha, don't you see how I came to be a teacher? In class one has to act, ha, ha! Some years ago, in the summers of '57 and '58, in Leipsic, Ohio, I worked with the National Council of Churches as a social worker among Chicanos who harvested tomatoes in Putnam County. In Harlingen, Texas, in 1951–52 for the first time I had been with the Raza, the people who kill themselves working in the sun for the few pennies the ranchers pay. I loved that work, although it only lasted six months. From there and from South Texas and later East Austin, my heart filled with affection for the people, almost all of them poor; from that also came, in part the anger people say they see in *Perros*, but in truth it is more than simply anger. *Perros* is nothing more than a long story, with many small stories between the beginning and end, although the ending, as in the old-time carpas [traveling theatres], is a *fin a palos*, a satire, a ridiculing, a great laughter. Writing *Perros*, I remembered what most of us, Raza, have done as children at night—tell stories, take imaginary trips, kill the dragons we have inside ourselves, and not even death gets away. *Perros*, as you know, was the first work I wrote with purpose and seriousness, although the reception it has been given since the first has surprised me. It has been a small weapon with which, in public, I throw rocks at the giant.

What kind of books did you read in your formative years?

I don't remember much of what I read in my formative years in Mexico. My father had a library at home and I read European books. I remember it all vaguely. I know he had a Bible and with great fear I read it in secret. I was not a very devout Catholic and did not go to church. My father was an agnostic and my mother, very Catholic. I do remember that in secondary school, between fourteen and seventeen years old, I read Oscar Wilde.

It has been years since I have read Wilde, but I still remember what I felt, in the school in Culiacán. *The Portrait of Dorian Gray* fascinated me; who would not want to be young forever? But I extended that fantastic idea—to be all powerful all my life, to put the world in order. It was during World War II, and I was well informed on the events in Europe, North Africa, and the Pacific, although I preferred reading about the European Front. This gave rise to my strong interest in geography, history, art, and music; the latter remains the most beautiful vehicle I possess. Every day I listen to some eight hours of classical music, especially the European composers.

Wilde powerfully touched my heart, with a type of modern romanticism which fed my adolescent fantasy. It was something beautifully exotic, and then, well I read him in English.

Wilde was an open, sweet man, like a friend incapable of doing one harm.

Once I read a book, written by an Englishman or American named Marden, entitled *The Silent Crime*; it was translated into Spanish. I liked literature very much, especially Spanish literature. In secondary school the Spanish Romances were a favorite, especially *Los siete infantes de Lara*. I remember well that book used in secondary school—it still is—*Corazón diario de un niño*. After my father's death, I did not have much chance to read. In the public library of Culiacán, Sinaloa, I read geography and world history. During my adolescence I read Immanuel Kant's *Critique of Pure Reason*. Philosophy interested me. It bothered me not to have my thoughts in order at that time. Mexican literature bored me, especially the pre–Twentieth Century works. It still bores me.

What is the extent of your studies?

I received a B.S. in sociology from Findlay College, Ohio; Master's in Romance languages from the University of North Carolina at Chapel Hill, 1961; and my doctorate also from North

Carolina in 1964. I had studied at the National Polytechnical Institute in Mexico City and, later, a year at the Sinaloa Normal School, which I did not finish for reasons of illness.

***

Has formal education helped or hindered you as a writer?

I think that my formal education, all of it, and my studies of Spanish, French, and Italian literature, and the nineteenth-century American Transcendentalists have especially helped me intellectually and emotionally. In medieval Spanish literature I especially like the epic poems, Juan Ruiz, *La Celestina*, Luis Vives; of the Renaissance poets: Fray Luis de León, San Juan de la Cruz, Garcilaso de la Vega; the dramatists: especially Calderón and Lope de Vega, and particularly Tirso de Molina. Eighteenth-century Spain bored me—deadly. From nineteenth-century Spain: García Gutiérrez, Galdós, Larra. Bécquer has been a model for me. Some of the Generation of '98 writers I like—Baroja. Twentieth century: Valle Inclán, Benavente, and, greatly, García Lorca. In France, medieval literature, I like *The Song of Roland*, *Lais de Marie de France*, François Villon. Then *précieuse* literature. From the eighteenth century, Montesquieu, Rousseau—a lot—the Encyclopedists like Diderot; Voltaire in particular; Saint-Simon. From the nineteenth century, poetry from Romanticism to Maeterlinck, including Hugo, Leconte de Lisle, Heredia, Baudelaire, Verlaine, Rimbaud, Mallarmé. I know nineteenth-century French poetry rather well. Drama, especially the thesis plays; Maeterlinck, with his poetic, symbolic language, as in *Pelléas et Mélisande*. I studied twentieth-century theatre quite well. Artaud and Claudel were a passion. The poets, among others, the existentialists. I studied Provençal poetry very well and I think it has inspired me. I read in depth the poets of the court of Federico II of Sicily, the thirteenth century. I know Dante rather well. Of the Germans Goethe has been my teacher. Philosophers like Schopenhauer and Nietzsche; and among the Dutch, the Spanish Jew Spinoza. Among the North Americans, very especially Emerson and Edgar Allan Poe. From among the contemporaries there have been no great models. From twentieth-century Mexico, Carlos Fuentes, Rulfo, and Paz.

It is difficult to say that the formal literary study has hindered me in my work. Critics would have to judge. But sometimes I look at how I write in Spanish and I see the form of the ballad, its versification. I think I have originality, and I try to avoid repetition; and if I do repeat unknowingly, I try to modify it, which is one of the phenomena of literary creation.

I was born in a very old town founded by Zuaque Indians; in 1562 Nuño de Guzmán arrived. El Fuerte de Montesclavos—the Spanish name—has not changed much, or at least that is the way I see it. In the bars and the market, one still sees guitarists singing *corridos* of all types and periods, though all of them are Mexican compositions. In our family fiestas, picnics, jail, the dances, they sang and still sing *corridos*. It is an intimate part of our lives. The first time I read a ballad from the series of the *Siete infantes de Lara* it thrilled me because I could not see any difference from the *corrido* of Valentín de la Sierra. It is all the same; in the medieval ballad I see our *corrido*, a natural way of telling stories, and, as we know, still used here by Chicanos. Here in New Mexico we dance *corridas*, but we sing *corridos*. In our Chicano literature the *corrido* has always been written as such, but I see it, also, in the serious poetry, like very personal poetry, if not in the ballad form, most certainly in the musical rhythm of that very old poetry. In Alurista, Abelardo, and Ricardo Sánchez, among the best known, one observes it. Our people understand and enjoy that popular poetic form. I don't think it is anything special, it is so common. Lately, in New Mexico, Roberto Mondragón, a distinguished politician and educator, has composed *corridos*; he also sings and has recorded several records. He is an influential person; but just as he writes *corridos*, any kid or adult could do it.

However, for formal works it is better to know something, know life, read, and read everything, not only literature, but anything, and, of course, write a lot and revise, rework, make changes until what you want to say comes out well. This discipline is perhaps the most important thing for any writer, new or experienced. I also see that as Chicanos and renovators of something we have always done (the *corrido*), we have the real opportunity to achieve new forms, techniques, styles, and to utilize unexploited sources; the masters of this are Miguel Méndez, Alurista, Luis Valdez, Rolando Hinojosa, and Tomás Rivera.

Which was the predominant language in your home as a child? Which do you speak more fluently now?

Having been born in Mexico, I spoke Spanish. Frankly I do not know if now I speak Spanish or English better, but I am sure that

my true personality comes out more clearly when I speak
Spanish.

Does Chicano literature have a particular language or idiom?

I consider myself a nationalist and write in Spanish. It seems to
me that the literature of the Chicano has the language that is
most suited to the writer, the one he feels more comfortable
with. I deplore, however, that there is not more literature in
Spanish.

They tell me that bilingualism is a characteristic of Chicano
literature. We know, however, that bilingualism is a complicated
sociolinguistic phenomenon—well, also psycholinguistic. I
could not say that, because to accept it would impose limitations on Chicano literature that in truth do not exist. The literature of the Chicano people is written in any standard or sub-
standard dialect of Spanish or English; of course there can be
interference from Spanish in English and vice versa. The term
interlingualism is acceptable in a work where there is interference. The linguistic variants within Chicano literature simply
reflect our linguistic reality, in spite of the purists. This reminds
me that many universities and colleges have special Spanish
courses for Chicanos in which the student receives credit for his
degree of proficiency; that is to say, the linguistic situation and
reality of our people finally is being recognized. On the other
hand, there are those who insist that we should speak the "language of Cervantes," when we very well know that that glorious
personage died in 1616, but his language has kept evolving. I
think Chicanos are in the vanguard of the linguistic change taking place in so many countries where Spanish is spoken. I cannot say whether interlingualism in Chicano literature has a
future or not; whatever is done well has a future, the relative
"purity" of the expression aside.

*How do you perceive your role as a writer vis-à-vis: (a) the Chicano
community or Movement; (b) U.S. society; (c) literature itself?*

In my two books and other poems, the work I have done mostly
is directed at the Chicano people as an educational instrument.
What the North American society thinks does not matter to me;
I do not write for it. I do not think I write for it. Lately, in *Libro
para batos*, I think I am writing more literature than Chicano

literature, although there are some social poems in it. I would like to see more literature written for the community, but also, that it be written as art.

First, I would like to tell you that although I have written and published some works, I do not consider myself a writer at all; that is to say, I am a professor first, a professor who writes. I am not avoiding responsibility for my writings; I am simply saying that I am not just a writer. I say this modestly.

With respect to my role and the community and the so-called Chicano Movement, my ideas, dreams, and aspirations precede the Movement; for me the Movement has been more a cultural or political explosion, or an "awakening" or even "renaissance." I would like to say now that my role in the community and the Movement has been that of active participant, though I had already been active before it came to be called a movement. My writing is only a part, one aspect of my work in favor of our people's betterment. It pleases me, of course, that some readers see my work as a contribution to the Movement. It recalls what Ruiz de Alarcón said to the readers in the preface to a collection of plays. My little works sell in spite of being poetry, and, well, it gratifies one to know that what one has written is purchased and read. Apparently the majority of the readers, up to now, are Chicano or Hispano. I doubt that what I write has interested the U.S. society; and what the Gringos say, well, it really matters very little to me. Now, Gringos read very little of what Chicanos write; Rudy Anaya's work is an exception, because he writes well, and because he writes in English.

As a participant in the literary process of the Chicano people, among the minority cultures in this country, I jealously guard my intellectual freedom; I would prefer to go unnoticed by the majority of the public, to not see myself in the embarrassing situation of having to recognize that "I am a writer," because if I accepted it I would have to assume the responsibility of an artist of the pen; accepting it, I would then find myself in the same situation in which I daily find myself—doing whatever possible to be sincere, frank, and at the same time maintain the highest level of intellectual honesty possible. It is difficult. Among other things I consider personally valuable in my work, I write; I write because I like to and I have something to say; it is one of my contributions in life to support an effort, perhaps universal, of putting my grain of sand in the way of the torrent of insensitivity and materialism, especially in its very source—this country. Presumptions perhaps, but my work is serious, including what I write. In this way, *maestro*, with an interior effort, I reject, with great success, the greatest presumption I could suffer, that of wanting to be a famous author. My ego gives me enough trouble without worrying about kissing the fantasies of a society which, in general, bores me with its materialistic incontinence, its disdain of whatever is not white or native or, of course, Gringo.

My role in *literature* is only part of my role as teacher and, modestly, thinker, which I have been for a longer time, much longer than I have been a contributor to the literature of the Chicano people. Only too well do I remember daily my colleagues in this profession, the most conceited, fatuous, and egotistical people. For the rest of my life I will continue *asking* myself if perhaps I have managed to discipline myself enough to satisfy myself. I am lazy about revisions, and, as you know, *maestro*, that is the most difficult part of this beautiful exercise we call literature. I repeat it again clearly: I do not hope to become famous as a writer; I have other things to do.

What is the place of Chicano literature within U.S. literature?

It seems to me that Chicanos' literature academically belongs to the corpus of U.S. literature, but even so it preserves its identity, revealed in many ways, but culturally separated from the North American literary or cultural current; except, maybe, some works in English by some Chicanos, that could fit within U.S. minority literatures.

The success of Chicano literature not written in English surprises me. Considering that Gringo society has systematically tried to suppress our language, I see that the literature of the Chicano people has survived on its own merits. Though I recognize that it is mostly read in colleges and universities, one cannot negate its appeal. Remember, for example, that *Peregrinos de Aztlán*, by Miguel Méndez, written in Spanish, has been sold out for several years; I think the first edition was of 2,500 copies. A second edition is about to be published by Justa. My optimism for the survival of Chicano literature in Spanish is firm, because I believe that the future reader will be more educated. Now we have two or three hundred thousand Chicanos in college. The worst is over; they haven't Anglicized us completely. Our economic situation itself is improving—not much, but it is better than when the wetback Sergio Elizondo washed dishes in the Harlingen Hospital for Consumptives, seventy hours a week for twenty dollars. Moreover, I think that our serious writers are producing more beautiful works; I see it in Hinojosa, Brito, Arias, Méndez, and Ulibarrí. The success of Arias, Anaya, Soto, and Villarreal (who write in English) can support the Spanish portion, at least, because we are all from the same stable. Though this is merely speculative, I see that our sisters are producing excellent works. Mireya López, Inés Hernández Tovar, Lin Romero, and others have realized good works. We have had five Floricantos since 1972, not counting other festivals in which no less than one hundred writers and artists have participated, and more than half of them youngsters. As you can see, my view is optimistic . . . I remember when we didn't have anything, or hardly anything; I see what is happening . . . and it heartens me.

What is the relationship of Chicano literature to Mexican literature?

I am not sure I can answer this question. I am not very close to Mexican literature. I think that the literature of the Chicanos is separate from the Mexican, although I recognize our cultural roots and, of course, that we belong to the same literary current because of the language, symbols and other factors that intervene in our literature. For the present I think that the literature of the Chicanos is being formed and that this question cannot be answered well.

Some serious critics have spoken about Mexico's literary transcendence with respect to the works of some Chicano authors. Well, this phenomenon is natural; the blood call, let's say. In general terms I would say that our literature reflects, socially and linguistically, the popular human condition in Mexico, be it rural or, recently, urban, although only in a minor tone. In Miguel Méndez I note a very clear tone of the Mexican people's ingeniousness and picaresque spirit; but then, perhaps it was the author's intent, considering that he is very "Mexican" and *Peregrinos [de Aztlán]* is a work that transcends the border in both directions. *Maestro* Alurista excels in Mexican indigenous metaphysic, so much so that in *Floricanto en Aztlán* and *Nationchild Plumaroja* he seems to construct an entire bifacial indigenous theogony that looks in both directions: north and south. I would say that these two works, at least for their didactic utility, have contributed to the appreciation of a deep and extensive pantheon of Mesoamerican deities, symbols, and ancient values. Alurista has managed to make the reader look south, as he himself looked to his ancestors to produce an interpretive-literary art for the descendants of those tribes, which some time back made a pilgrimage to the south from their prehistoric home in Aztlán. Be it truth or fantasy, I think the evidence is in the impact it has made on the minds of young Chicanos.

[*B.-N. asked S.E. about a meeting with Miguel Méndez in which they played at albures, Mexican punning, often with sexual connotations.*]

Now, with respect to the *albures* Miguel Méndez and I played, well a few years ago we saw each other in San Diego, and, noticing a spark of wit in the vernacular speech of the *maestro*, I threw out a key word, and he immediately responded. We tangled in an *albur*. And how that old Yaqui can do it! On another level, I see in *Peregrinos* a true linguistic treasure. There are aspects of Miguel's style that recall the humorous intent of the picaresque-alburesque—in some of his male characters; in addition, he is an excellent manipulator of the word in more than one dialect.

As you can see, Maestro Méndez has outlined a very realistic panorama of the social condition of the Raza on both sides of the border, but he is not the only one who reveals the people at work, because the majority of the writers are doing that, although, as we know, some do it better than others, but each in his own way. Alejandro Morales has managed to capture the anguish and joy of the metropolitan barrio. Sabine R. Ulibarrí recalls the old times, describing them with talent in *Mi abuela fumaba puros*. Both of them are like the old minstrels. I think some of our people do it also.

Do you perceive yourself and your work as political?

It seems to me that in part my work is political, but I am moving away from politics. To clarify that, my work is more than political. I said earlier that it is political in the sense that it is like a weapon, and thus *Perros* is a literary work of struggle. Its socio-political stridency seems to have suggested to some people that it is only that. We also know that if analyzed correctly, up to our time, the majority of literature has social content.

Libro para batos was written with a dual intention, as is obvious in the two principal parts of its structure. "The Night of the Berets" could be in *Perros*, for example, but the *chavala* poems, no. What I have published in *Revista Chicano-Riqueña*, *Tejidos*, *Plural*, and *Riversedge* illustrates that, since 1972, I have wanted to achieve something different from *Perros*.

Lately I have experimented with the short prose form. One of my stories came out recently in *Riversedge*, besides the one you know from the *Latin American Literary Review*; they are part of a small collection that I am finishing now. I have not decided what to call it yet, but I like the title of one of the ten stories—"Rosa, la flauta." This is new for me; I am very satisfied with what I have done and I will continue trying to write in the form. In these stories, two tendencies stand out: our people's realism and the fantasy that often occupies our imagination in the most intimate moments. Those stories are forms of interior and exterior life that I think are aspects of human nature, but more than anything I wanted them to be entertaining.

Does the Chicano author have anything in common with the majority group writers? Differences?

It seems to me that what the Chicano writer shares with the majority group in the United States would have to be the discipline of the writer; that is very difficult. But I insist on the cultural differences that distinguish them.

Does Chicano literature share common ground with Black literature? Differences?

I don't know the literature of the Blacks in the U.S. very well, but if it is, in part, a literature of struggle, then the literature of some Chicanos has that in common with it.

Is there any relationship with the literature of other Spanish-speaking groups?

No comment.

Does Chicano literature have a distinctive perspective on life? What effect does it have on the literature?

I see a lot of anguish in the Chicanos' literary works. An anxiety, also, which comes from the emotional uneasiness that North American domination has created in our life. I think that protest, anguish, the peculiarly Chicano worries hurt the literature being written, because there is more protest than writing with the intention of contributing to art.

Does Chicano literature improve communication between Chicanos and Anglo Americans?

It seems to me that the literature of the Chicanos improves communication and brings the majority Gabachos [Anglos] and the Chicanos closer. Because it is a way in which the Gabachos can perceive something of what we are doing, when they usually do not pay attention to us. There exists a lack of communication. The Gabacho considers us not yet legitimate, but he hardly reads us. From this he will learn about us.

Does Chicano literature reevaluate, attack, or subvert the value system of the majority society? Is it a revolutionary literature? Thematically? Technically?

The literature of the Chicanos does reevaluate and attack the system; Alurista, for example, basically does it. Others do it more subtly. I think Tomás Rivera does also. It is done more thematically than technically. To date, I don't think there are technical innovations in the literature of the Chicanos.

What problems have you encountered in publishing? Were they racially founded?

I haven't had problems with the publication of my work. Up to now I have published with Chicano publishing houses, although some non-Chicano magazines have published my poems. I think that this problem will end someday.

Are Chicanos at a disadvantage in trying to practice the art of writing?

I don't think that Chicanos suffer more than anyone else if they want to write. Whoever wants to write can do it. I would say that we are, perhaps, in a better situation to write, because we have so much to say. It seems that our world, our way of seeing the world, has not been exploited yet, so the field is open.

What are the most outstanding qualities of Chicano literature?
Weaknesses?

The principal advantage is newness. This newness consists in
that Chicano literature is now filling one of the many lacunae in
this country's civilization. Its newness is nothing strange; and
even if it were, that would prove its truth. Chicanos are singing,
singing and revealing the reality of our lives and our artistic
presence that we have always kept relatively hidden. I previously referred to our situation vis-à-vis or within the major
and dominant part of this nation. I do not think that it is new
that there are good Chicano writers; it is only new for those who
did not know us (including our own people).

Its weakness is that there is a lot of literature that is more
personal than anything, and it should not be published. There
are many writers who do not write carefully; they have not yet
learned to be discriminating. Some time ago I stopped thinking
that in literature, as in other disciplines, we are like children
who are learning to walk. Nevertheless, we have a need for analytical criticism of what has been written; we lack truly analytical critics, although there are one or two who already stand out
among the best of the best. Our Gringo colleagues continue to
shine for their lack of criticism; I wish that they would participate in this truly new experience that is the literature of the
Chicano people. I think that the literature of the Chicanos in
our day merits the proof of approbation or rejection by the people who read it, as well as the investigation by the serious critic,
be he Raza or not. In this I see, at the present time, a kind of
weakness, but only with respect to the science of criticism, and
not its relative literary value as a natural part of the value system of the Raza.

What are the milestones so far in Chicano literature?

The principle works of literature of the Chicanos, more or less,
are the following: Alurista's *Floricanto en Aztlán*; . . . *y no se lo
tragó la tierra* by Rivera; *Peregrinos de Aztlán* by Miguel Méndez; Rudy Anaya's *Bless Me, Ultima*; *Estampas del Valle* de
Hinojosa, without overlooking his *Generaciones* [earlier title of
Klail City y sus alrededadores]; and, of course, *The Road to Tamazunchale* by Ron Arias. Do not forget the foundation of Quinto
Sol [Publications], Editorial Justa, and Editorial Pajaritos, our se-

rious publishing houses. These seem to be the most important until now, although there are many talented writers besides the ones I mentioned.

What is the future of Chicano literature? Distinctiveness, or the de-emphasis of the distinctive characteristics?

I cannot say anything in this respect. I do not know what will happen in the future. I hope that more people will write and that they will do it with more discipline.

Who are the leaders among Chicano writers, and why?

The leaders are Tomás Rivera, Alurista, Miguel Méndez. I think I have a small part among them. The most influential are Alurista, Rivera, and Hinojosa.

Miguel
Méndez M.

In the first edition of *El Espejo* there appeared two poetic prose
pieces, "Tata Casehua" and "Taller de Imágenes," the works of
Miguel Méndez, a Tucson construction worker with a sixth-grade
education, an extraordinary gift of imagery, and an obviously
mythological sense of time. Since then Méndez has released a
novel, *Peregrinos de Aztlán* (1974), and a lengthy narrative poem,
Los criaderos humanos (épica de los desamparados) y Sahuaros
(1975), both published by Editorial Peregrinos, Méndez's own,
now defunct publishing house.

From the beginning Méndez displayed a penchant for hybrid
language, mixing Yaqui words with Mexican Spanish in "Tata
Casehua." In *Peregrinos* he juxtaposes sections written in distinct
forms of Spanish, while *Los criaderos* is written in a more standard, though difficult, poetic Spanish. All three are linguistically
taxing for the average reader, requiring careful reading, no little
amount of dictionary work, and a rereading or two, all of which
seems paradoxical in a writer to whom the loss of the oral tradition is a major concern.

Méndez sees a breakdown in traditional communal communications—the young no longer listen to the old, neighbors do
not speak to each other; familial, communal, ethnic, and national
heritage, which once was preserved by word of mouth, is disappearing into silence. At the same time, written history represents
only the elite classes' vision of the past, ignoring the existence of
the poor. Thus, as the poor abandon the oral preservation of their
heritage and simultaneously embrace literacy, alienation and a
sense of diaspora possess them. Méndez counterattacks through
his writing, not only by revealing the threat to the oral tradition,
but also by filling his written texts with oral tradition. Yet, believing that tradition should not be shared frivolously with outsiders, Méndez makes his texts difficult to read. The result is the
contradiction—a concern for the preservation of oral tradition

and a style of writing accessible only to the highly literate reader. Méndez's proletarian sympathies, as well as his explicit and bitter attacks on capitalism, have made him a favorite of the Chicano intellectuals of leftist persuasion. However, in his interview one finds little of the bitterness and class consciousness of his works, and according to Méndez his next publications will mark a departure from the proletarian themes that dominate his literature up to this point. But then, too, this interview will seem a departure in stylistic terms for those familiar with Méndez's prose or poetry: absent are the dense, baroque passages and the esoteric language. The prolific writer—at this time he awaits the publication of two more books written some years ago—preoccupied with the oral tradition proves a rather laconic interviewee.

Miguel Méndez responded to the questionnaire in writing in 1976, and revised the interview in August 1979. I have translated his answers, originally in Spanish.

When and where were you born?

I was born June 15, 1930, in Bisbee, Arizona.

Describe your family background and your present situation.

There are three brothers and three sisters in my family; I am the oldest. The same year I was born, my father lost his job in the mines of Bisbee, due to the famous depression of the 1930's, and he returned to Mexico, becoming part of the ejido [communal farm] called El Claro, in the state of Sonora. Along with our family there arrived many other families to take part in El Claro. They came from different parts of the country, including several families from the Yaqui territory. Plutarco Elías Calles, the president of Mexico, was especially interested in the formation of that ejido, which in the past had belonged to León Serna, a rich feudal gentleman overthrown by the Revolution. My parents died recently, my mother in an automobile accident in 1977, and my father in 1978.

My present situation is pleasant. I enjoy my work and I also write. [Méndez teaches full time in the Spanish Department of Pima Community College, Tucson, Arizona. He teaches language, literature, and creative writing. He has also taught at the University of Arizona. As of September 1979, he has two books about to be published with Editorial Justa.]

When did you first begin to write?

I began to write early. When I was eighteen I wrote a novel as a training exercise. It was somewhat autobiographical, focusing on my experiences in the United States, since by that time I had been in this country for three years. My life in Mexico was shown in a retrospective fashion, as a background. Naturally, fantasy played a great part in that first attempt. In addition, I entertained myself writing poetry and short stories. When I now examine those first attempts, I find that certains parts are laughable, and, of course, some show promising qualities.

What kind of books did you read in your formative years?

Since my mother taught me to read before I was five years old, I covered the classics very quickly. I was always bothering my mother, distracting her from her chores, trying to get her to read me the comics in the papers. She would explain the letters to me, while I constantly asked her questions. I never knew how I learned to read, only that it was very early. Among the modest belongings that my parents had taken to El Claro, there were several boxes of books, an RCA Victor phonograph, and many records: popular music, semiclassical, and a few classical.

My favorite author was always the one I was reading at the moment. Among the first ones, I remember Edmondo de Amicis, Enrique Pérez Escrich, Jules Verne. I was eleven or twelve when I read the nine volumes of *Rocambole* by Ponson du Terrail, and then came the Russians. I read Juan A. Mateos, *El sol de mayo*, *El cerro de las campanas*, and *La majestad caída*. I also read *El fistol del diablo* and *Los bandidos del Río Frío* by Manuel Payno, *Astucia* by Luis Inclán, and Lizardi's *Periquillo sarniento*. Later I read the majority of the novelists of the Mexican Revolution, as well as other groups: the Contemporáneos, the Modernists, etc., etc. Nor have the South American authors escaped me. Also, in those days, I read many European writers, along with the Russians, Victor Hugo, Dumas, and others. And of course I got all tied up in the medieval writers, those of the Spanish Golden Age, the Generation of '98, and the contemporary Spanish authors. Frankly, I have read many books whose authors I cannot even remember.

Curiously, in those years I read in a tireless fashion in an environment in which the majority of the people were illiterate, absolutely unaware of any literature.

What is the extent of your studies?

I have six years of formal education, those years of study on the ejido El Claro I mentioned before. With the base of those six years of primary school, I continued my own education through readings and experience.

Before I turned twenty, when I was working as a laborer in the agricultural fields and in construction, I already had a vast knowledge of the language and literature. Nevertheless, with my fellow workers I spoke the same as they did, in the language of the pachuco. For some twenty-four years I worked in rough jobs, almost inhuman ones. Believe me, before being a writer, teacher, or intellectual, I am still a farmworker or a laborer, or both, perhaps.

An interesting point is that during my childhood I heard many stories from those people who came from different places, and, like my family, were newcomers to El Claro. They would tell anecdotes about the Revolution, the Yaqui wars, and innumerable other themes, among which there was no lack of apparitions and superstitions. Those days were extremely dramatic. I learned about tragedy, at times in the flesh.

Has formal education helped or hindered you as a writer?

In my literary career those years have been fundamental, naturally.

Which was the predominant language in your home as a child? Which do you speak more fluently now?

In my home only Spanish was spoken, which is only logical, since we were living in Mexico. The language I speak best is Spanish. Spiritually, I identify totally with the Spanish language. I believe that language is the structure on which all culture rests. If the language disappears, there remain memories that, as they slowly fade away, take the ancestral culture into oblivion. In our case, the Spanish language is the most powerful factor with respect to a means of identity. I believe that Spanish is essential to us; if we leave it behind, we risk developing an unsure character. Spanish is our genealogical language, in a manner of speaking; if we forget it we will lose many memories that are proper to our historical nature and then we will be culturally poor, without the authenticity that a culture gives through the centuries. In exchange for what? To become unskillful newcomers in another culture, in which it would take us a long time to achieve a complete fusion. It is definitely to our advantage that we remain bilingual.

Does Chicano literature have a particular language or idiom?

Given our Chicano experience, such a particular experience, our literature appears in diverse languages. I think that the language most adequate for giving expression to our literature should be the one which each author commands best. Because the command of a literary language is essential for every ambitious work. Spanish suits me best because it reaches me with a great wealth of experiences and knowledge from across the centuries through countless generations of my same nature.

How do you perceive your role as a writer vis-à-vis: (a) the Chicano community or Movement; (b) U.S. society; (c) literature itself?

My experience within the society has been the same as that of the average Chicano, and for that reason my literature proves to be attuned to the Chicano Movement, I believe. I don't know how to evaluate my literature within the Movement. To do that there would have to pass several years and I would have to publish a half-dozen books. In any case, it will be others who will be able to state my role in our world, and in a more objective manner. With regard to the society of the United States, I believe that my writings show perspectives that arise from the Chicano mentality; thus, they are different from the stereotypes coined by that society. As a writer I put the maximum effort into giving intrinsic value to what I write.

What is the place of Chicano literature within U.S. literature?

The place conceded to Chicano literature within the United States is the lowest, but the one which it deserves legitimately is that of great importance. It should be noted that we are very little favored by the attention of critics, who strictly pursue commercial and political objectives, because those are the dictates of the publications that employ them. Keep in mind that, within university circles, the professors with old ideas reject our literature without even knowing what it is, somewhat due to analytical impotence and also out of a conservative tendency to repeat, like recorders, the old works that have served them as faithful battle horses. Our literature is not recognized because the Anglo American writers as well as the Latin American ones, with rare exceptions, are egotistical to the point of perversity, and, as can be humanly understood, they do not accept any threat of competition. In spite of everything, Chicano literature will impose its values.

What is the relationship of Chicano literature to Mexican literature?

Chicano literature, particularly that which appears in Spanish, to a great extent derives from the antecedents put forth in Mexican literature. Although when we look at it more closely, its freshness lies in that its veins of material arise from the anecdote that springs from the daily struggle of our people; from the oral narrative that is transferred, through the immigrants from northern Mexico, from an entire tradition unexploited by the writers from the Mexican highlands. We could affirm, furthermore, that the essence of Chicano literature flows from the socio-historic problematic, with the sum and total of circumstances that have been determining the character and activity of the Chicano man.

I have read most of the Mexican contemporary writers, including Yáñez, Rulfo, Juan José Arreola, Fuentes, Spota, Sainz, Paz, Monsiváis, etc., etc. I do not think that there is any writer that does not influence us, since from many readings we search for a synthesis to mold our own style. I have never tried to imitate any writer in particular.

Do you perceive yourself and your work as political?

Political passion is latent in every artistic work, to a greater or lesser extent. My literature is no exception. Nevertheless, the mere thought of living from politics makes my hair stand on end.

The part of my writing that is known to people has a very close tie to the proletariat. It has been an obligation to put forth my experience in that environment. Nevertheless, in my next books other subjects will predominate. If it were not that way, you couldn't explain my insistence in continuing to publish.

Does the Chicano author have anything in common with the majority group writers? Differences?

What there can be in common between Chicano and Anglo American writers is that both of them reflect their epoch and the society in which they live according to their own experiences; the differences also come from that. Although I dare say that their literature, with honorable exceptions, is highly commercialized.

Does Chicano literature share common ground with Black literature? Differences?

Chicano literature and that of the Blacks of the United States have in common that they both spring from the imperative of social protest, differing in their context, because that is how the historical and culture differences have determined them.

Is there any relationship with the literature of other Spanish-speaking groups?

Chicano literature relates to that of other Spanish-speaking groups in a partial way, in regard to language and cultural similarity. The Puerto Ricans I like very much, though I have read relatively little of their work.

Does Chicano literature have a distinctive perspective on life? What effect does it have on the literature?

Chicano literature obsessively tends to look at life retrospectively, because it is not healthy to obstinately insist on our historical roots and also go over our history in the United States. I do not know if it is the correct answer to your question, but I think I glimpse in our literature a perspective of life in which are mixed a longing and a nostalgia for the past with the hope for an undefined future. As a characteristic that binds our literature, one could well cite the acknowledgment and full acceptance given in it to the Indian, in the glorification of his past as well as in the pride taken in inheriting his color. The dignity of the Chicano augments gigantically because he has realized a reconciliation that still has not come to be in Latin America, including Mexico.

Does Chicano literature improve communication between Chicanos and Anglo Americans?

The communication that might be derived from the reading of Chicano literature by Anglo Americans would be purely incidental. It is only logical that those who would read us, should understand us better. So, indisputably, Chicano literature would improve communication with Anglo Americans and with any other readers. It follows that if many people would read us, then they would understand us better. Without it having to be one of its goals, it proves a happy coincidence to the literature. However, I believe that the reality is another thing.

Does Chicano literature reevaluate, attack, or subvert the value system of the majority society? Is it a revolutionary literature? Thematically? Technically?

Chicano literature actually is revolutionary in its themes and its technique. That is why the false critics do not understand it, since the old molds for judging it prove obsolete, and they are not capable of creating new ones to frame it adequately. Chicano literature manifests its own concept about the value system that motivates our people. So that if the reader sees, on his own, subversion, attack, or reevaluation of the value system of United States society, it is because those are the dictates of his own beliefs, experiences, or prejudices.

In every Chicano work we see a language which is not precisely that of the academic model or standard, so in that sense they are innovations in the area of linguistics and they manifest also the personal experience and language of the author. This disconcerts those who persist in ignoring the fact that there now total millions of us living in this country who speak Spanish or a variation of it. At the same time, I think that the structure of the contemporary novel has a lot to do with the form or the style of life today. The novel has reduced its context, while presenting itself in episodes, so that through a fragmented form it might encompass a more extensive panorama of the extremely complex world that we confront. The reader must spend his time in multiple activities. For his recreation there are television, film, comics, pamphlets of all types, the daily newspapers, etc. So his attention is focused on many things and he is not willing to read voluminous works, with slow, lineal action. The literary work, in our case also, is an experiment in each attempt, because it is an effort to manifest a society alienated by multiple anxieties and afflictions, which have become more acute because of the extraordinary efficiency of our means of communication, the media, which inform us instantly about what is happening in the whole world. The complexity of contemporary literature is not the caprice of the author. The critic, on the other hand, sometimes does not want to understand these things, or he simply cannot, and he continues obstinately tied to literary models that correspond to another period and other circumstances. But since our literature is in its initial phase, we will learn.

What problems have you encountered in publishing? Were they racially founded?

The problems I have had in publishing are related to economics. Perhaps because our literature is not highly esteemed and editors are afraid of losing an investment they might make in us. To be frank with you, if I do not publish more frequently it is not for lack of material, but rather because my time is occupied in writing, with the intention of publishing later.

My novel *Peregrinos de Aztlán* was rejected by a well-known publisher, so we had to invent a business to make its appearance possible. Editorial Peregrinos published it and my book *Los criaderos humanos (épica de los desamparados) y Sahuaros*. However, it went out of business, due to a lack of funds, among other things. Right now I am waiting for Editorial Justa, Herminio Ríos's publishing house, to release any minute now two books: *Tata Casehua y otros cuentos* and *Cuentos para niños traviesos*. By the way, they will be in a bilingual format, Spanish-English. I think that now I am well established and publishing should not be difficult for me.

Are Chicanos at a disadvantage trying to practice the art of writing?

There is absolutely no disadvantage in being a Chicano author; on the contrary, we have the advantage of a vast range of themes. What is a disadvantage is wanting to be an author without having the necessary qualities.

**What are the most outstanding qualities of Chicano literature?
Weaknesses?**

The weak points reside in the linguistics employed in its formation; paradoxically, in the linguistics also reside its outstanding
qualities. I mean to say that many readers do not read our books
because they claim not to understand the Chicano language.
This can be explained if one keeps in mind the divorce there has
been between the university world and the Chicano people. This
situation has proved that if an author needs language as an instrument to bring about his work, mere language, without the
knowledge of the soul of a people, will not guarantee the creative phenomenon. However, since the demographic factor is
now powerful, and a very numerous population needs to reflect
its social phenomena in Chicano speech, it is overflowing and
forcing its comprehension on even those who have not held us
in high regard. The in-depth study of Chicano literature will find
that the language is one of the most important qualities upon
which depend the value and originality of the content itself.

What are the milestones so far in Chicano literature?

The most important events are still to happen. However, it is
encouraging that several authors are writing about a common
subject, seeking the same goals. One could point out as an important fact that we are producing literature to form a tradition,
although some unscrupulous publisher might have taken advantage of it.

**What is the future of Chicano literature: distinctiveness or the de-em-
phasis of the distinctive characteristics?**

Chicano literature will continue being legitimate as long as it
has distinctive elements.

Who are the leaders among Chicano writers, and why?

I do not see leaders in Chicano literature. The fact that several of
us have published, if it can well serve as an example, should not
hinder the originality of those authors who are beginning to
appear.

Abelardo Delgado

One of the most prolific of the quality Chicano poets, Abelardo, as he is usually referred to, has published to date four books of poetry (*Chicano: 25 Pieces of a Chicano Mind*, 1969; *Bajo el sol de Aztlán: 25 soles de Abelardo*, 1973; *It's Cold: 52 Cold Thought-Poems of Abelardo*, 1974; and *Reflexiones*, n.d.); has contributed a major portion to *Los cuatro*, 1970; has published pieces in many magazines; and has been anthologized in several Chicano collections.

If his books have not become as widely known and read as those of Alurista, Sergio Elizondo, or Ricardo Sánchez, it is surely due to the problems of poor distribution inherent in small-scale publishing, because several of his poems, found in anthologies, must be included among the most popular and most often quoted in Chicano literature. "Stupid America," "La Causa," "The Organizer," "El Vendido," "El Chisme," and "The New Cross" are now classics. Among Chicano poets Abelardo is often spoken of as a model and inspiration, and in my conversations with them, several have called him an influence—thematic, technical, and spiritual—on their work. At another level, his enthusiastic readings still excite and move audiences as they used to in the late 1960's, when no mass demonstration of Chicanos in the state of Colorado was complete without Abelardo's voice screaming his poetic synthesis of the Chicano Movement at its emotional peak. As Alurista says, Abelardo's true genre is declamation.

For some years Abelardo has been writing a type of epistolary essay (which someone should study as a possible influence on Ricardo Sánchez's particular hybrid writing). His prose manuscript was awarded the first annual Tonatiuh Prize for literature in 1977. The work, *Cartas a Louise*, is made up of a series of writings in the vein of Abelardo's letter/essays, with the difference that now he has created a fictional character, Santiago Flores, who bears more than a casual resemblance to Abelardo. Flores's

letters, with some poetry interspersed at times, are presented as if
Louise had given them to Abelardo, who then enters them in the
Tonatiuh contest with the hope that by winning, Santiago Flores
will be drawn back into public life, after having disappeared into
despair and anonymity. This award may bring Abelardo his long
overdue recognition.

A first draft of this interview was published in the *Revista
Chicano-Riqueña* 4, no. 4 (Fall 1976). It appears here completely
revised and greatly extended. Abelardo's responses can be dated
from the summer of 1978. The translation of Spanish portions
was done by Maricela Oliva.

When and where were you born?

I was born in La Boquilla de Conchos, Chihuahua, Mexico,
November 27, 1931. Funny how one always seems to find the
time to talk about oneself . . . I would lie if I were to say I remember La Boquilla, the little village where I was born. Because
of that I made it a point to visit and get a grown-up view rather
than a child's memory. It is a church and a few adobe houses
plus the customary kiosk. It is a tourist place because of the
famous Boquilla bass which can be caught behind the Boquilla
dam. My padrino [godfather], if he is still alive, has a boat for
rent in a restaurant-bar called El Tigre. My two abuelas [grand-
mothers] constantly would talk of La Boquilla and consequently
I believe myself to know it. It does occasionally and subconsciously emerge in some of my versos [poems] or prosa
[prose]. Because the images of what is true are so blurry they
become fantasies at times.

Describe your family background and your present situation.

All of my family consisted of two females, an abuela
[grandmother] and a mother. I'm an only son on my mother's
side, and have seven half brothers on my father's side. They and
my father live in Mexico. Never had a real father but had my
share of those who assumed that role. I did get to be greatly
influenced by a great-grandmother a lot. I have tried to capture
these two abuelitas [grandmothers] in a couple of poems. My
mother lives in Santa Paula, California, but is still a Mexican
national. She and I came into the U.S. in 1943. Since 1943 to
1969, plus one year that I came back, sums up my actual time

spent in El Paso. This bridges the tail end of the Pachuco era. The caló [slang] fascinated the hell out of me and I made it a point to study it even at that early age, even though I did not know that was what I was doing. I would ask people, my Pachuco carnales [brothers], why they used this word and what meaning lay behind it. Most certainly such a huge chunk of my life is the bulk of my pool of experiences from which episodes can be drawn plentifully. Ten years of heavy influence by the Catholic Church, as I worked for a Jesuit priest for that length of time. That religious influence, which ranges from the fanatic to the very pragmatic (the Jesuit priest is German), constantly shows up in my writings. I can very easily use all kinds of space elaborating on my various involvements and present activities, so I hope you bear with me as I try to capsule them out . . . I presently am doing research on farmworkers, computers and all of that . . . we are gathering data on one hundred thousand farm-workers. This work keeps me moving throughout the nation. I work with the Colorado Migrant Council; back in '69 and the next two years I was the executive director of this outfit. I have taught three years in Utah, one in UTEP [University of Texas at El Paso], and some summers here in Boulder. I have also worked in the northwest getting a health consumer corporation off the ground. I do a lot of readings and a lot of training work plus involving myself with all kinds of pertinent issues . . . such as the undocumented workers' struggle and the Bakke thing. Basically I show and share a lot of enthusiasm in trying out new ideas and that is where I feel more at home, thus creating pro-grams, alternative education options, dreams that at times crumble into plumitas [feathers] . . . I have come to the con-clusion that much value lies in merely gathering and dissem-inating information, so that I have been doing that on the side.

Presently I'm married to the former Dolores Estrada and have eight children. The eldest, 23, is married and lives in El Paso, Texas. My youngest daughter is seven years old. I have two grandchildren.

When did you first begin to write?

I think the earliest I can pinpoint my writing efforts dates back to my elementary school years when I edited a newspaper in the third grade and wrote short cuentos [tales] and verses as well as essays. Later on in junior and senior high school I began to win some prizes for essays and letters, as well as to collect some of my poems. My early experiences in writing were mostly all Spanish or all English. I did not think mixing both was cool.

What kind of books did you read in your formative years?

If by my formative years you mean my childhood years, they were spent in Mexico, where I taught myself to read and write in Spanish. During these years my readings were limited to two daily comic books with continuous stories. They were *El Pepín* and *El Chamaco Chico*. Once in the U.S., I hurried up to learn English to enjoy the variety of comic books of those days, '43 to '50 approximately. I did not have preferences when it came to comics; I took them all. I did go after Classics and others that showed more depth in their plots; without knowing it then I was yearning for literary satisfaction out of those monitos [comic books]. I do not see any influence from those comics. I have always been drawn by the human dilemma, which is plentiful now as it was then.

In school I was exposed to the regular assigned readings: ". . . And Tell of Time," *A Tale of Two Cities*, and Shakespeare. My sister gave me *El Quijote* about then, and another friend, *The Brothers Karamazov*, which I read previous to my going to college. I got interested later on in Mickey Spillane and other paperbacks. I always read particularly that which was prohibited, like *The Tales of the Decameron* and *Forever Amber*. When it comes to books, I cannot honestly say that much remains, as I believe I have always read for the sheer enjoyment and not to see what I get out of books. It is obvious that all that reading has helped me to augment my expression, literary as well as simply communicative. My taste range is so weird that I cannot single out specific books. I go from pornography to religious and I guess the only thing that turns me off about books in general is the darn time it takes me to read just one. I am a very slow reader and read thirty or so pages at a time. I would advise my Chicano carnales [brothers] in general to match their taste to some set of authors and to exhaust their material so that the influence can really be beneficial. Those with inclinations to be poets or writers I would advise lots of care that you do not get into the trap of wanting to be like so and so, and that you develop your own style and say what is really yours to say and quit any attempts at imitation. The world has enough mimics; we need more creative minds.

What is the extent of your studies?

I have gone through a Bachelor of Science degree and some postgraduate courses, as far as my formal education.

Has formal education helped or hindered you as a writer?

I would say education has helped me in two great ways, by expanding the necessary vocabulary in both English and Spanish, and secondly by giving me a general range of challenging basics to write about and exposing me to a few stimulating professors with beautiful minds and hearts as well as a creative spirit. Other than that, my own life experience is the basic source of inspiration and material from which I draw, as well as a vocabulary I would not necessarily have picked up in my formal education.

I would recommend to those who want to indulge in the curse of the pen to write and write every chance they have. Rather than any specific subject I would recommend exercises which can be done without maestros [teachers] or schools, such as doing profiles of people, trying to describe their manners, their physical highlights, their moods, etc., etc. I find driving in a bus much more creative than the whole bunch of creative writing courses I have seen. The writing and writing bit I recommend is for writers to arrive by that process at their own style and their own forte and then cultivate that strength. Of course as you write and write you will also notice your weaknesses. Rather than asking anyone what they think of your writings, just share them and learn to read their expressions as they read it.

Which was the predominant language in your home as a child? Which do you speak more fluently now?

The predominant language in my home has always been Spanish and I'm certain that continues to be the language in which I express myself best; yet my command of English is such that comparatively speaking the vocabulary inventory in English may be as extensive.

When I write it is a very special process. I literally give birth to the ideas which wiggle in me wanting to come out. To see in front of you, on paper, ideas that were but moments earlier all disarranged in your mind is quite a feeling of accomplishment which is more fuel and more inspiration for those of us who write. We have our dry spells in which for whatever reasons nos tapamos [we block ourselves] and nothing comes out. Those moments, long as they may be, are also part of the total process. The spirit is creative and spontaneous, at least it is that way in me, and when you gotta write you gotta write even if the tools are an old crayon and a napkin. I have just said that when an idea is ready to out and become a short story, a novel, or a short verso [poem] it is almost kicking out of me; thus it has already its gender. We can ovulate as well in English or in Spanish, or mixed . . . you can say the genes are there and we at times do not know what we will be creating until it is in front of us. It is like a pregnant woman who knows she has a baby en la panza [in her belly] but does not know if the baby will be a boy or a girl and prieto or quero [dark or fair]. The background I can give you about my personal writing habits is that I tend to be prolific and turn out great quantities of stuff. In doing this I sacrifice quality and turn out a lot of junk; among the junk once in a while, sometimes, I turn out something that impresses even me. I know I will never be a good writer because I am basically too lazy to polish what I do, but I also know that few people have the ability to present so many ideas in so many ways as I do. I began to learn to speak English at the age of twelve when my vocabulary was actually zero, despite the fact I used to love movies (with subtitles in Spanish; thus I never paid much attention to the sound). I started at the age of twelve and now at the age of forty-six I am still learning. This was in El Paso along with other Chicanos chorreados como yo [bedraggled like myself] who really did not realize that learning the language well could have some payoffs in the long run.

Does Chicano literature have a particular language or idiom?

Chicano literature's main characteristic is that it is a literature that is naturally at ease in the way that Chicanos express themselves, and that is a natural bilingualism, with the influence of English naturally predominant, as that is the language in which all Chicanos are educated. As far as an idiom, if I can detect the thin difference applicable to Chicano literature, we can say that Chicano literature is heavily spiced with caló [slang] and a sort of regionalism, and even ungrammatical standard expressions

which give it flavor peculiar to Chicanos. To write using natural
bilingual style is a very vivid affirmation that we are here, that
we are alive and well, thinking and writing in both idiomas
[languages], and that there are many like us out there in that
mythical Aztlán who also think and talk and write as we do. To
list writers and explain by examples of their writings this phenomenon is a bit redundant and causes a problem of saying that
those carnalitos and carnalitas [brothers and sisters] writing
monolingually in either Spanish or English no andan en la onda
[are not in step]. Among Chicano writers some of us tend to
favor mixing the two languages, at times naturally or at times
calculatedly, for effect, and se vale [it's O.K.], but it is no big
deal. Let it suffice to repeat that in the total sum of Chicano
literature, bilingualistic mix, even more than two languages at
times, is a trademark too big to ignore.

---

*How do you perceive your role as a writer vis-à-vis: (a) the Chicano
community or Movement; (b) U.S. society; (c) literature itself?*

The way I perceive my role vis-à-vis the Chicano community
(Movement) is in a triple-whammy manner. One role is that of a
recorder for Chicano events, happenings, victories, defeats,
struggles from a poetic perspective absent from newspapers and
prose journals. The other role is that of "animator" to give spirit
and even at times philosophical direction and criticism. And yet
a third role is to serve as a model in our own communities for
other writers to follow in developing their own creative spirits. I
could say that not all writing that I do can be considered literature per se, but a lot of my efforts have been dedicated to writing
proposals, evaluations, letters of recommendation, teaching
modules, etc., etc. I certainly do make a distinction between the
Chicano community and the Chicano Movement. Therefore the
role of a Chicano writer may very well be viewed from various
perspectives. When I write I keep them all in mind.

As far as my role in relation to U.S. society, I do not see how
the dominant segment affecting our lives can be ignored either
as an audience or as a subject. It is not necessarily the intent, at
least mine, to limit my literary expression to theme or audience.
The thing is, we as Chicanos are very much a part of U.S. society, and being absent from the literary scene is but one of the
calculated, forced exclusions we have experienced and are trying
to correct.

As far as literature itself, it must be considered from an artistic and universal perspective, and my role is to introduce myself as part of the continuous process and even impose myself as a contemporary and future influence.

What is the place of Chicano literature within U.S. literature?

The question bothers me, since U.S. literature is not an abstract box which other literatures are fitted in; but Chicano, Black, Native American, and Asian American literary expression, long absent from American literature, have designated by their absence American literature as an incomplete representative of American literary efforts. A true fact is that Chicano literature is an emerging and imposing form needed to make American literature truly complete. Chicano literature does not bring anything to American literature because it too is American literature. This was not a good question, I am afraid; I cannot field it without getting a bit angry that you would even ask it. What it brings, not to literature but to the dominant world of Anglos, is a chance for them to look at us as we look at ourselves, and that is a minor part of the total Chicano effort to be acknowledged as equals in the full sense of the word without the bullshit of affirmative action.

What is the relationship of Chicano literature to Mexican literature?

The relationship is a very natural one, as among Chicano writers a great portion of us have our native roots in la Madre Patria [Mother Country]. Some Chicano writers are Mexican or at least extensions or descendants of Mexicans making great literary contributions. Again the question of the movement is relevant here in that a stronger bondage is felt by those who have dedicated themselves to the question of using literature as a vehicle of social protest, whether Chicanos or Mexican nationals. Some of us Chicanos envy the way our brothers to the south handle the Spanish word, and they must laugh at times at our shortcomings in that respect, but all in all the brotherhood is a felt and real one. Lately, exchanging articles, poetry, and publications has become a more extensive effort. I would have to say that of all the carnales and carnalas I know who write, very few, if any, are influenced by Mexican writers. I for one do not even know who they are. Not that they are not important and that we should not read them, make efforts even to read them, but right now those chains are not too well built. The fault may lie in the crazy Spanish departments of all U.S. institutions of higher learning who have a bias against Mexico and pump us full of Spain and Latin America before they acknowledge the literary forces of Mexico.

The question of "crítica" [criticism] is a valid international question in which we can develop international critics in both English and Spanish. By international critics I have in mind first of all creating a bond between writers and poets from here and writers and poets from Central and South America, and then exchanging books and material for comment, and ultimately identifying people who can offer crítica [criticism]. The function that they would serve would firstly go to weeding out bad material from quality works and relating Chicano literature in a much wider, international, context. It would be understood that from among Chicano writers some critics would emerge. By now, that I write this, there are already a good dozen individuals whose specialty of work is criticism of Chicano lit and among them some who also criticize works of writers south of the border.

Do you perceive yourself and your work as political?

Whether I do or do not see myself and my writings as political is really not important; the truth is, all writings and all persons are political in one way or another. In my case it certainly is a more calculated way of life, and my work can easily be identified in the areas of raising questions both inside and outside the Chicano community which are socially and politically motivated. When I inspire my Chicano brothers to rid themselves of all oppression and to rid themselves of hang-ups and complexes, when I speak directly to the dominant oppressive society and point to their neglect and abuse, I am being very political, but you could easily substitute the word "Christian" for "political."

Does the Chicano writer have anything in common with the majority group writers? Differences?

Some of us Chicanos have had some occasion to share expressions and jointly do readings, conferences, or seminars with other writers, with the majority group writers. These occasions are yet few and far between and most of us continue very much on the fringe, some by design and some by choice. We have found that the majority of Anglo writers are very much in tune (or us with them) when it comes to using literature, poetry in particular, to criticize the obvious abuses that are committed world-wide by our country and all the social neglect, insensitivity, and racism. They too write of a better America, a better world, a real humanity, a start for the use of our divinity. The differences we have, at least those I have noted, have to do with the styles, handling of subjects, and of course the different cultures, values, life styles, and experiences, and most certainly the vocabulary. By being Chicanos, writers contrast with Anglo writers in that certain themes can only be handled vividly by them and Anglos would be at a disadvantage at trying to refer to them with realism and feeling. One obvious one would be the experience of discrimination by Anglos themselves. Most certainly Anglos do not discriminate against other Anglos. There is the white goddess complex, or racially mixed love affairs; only the Chicano can feel and write about such experience and describe what Chicanos feel. The barrio growing-up thing is netamente [genuinely] a Chicano subject. The styles in which these themes are handled are again subject to phrases and words which are part of the Chicano totality of experience and which are used by Anglos only as second-hand observers. When it comes to values it is a new ball game. Chicanos and Anglos both bear the brunt of society in general and both at times have the same value outlook on things and both can write about love, war, life, death, success, and, depending on the degree of acculturation of the Chicano, writers offer us a different interpretation of similar episodes. Three novels exemplify this: *Bless Me, Ultima, The Revolt of the Cockroach People,* and *Peregrinos de Aztlán.*

Does Chicano literature share common ground with Black literature? Differences?

Chicanos and Blacks, Native Americans, too, for that matter, have in common the obligation of amplifying in their literature, of dramatizing, las quejas de su gente [the protests of their people], the misery, the struggle, and the heroic survival they undergo. The style of writing and the degree of imitation of the whiteman's literature as a model varies. Most of us do not go around just reading other Chicanos, so that we tend to read what those writers from the dominant culture are writing. Some of us knowingly or subconsciously get influenced by what we read. After all the English language is no sole domain of theirs and whatever we write is bound to look like what someone else wrote. I would say because Blacks do not have another language pool to draw from other than English, in contrast to Chicanos and Boricuas, they would be subject to greater influence from Anglo writers on the pure use of language and plot than we would. The influence is neither positive or negative but depends on what it is we copy or use from any particular Anglo writer.

Another major difference has to do with our own audiences and the degree to which our literature is appreciated and well received by our own people in contrast to the dominant society. People who read what we Chicano writers write are either other Chicanos or minorities or the dominant society in general. It is obvious that the two audiences or readerships are looking at what we create with different eyes and minds. Even among those Chicanos who read what we write there are degrees of acceptance, rejection, relating, as they come from various strata in our own communities. You cannot expect a Chicano banker to relate to a campesino, or a businessman to a pinto [convict] or tecato [drug addict] poem or story. The question of art and the question of how effective we are with what we create are two questions which determine the impact we have. The truth is that we can make classes and races relate to each other and use our works as bridges for them to meet.

Is there any relationship with the literature of other Spanish-speaking groups?

The literature of Portorriqueños is quite similar to that of Chicanos in theme and style. There is a great resemblance to that of other revolutionary people in South America. Some of the Chicano writers, having been educated formally, pick up Spanish (from Spain) poets and authors of the magnitude of Cervantes and Lorca, and, consciously or subconsciously, go on to imitate those styles. The short cuento [story] and the poetry have more in common with each other than do novels, generally speaking. Rather than give you examples I will only refer you to *Revista Chicano-Riqueña*, in which the Boricuas and the Chicanos are often placed page to page and one can immediately find the strong resemblances of styles and themes. In the recent Canto al Pueblo festival in Corpus [Christi, Texas, 1978], about five Portorriqueños got up to read, and for some of us who do not get a chance to listen to them it was quite a treat. They take characters from the barrio, or from the drug culture, or the struggle, who are easy to interchange with Chicanos. In exchanging opinions with those who have traveled to Cuba and to other parts of S.A., as Morton and Raúl Salinas do constantly, they rediscover a direct relationship with revolutionary poets and writers. The other art form of canción de protestas [protest songs] brings forth these relationships much better.

Does Chicano literature have a distinct perspective on life? What effect does it have on the literature?

The main criterion from which to recognize Chicano literature, other than the author having told you he is Chicano, is the very distinct perspective on life; our culture, which is, after all, our values or perspectives on life, is different, so we naturally have to express those differences. Because of the great dominance and influence of the Anglo value system, some of our literature cannot help but reflect warped perspectives at times and speak of this cultural struggle constantly.

If you are a Chicano writer you are bound to be in a constant struggle with yourself to sort out what it is that you say that has actually been influenced by the way the Raza you represent thinks. The other side of that coin is that we are constantly influenced, and to a greater degree at times, by the way Anglos think. That struggle is bound to be reflected in what we write. If it is about suffering; the dolor [pain] of the people who lose children at the hands of uncaring schools, prisons, medical systems, the army, has got to be a unique Chicano experience. The humiliation of having to be at the mercy of a crumb-throwing society and even the acceptance of the role of adopting nueva lengua [a new language] and the idea of being on your own soil as a foreigner . . . all of these things have to be a set of themes with universal relationship, but with a very peculiar Chicano flavor. We drown in two cultures and when we come up for air for a third time we do not know whether to yell for help or auxilio [help].

Does Chicano literature improve communication between Chicanos and Anglo Americans?

Because of the intimate nature of communicating with other people via literary efforts, relationships do tend to improve, to increase our levels of tolerance and understanding. There is the danger that those with no minds and no hearts, bent on racist, oppressive, and elitist ways, will see our literature as a polarizing medium which works away from their aim of Americanizing everybody and everything. To these people Chicano literature is an opposing, threatening, and dangerous force.

We as writers carry an added responsibility. Some of us are even very dangerous individuals in that we can confuse readers and speed up the acculturation which often appears in our own writings. This was the subject of some of the crítica [criticism] presently leveled at some writers. If they write and tell people who are suffering that it is cute to suffer and that we must be machos and aguantar las jodas sociales bajo las cuales vivimos [bear the social ills under which we live]. We are worse than sellouts, we are the vocinas [spokesmen] of the dominant culture, the agents of doom and acceptance, we are the social tranquilizers. We are not any longer talking of making people accommodate or survive in an Anglo world, we are talking about revolution, about us not having to change to live in dignity and get our due as true contributors of this land of plenty. Communications are improved all over if there is honesty in the writers. If we are truly artistas and we paint with words fantasies or realities, we are mirrors in which many can come and look at themselves. If we are phony, those mirrors are tinted and no one can truly see himself in us. Thus, communications can improve internally among our own Raza first and secondly we can begin to dialogue with el enemigo [the enemy].

Does Chicano literature reevaluate, attack, or subvert the value system of the majority society? Is it a revolutionary literature? Thematically? Technically?

Both technically and thematically Chicano literature is a revolutionary force in that it advocates a change not necessarily solicited, welcome, or wanted, by the dominant culture. Chicano literature is revolutionary in that it imposes itself forcefully rather than sit back for natural evolution to invite it in. Most of our initial efforts took the shape of attacks upon a system that has historically been abusive, oppressive, insensitive, and closed to us and our needs. It is cowardly and unnatural for a true artist not to use his talents for this purpose.

One technical revolutionary theme or element presently identified in Chicano literature is that a negation of the "realist" school is strongly emerging among Chicano and other Mexican writers. It is as if we have a nation of people who are fed up with being fed realism and now want a menu full of fantasies. We can deliver fantasies with un poquito de chile [a little dash of spice] . . . but . . . there is danger there, too. Chicano wit, or humor, is found more and more . . . the cabula [word play] that is ours can be a major tool to also combat the hipocrecía [hypocrisy] found among us and certainly among those who profess to lead this nation. Chicano writers have matured significantly since the fifteen or more years that we have been macheteándole a las tristes [beating the sad] typewriters . . . We have weeded out clichés and slogans and now busy ourselves with another bigger mandate [order] than fighting the oppressors, and that is what do we offer by way of strategy to eliminate our social woes and what do we see as a possible Aztlán, rather than a mythical one. We have even directed a few word fregasos [lashings] among ourselves, Chicano leaders and other would-be poets and writers who compromise themselves a vuelta de esquina [just around the corner]. To go on narrowing down fictitious enemies so that we can truly destroy them and an oppressive system which tricks and connives the weak into staying weak—and the goal is to keep before us the beauty of our humanity and anything that is dehumanizing . . . pos a darle matarili [well eliminate it].

What problems have you encountered in publishing? Were they racially founded?

My personal problems in getting published have been and continue to be major ones. In my case I would not wait, so I created Barrio Publications to print my works and those of upcoming writers. Barrio Publications uses the financial support of those carnales who wish to see our works printed and invest their own meager resources. Although my poems appear in almost any existing anthology, major publishers are still afraid to invest in us. Other than a few breakthroughs, I would conclude that racist misreadings on the quality and need of our literature still govern the thinking of major publishers who have a commercial rather than a social concern.

Are Chicanos at a disadvantage in trying to practice the art of writing?

Chicano writers, and other minorities for that matter, are at a set of disadvantages when it comes to the art of writing. Most of us tend to be deficient in two languages rather than proficient in both, as we should be, or as hopefully bilingual programs will prepare us to be. This tends to give us a sense of insecurity when we express ourselves orally and in written form. This tendency to feel unable is reinforced in schools, where our sparks of creativeness are often suffocated. Our homes do not often have the abundance of books, periodicals, and magazines, to inspire in us a love for the written word, and even the beautiful Chicano art of conversation lacks as our parents struggle for mere survival and are often too tired or worried to tend to it. Later on in life, as is the case with some of us, time becomes our worst enemy in that I do not know any Chicano writer who gives writing his best attention; rather we have to do it when we can. The costly question of having our work typed, xeroxed, or properly edited is a luxury. As long as writing is but one of our sidelines, as we work and involve ourselves in El Movimiento [The Movement], it will suffer a bit in that we really do not give it our best effort. Sacrificing time and energy and being involved have a positive side, too, as our work is more relevant and also more precious in nature as it is an artistic birth of our struggle, so that what I state is not truly a complaint but a set of facts.

What are the most outstanding qualities of Chicano literature?
Weaknesses?

The most outstanding qualities of Chicano literature have to do with introducing in greater quantities a set of values and perspectives on life so long admired and misunderstood by the dominant society, while at the same time sharing them with our own community, who at times are on the verge of forgetting or ignoring them themselves. These values are in strong contrast with those of the dominant society, and this clash is a healthy one which is long overdue to produce a rainbow of values in the pluralistic society in which we live. Many Anglos have told me personally that they admire our way of life. I am sure others have confessed such. What is it that they admire—our poverty, our misery? No. They admire the way we cope with life and enjoy it. They admire our capacity to suffer and to enjoy. In a way they admire our freedom to be not so concerned with the damn future and with all these material possessions and trinkets which abound. The sense of loyalty to our familias and to friends. Even the rascal qualities we seem to have are at times admired, because we can be dishonest with flair rather than in the dark. They are coming around, with the energy crisis and with the ecological movement, to where we have always been, to a love and respect for mother earth, to a way of using solar energy . . . los tendederos, ese [the clotheslines, man]. Some of our writings express well Indo-Precolumbian thoughts, which ecologically speaking are so in tune with today and offer answers to our personal anxieties and fatigues, so that we can, in fact, say that Chicano literature has in itself a curative effect for our present confusion and despair. Since our raíces [roots] are in themselves indo-ecological, we carry in us a sacred admiration of food and food-producing earth. The idea of poisoning water and earth which give us life is certainly not in our culture. While we acknowledge death as a very natural part of life, we do not go around bending backwards to create it in mass with nuclear plants. The curative effect of Chicano literature frankly is that it offers us a bit of healthy insanity, a valve to let out some of the frustrations of living as we do in America, nay, in the whole world, today. Not many other carnales have picked up on the onda [the notion] that we can be remedial with our works. Dig on how poetry is part of a psychotherapy now . . . we've known that all along and say it jokingly que de poetas y locos todos tenemos un poco [there is a little bit of poet and madman in everyone]. Unless we know this we are bound to be creating the same kind of anxiety in our works and that same feeling of apathy and hopelessness so abundantly present nowadays. To weave these philosophies into our poetry and our cuentos [stories] without having them appear as moralizing messages is art.

The only weaknesses in our literature that I presently see are by way of danger, that is that we as writers drown and perish in a sea of hate created by ourselves for our lot and against our oppressors. This translates in making every piece we write a slogan, a chicote [whip] to whip our enemies with, a cry, a bellyache for our hunger and misery, leaving out the artistry of expression and the universality of our message. I'm not saying this should not be done, but that it should be done in the medium we have chosen ourselves, which is "literary art."

Critics are not superhumans, they are as desmadrados [messed up] as the writers at times, if not more, in that they have Anglo measuring sticks, or European ones which they were given in academia, and if we as writers had been trained to write in academia also, all would be cool. They are measuring oranges with a tomato scale, and that just won't do. The other set of critics are on a political onda [trip] that overblinds them to writing as an artform; everything is measured by a Marxist yardstick, and if what you are writing does not have gunpowder and lead all masses to overthrow the burgueses [bourgeoisie], olvídate, porque ni te van a criticar estos carnales y admirables carnalas [forget it, because those brothers and admirable sisters are not even going to criticize you]. I have challenged critics to develop their own standards in keeping with what they are trying to criticize, and they think I am nuts. They are right, as that thing we call literature must of necessity have some universal standards to be measured by, or else a bunch of different measuring instruments would be quite confusing. Chicano literature is bound by these universal standards and by the art standards established long ago . . . those standards, I believe, are subject to revolution also.

What are the milestones so far in Chicano literature?

Oddly enough they have nothing to do with literature per se but with the taste for it aroused, with the demand for Chicano literature courses which constantly grow and demand new materials, new works from us. The biggest milestone is that our barrios, our farmworkers, our pintos [brothers in prison], our still uneducated and impoverished masses have accepted our work. How it happened that Chicano literature emerged and that some became interested in creating it and others in accepting it and even demanding it is the question of the steady diet of Gabacho [Anglo American] literature to which we had been subjected for many years. The item suddenly appeared on the literature menu and people started to taste it and order it again. It is obvious that certain conditions had to exist; the question was one of an explosive readiness on everyone's part. What has been extremely difficult is that we have no Wall Street backers or Madison Avenue promoters, and the few garage printer efforts are few and far between. Since I personally have been in the business of disseminating, I know first-hand how hard it is. Presently I am getting a book out which costs thirty-eight hundred bucks . . . not many of us, none of us have that kind of bread to invest in books, even if they do sell. Los festivales como [the festivals like] Flor Y Canto and now Canto al Pueblo have done much to inspire new writers, particularly young writers, women writers, and the many other art forms from our communities. These festivals have some built-in dangers; they can become too phony and too commercial, too much entertainment and not enough concern for who we are and what we are all about, too much of a forum for all the old prima donnas to promenade in a non-Chicano spirit competitively among each other. As for publishing houses, pos cuales [which] other than Quinto Sol and now the other one [Justa] . . . that is not enough and the dumb Chicanos running Chicano studies, who are in a position to help, continue to buy Gabacho products and foreign, so it is a wonder that they are still operating. If it is not possible on the part of eight million Chicanos to create literature for themselves and to promote it, I say we are in a damn sad state of affairs and maybe ready for another few hundred years of silence and obscurity. There are many things we can do to prevent this self-created doom.

Rayas is one answer. Three or so years ago some of us thought of creating a vehicle to promote Chicano literature in all levels and aspects. It plays a role in identifying writers and doing críticas [criticism] on them. It seeks to identify markets and resources; it seeks to establish communications on an international level and to begin to address ourselves to the question of turning out quality works and doing them in a professional way. Just because La Raza está pobre [the Chicano People are poor] is no excuse to give them crap . . . they themselves deserve the best we can produce, and they know quality from crap as well as any critical genius. We suffer from the same mickey mouse regional and personal tirades that others in the Chicano communities suffer, and so we move slowly and carefully and defensively.

What is the future of Chicano literature: distinctiveness, or the de-emphasis of the distinctive characteristics?

The future of Chicano literature is precisely dependent on what I have just said. If it continues to be relevant to our gente [people], it will continue to live and give fruit and flower. The danger is also eminent that if we make it a mere toy of the elite or the academician, or bury it in libraries and bookstores, it may not receive the necessary sun, it will die. I take the action of de-emphasizing or modifying the characteristics of Chicano literature as equal to accommodating ourselves to the norms of the dominant society and losing ourselves in the process.

Who are the leaders among Chicano writers, and why?

There are by now a good number of Chicano authors well recognized throughout Aztlán. They are liked and oftentimes imitated and even surpassed in effort by young writers. A recent Flor y Canto brought many of us face to face with each other, and yet many remain unread, undiscovered, with shelves full of beautiful manuscripts. To say who the leaders are in our fraternity of artists and writers is a dangerous task, as it only indicates preferences and like, and is not truly reflective of in-depth comparison and crítica. Also, since Chicano literature can be said to be in its embryonic stage, it may now be very easy to be among the first and best, whereas in years to come this might well be a giant task for experts. Three names come to mind who are generally considered geniuses in the art form: Ricardo Sánchez, Rudolfo Anaya, and Oscar Zeta Acosta. We had for a long time the genius of John Rechy from El Paso, Texas (*City of Night*), whom few knew to be a Chicano novelist of great stature. Poets like Alurista and Nephtalí are now giants in the field, while the most-read poem, "Yo Soy Joaquín," cannot be ignored and places its author among these creative brothers. There are technical writers like Rudolfo Acuña, who treats history to our advantage, who can easily be considered great. I'll conclude by giving my own preferences regardless of stature: Miguel Méndez, *Peregrinos de Aztlán*; María Mondragón, unpublished poetess from Alamosa, Colorado; the late Heriberto Terán and Magdaleno Avila, who writes with the pen name of Juan Valdez; Pacheco, Contreras, Raymundo Pérez (El Tigre), and Tep Falcón—only some of those I myself consider leaders. As to why I consider them so, the answer may be found in the beauty, the sensitivity, the simplicity, the craft, the heart, the fidelity to our cultural values, the enojo [anger] I find when I read them. Javier Pacheco, José Antonio Burciaga, Lorna Dee Cervantes, Amy López, Bernice Zamora.

I would like to conclude by emphasizing what I consider terribly important. I'm referring to instilling in our young Chicanitos a love for the written word. This word in itself, when it is truly their own and not someone else's, has a liberating power equal to none. In the school and in the home we should do all we can to expose the child to the written word, to equip him with an ample vocabulary and to add variety to his expression and give free vent to the creative spirit so naturally inherent in most Chicanos. Secondly, I foresee a need for developing our own literary critics who can assist in evaluating and prompting our works as well as adding to our improvement by criticizing and pointing out areas of weakness. Thirdly, I would like to see a few more Quinto Soles (a Chicano owned and run publishing house in California), who would help us publish and recognize our works, and more distributing houses and a whole front of educators fighting to crash the racist barriers which continue to keep our materials out of textbooks and out of the schools. The Chicano book belongs in primary and secondary schools and not only at the college and university levels. By the same token, some of us must begin to write for children and put the beautiful cultural values we have into our writings.

José Montoya

In Montoya we have the case of a poet who is respected as one of the most important among Chicano poets mostly on the basis of one poem: "El Louie." Of course, it happens to be the most widely known, most popular Chicano short poem and, in my opinion, the best. "El Louie" is an interlingual elegy to Louie Rodríguez, the leader of a Pachuco group from Fowler, California, in the 1940's and 1950's. Louie, the epitome of the positive Pachuco, rejects opportunities to ingress into the majority society and finally dies, a drug addict alone in a rented room. Its essential theme, the threat of disappearance, and its deep structure—threat to vital image→rescue of image in the text→text as response to the threat—are those of Chicano literature itself, and "El Louie" is thus an excellent paradigm of that literature.* This could explain its success among widely diverse segments of the Chicano reading public.

A selection of Montoya's poetry appeared in the first *El Espejo*, and "El Louie" has been anthologized and pirated countless times. Montoya also published a book, *El sol y los de abajo and other R.C.A.F. poems*, printed in a back-to-back edition with a text by Alejandro Murguía. This arrangement has proved unfortunate, for the book has been almost impossible to locate since the beginning, though apparently there is a large stock of them being held by the publisher. Montoya talks about beginning his writing with short stories, and recently he has published in that genre. At the present time, La Causa Publications is preparing a second book of poetry, a joint project with the artist Estevan Villa.

By profession Montoya is a painter and professor of art. His paintings have been widely exhibited. His innovation of Tortilla

---

* See Bruce-Novoa, "Literatura chicana: La respuesta al caos," *Revista de la Universidad de México* 29, no. 12 (August 1975): 20–24; "The Space of Chicano Literature," *De Colores* 1, no. 4 (1975): 22–42.

art—images burned onto tortillas, which are then displayed as paintings—can be taken as a joke, or as an intuitive stroke of genius in that it aesthetically transforms the staple of Chicano life into an object of art. More accurately, it is both, and here is the key to Montoya's real genius: a sense of perspective, based on humor, constantly undercuts the grandiose pretentions of the arts, while never hindering their progress. Montoya's work is never pretentious. He avoids the preachy didacticism and the precarious righteousness of some of his peers, never reducing life to simplistic dichotomies. This same healthy, ironic humor is found also in the term RCAF, which Montoya utilizes several times in the interview. It stands for Rebel Chicano Art Front, though hardly anyone knows that; rather, what began as a joke has imposed itself on reality: Royal Chicano Air Force. Under that name work a group of artists and poets who have gathered around Montoya in Sacramento, California. They are a highly respected, model artists' cooperative and community-action group, whose art has attracted national and international attention.

What is conveyed in Montoya's poetry, besides the balanced sense of healthy objectivity, is the natural, down-to-earth tone of a sincere, candid man. Everything in Montoya rings natural. His poetry flows like spontaneous speech. And while Alurista may have been the first to publish interlingual poetry,* Montoya is the master, utilizing the two languages as smoothly as if they were one. Perhaps in Montoya's case we should speak of *intra*lingualism, one language encompassing both Spanish and English, instead of *inter*lingualism, a language that moves between Spanish and English. And always there is the sharp eye and the ironic tongue of his Manito forbearers from the New Mexico mountains.

I recorded the interview with José Montoya in March 1977 in New Haven. I wish to thank Orlando Ramírez and Isabel Barraza, who assisted me. Montoya reviewed the text in October 1979.

When and where were you born?

May 28, 1932, on a ranch called El Gallego, which is no longer anything, but my birth was registered in Escoboza, in the Manzano mountains of New Mexico, northeast of Albuquerque.

---

* See the section on language in the Introduction.

Describe your family background and your present situation.

My family had been in New Mexico a long, long time. Originally they came from Parral, Chihuahua. On my mother's side they went way up towards the Colorado border. On my father's side they settled in Tierra Amarilla, where my father was born, which I just found out last summer. I always thought he was born in Parral, but, apparently, from my grandfather on they were born in Tierra Amarilla. Ranchers on my mother's side and sheepherders on my father's. My grandfather José Montoya had sheep; Santiago Saiz, on my mother's side, had a farm.

We lived on the ranch until I was six, when we moved to Albuquerque. But I spent a lot of time in the mountains, because I couldn't adjust to the whole city thing. Consequently, I was always being shipped back to stay with my aunts. Of all the people I used to stay with, the ones I liked most were an aunt on my mother's side and my grandmother and stepgranddad, who was the Justice of the Peace in that area. That always blew me away. Like my cousin was the sheriff. It was a kind of law and order very different from what I grew up with later on. The *real* law men I remember law and order from was when the Treasury Department came down on the still. My father made corn liquor for some Italians in Albuquerque. He used to distribute it all over, but he ran the still in the mountains. That's the first time I saw tommy guns. They actually opened up on the still with a machine gun. Blew everybody's mind away. I remember I couldn't understand what the hell was happening. Then they brought out the regular hachas [axes] and sledgehammers and destroyed everything. But they were different law people than Primo [Cousin] Sandoval, the main sheriff who went after drunks and sobered them up; a very different kind of thing.

Education was the same trip. All the teachers spoke Spanish in Escoboza and you never had to worry; going to school was fun, like going to a party. You looked forward to it. Never any trips about having to learn English. But when I went to Albuquerque, education became a drudgery. I started considering missing school and ran away to California from the first grade; got as far as the Río Grande. Didn't know there was a river to cross; headed back home. I was crossing the school grounds when I ran into one of my sister's boy friends, who told me,

"Your Jefito's [dad] looking for you and is he mad; are you going to get it!" I got the shit knocked out of me by my jefito.

When I was ten we moved to Califas [California], to Delano. My father and my brother had already gone to Delano on a reenganche [work contract]. They used to have contratistas [contractors] who came and recruited and loaded workers on the train. We got a place in Delano on the Sierra Vista Ranch. My father got the cookhouse, which was a way to get the whole family in there. That started the migrant trip up and down, all over Califas. But I always gravitated back to the mountains. Even when my family was in Califas I still spent time there, in Escoboza mostly; went to school there.

The family came back to Albuquerque and back again to Califas. After '47 we stayed. After that there was talk about selling the house we had in the barrio of San José in Albuquerque. I started high school, but we still moved around, all over Califas, especially the valley. We lived in Oakland during the war so everybody in the family could work in the defense plant; my jefita [mother], my dad, my two sisters, and a brother. I was too young, so I spent my time in the streets of East Oakland. Those were the good times. In early 1950 my jefito split out to New Mexico, but we stayed.

In 1951 I joined the Navy. I wanted to join the Marines, but I had this cross [tattoo] on my hand, so they wouldn't take me. The Navy and the Marines wouldn't take anyone with a cross tattoo because of the Pachuco riots. It's kind of ironic, because just recently people were doing anything to stay out of the service, and we were trying like hell to get in, man, because in the barrio there were just a few things that you chould choose from. The prison was about all you could look forward to. Peer pressure pushed you into activities that would eventually lead there. A lot of my partners either wound up in prison or O.D.'ed. So I changed the cross to an anchor. The Marines still didn't take me, but the Navy bought it. I wound up in a minesweeper in Korea.

I had some good people in high school who deserve credit. I got along with the art teacher, who helped me out a lot, but he still didn't think there was salvation for me. I was headed for bad trouble. But another guy from back east—Adrian Sanford—was really impressed with the Chicano students and the difference between us and the Blacks and the Japanese in that area of town.

They all hung around together, but there was a very distinct separation; no dating. Sanford was interested. He actually wrote a play. He attempted to do an all-school play for the first time in that area, and he included parts for Chicanos and Blacks. There weren't too many Blacks, just a couple. He asked me to participate. I told him he was crazy, I didn't go in for that sort of trip. You were in school because you had to be and it was better than working in the fields. If you were lazy, school was the better alternative. But after school it was down to the pool hall y dale huelo a la hilacha [have a good time]. I had an idea he'd ask me to cut my hair and change my way of dress; but the play wasn't that sort of thing. It was about a gangster type, but Sanford changed it to Joe Drako. That was my part. It was a musical. I had to do a soft-shoe and sing a little ditty: [he sings] "I'm the roughest, toughest criminal in town. Everybody runs and hides when I'm around." And I'm doing this little dance. The music teacher wrote the music and lyrics. [He sings again] "Life is what you make it, it can be happiness or trouble or harmony." Not bad, I can't believe it, I still remember. That was 1951. So Sanford got me turned around about a lot of things. Because of my art ability, he got me to run for the Art Commissioner, the position that handled all publicity. I won and found myself in the student council. My partners were all blown away. I had to have little sessions at the pool hall to explain. After that it opened up for us. The next year we had a Chicano student body president. From there I graduated in 1951 and then, Korea.

Now I'm an Associate Professor of Art at California State University in Sacramento. I've never taught creative writing. I've worked with many young poets, but not in any class situation.

When did you first begin to write?

Well, back to Sanford. I had written a piece for an English class on my father's experience in Leavenworth, on how the prisoners were processed into the prison, what they had to go through, how they were sprayed with a green mist to get rid of lice; everything from the time they got inside the gate until they went to bed that night. Two pages, I think. Apparently, the way I wrote it impressed Sanford, and he put this bug in my head about writing. Somehow, though, I took it like I always had meant to do just that.

I don't remember when I actually started or decided to. It

seems to me that I always was going to write. I never felt the urge to do anything else. I never aspired to become anything. Maybe I had fantasies about being a flyer; that started in World War II with all the flying movies at the time, but I knew it was out of reach for some reason. Becoming a writer was another thing and I never bothered thinking that it might not be possible.

After Korea, I took some writing courses at Berkeley, and that's the first time I ran into the question of my use of bilingualism. They tried to discourage me from doing it. I could never understand why they couldn't see that it was a legitimate way of expressing myself. I just went on writing. I continued writing and painting while I taught high school later on. I had exhibited with MALAF, the Mexican American Liberation Art Front, an artists' group from the Bay area, and through that I met Octavio Romano from Quinto Sol. He had heard that I wrote poetry, and he asked me for some for *El Grito*. He liked it and decided to hold it for *El Espejo*, the anthology. That's how I first got into print. *Espejo* came out and I started to be known, give readings and all that. But I had been writing for a long time before then.

What kind of books did you read in your formative years?

In the Navy I read a lot, because that's what the Navy is all about. There's a lot of work, but there's reading material, everything from Spillane to the best. I didn't read much before then, just what you read in school, most of which turned me off. Walt Whitman had excited me, but almost everything else left me cold. But in the Navy I read *Tortilla Flat*, and I got so pissed off at Steinbeck, man, that I wanted to find the ass-hole out. That stayed with me until much later.

After I started City College in San Diego, I went after Steinbeck and got hooked on his writing. I enjoyed the rest of it and understood why he couldn't write anything on Chicanos; but he could write. That animosity became an admiration. I got into reading philosophy. Also, the stock English stuff. I didn't read anything that made an impression on me until I came to Berkeley and started getting into poetry. Whitman, again. The one I could relate to most was William Carlos Williams. I liked the way he wrote, so I made an effort to find his work. By this time I had heard the beat poets read. They were so far out that it took the works of Eliot and Pound as well as Whitman and Williams to get me to accept their stuff early on. Now I consider them to have been an influence—especially Snyder and Ginsberg. I started reading the French poets, the symbolists, Verlaine. Rimbaud impressed me a lot. I like his rebelliousness. It blew me out when I found out he had stopped writing at 19. Started reading the existentialists: Kierkegaard, Heidegger, Jaspers, Camus, and Sartre. Camus is like my man. Wow! *The Myth of Sisyphus* blew me away. La pinche muleta que traemos todos. [The same damn problem we all have.] I thought that the Chicano really knew how to push that rock up there and let it roll down and enjoy the trip. The dealing with the search became, at that time in my life, very real. If existence is absurd, do you cope or commit suicide; and both solutions are legitimate, valid.

What is the extent of your studies?

I intended to use the G.I. Bill when I got out of the Navy, but I didn't want anything to do with college or anything that smacked of academic work. About this time I found out about art school. I conjured up an image of just doing art and writing. Why go to college? I didn't realize that getting an art degree entailed all that other stuff. But my mind was made up. I also came back with the idea of writing about my experiences in the Navy—some fantastic things that I would like to eventually put down. I ran into about twelve guys from El Paso in Pearl Harbor and we banded together. Some very interesting types, bien apachucados [very Pachuco-like]. We had good talks. There were some vatos [dudes] there who were into art and writing and we'd talk about it.

When I got out I got married and got a job in a window company in San Diego with the intention of saving money to go to the Art Center in Los Angeles. But I couldn't save because we kept having kids. Five years with that company and five kids, and I was no closer to college than when I graduated from high school. So I started night school at City College in San Diego. From there I got a scholarship to the California College of Arts and Crafts, which I had decided was the best for me. The Art Center at that time only offered courses toward commercial art or advertising art. I wanted to get into painting, but I also wanted a good background in commercial art in case I should decide to go into it. But the school in Berkeley offered more, so that was the best school. The scholarship, ironically, was for commercial art, and I lost part of it because I changed to painting. It was a lot of fun at Arts and Crafts. That's where I first met Estevan Villa and Salvador Torres, who became compadres [godfathers to his children]. There were people who started things coming at me and I changed from commercial art to painting. But, also, that was a little exaggerated, because I didn't see how I was going to make it as a painter with five kids. So I changed to Art Education and became a high school art teacher.

By this time I was writing and taking creative writing courses, along with the regular English and lit classes. My first teaching assignment was in Wheatland, California, up north, which was a real trip. A high school teacher! I never knew what to do with that one. Chicanos were a shock for them. There were only three Mexican families; they didn't even want farmworkers. They kept them out in the labor camps. Strange place. I was happy teaching, but I didn't enjoy the area, so I used to get involved with the farmworker activists a little bit north of there, in a town called Marysville. That's when Estevan Villa and I started taking our trips every summer. The first summer we decided to work in the fields, figuring anything we made on top of our school salary was icing on the cake. But we had been away too long. Like my wife, she was also a farmworker, but we just couldn't get into the thing any more. After that summer Estevan and I decided to just travel. Every summer we'd take off. I had the support of a tremendous woman; she put up with a lot of shit, man, that I didn't even know I was imposing on her. I was just doing my thing and she was home with six kids. Now she's having a beautiful time, enjoying life, and she deserves every bit of it. I'm home with the kids, but it's much easier than she had it. Those trips even got us here to New Haven.
Anyway, I got my M.A. and a teaching credential.

Has formal education helped or hindered you as a writer?

It's hard for me to say, because I can say no, it's helped not hindered, but I don't really know. It might have hindered me. I'm forty-five and I see many people like Orlando [Ramírez], Hose [José Saldívar], Isabel [Barraza], and Louie the Foot [an RCAF member], people in their twenties who are far ahead of where I'm at now. Then I can go with people who have rejected the educational system and they're talking the same things as these guys are [pointing at Orlando, José, and Isabel] who are at Yale, you know what I mean? So I really don't know how to deal with it.

When I first started the Barrio Art courses with high school kids, my intention was never to bring to those barrio kids anything that smacked of the shit I had been submitted to in art classes. I would say, "Look, this is paint, these are brushes, that's paper or cardboard, there's a wall, then que vuelen [let them fly], let's have a ball, get into it and push it around and feel it." But then they'd say, "I don't know what to do." Oh, they dug it, doing anything they wanted. "It's great. This is really education!" But there was something missing. They weren't producing—well they were, but they didn't feel satisfied or comfortable. They did things without knowing what it was or why it was done. No, no está bien la onda [that's not right]. You got to get in there and actually teach, explain why they have done something good, or bad. So last semester, for the first time ever, I had them come in and take a drawing board and paper and charcoal, and I started working with light, cast shadows, the effect of light on an object, reflected light, and the whole thing. They got really into it and everybody was excited. Something was being learned. Then somebody asked me that question, boom: "Do you think this is good for them? Isn't that what you went through? Do you think it helped you?" I don't know if it did. I don't know if what I know about color theory and the principles of design, and about writing or anything else came as a result of having come through that process, or whether I might have arrived at it earlier if I hadn't gone through it.

I look at Louie's poetry or Juanishi Orozco's [member of RCAF] art—they dropped out because they thought they were getting screwed over, but they're not really dropping out. They're well read. That's dropping out with a purpose, out of one thing to develop another. So I don't know. It sounds good when Louie the Foot tells young, aspiring writers, "Don't get into writing or lit classes. You don't need to learn about Ezra Pound or T. S. Eliot. Just feel it." But, god damn it, I can sit down and talk to Louie about Pound; he knows him. I don't know from where. So I don't know how valid that kind of advice might be. I always say to read them, everything, devour them. It's a difficult position to be in. How do you facilitate learning; how do you instruct? How do you know you're not doing more harm than good? I don't know.

Which was the predominant language in your home as a child? Which do you speak more fluently now?

I didn't speak any English till we got to Albuquerque; then I became bilingual. Now? Probably I speak—well, I don't know. I always felt that I was more fluent in English, but recently, in the last few years, forcing myself to speak Spanish with certain people, I find that I know more than I thought. I was more afraid of it. There really isn't that much difference. When you're groping for a word, you can look for it in Spanish or in English.

Does Chicano literature have a particular language or idiom?

Well, it has several. The bilingual expression of the word is probably the most important, but there are all kinds of ways, and it's coming out more and more. It's limitless in the creativity the young writers are using.

How do you perceive your role as a writer vis-à-vis: (a) the Chicano community or Movement; (b) U.S. society; (c) literature itself?

Till recently I hadn't consciously ever bothered to think of whom I was writing to, what audience. This goes back, I guess, to rejecting the early instructors who talked about that by using Spanish and English you were limiting your audience. Maybe from that stems the fact that I never considered an audience. Thinking back to the places I've read, to the large community segments—fiestas patrias de mucha raza [patriotic festivals with lots of Chicanos]—the poems that excited people at Stanford turned on the people in the communities. I don't know if that defines my role or what it does to my having to think about what my role is.

Then, last summer I met with the people at the Academia [de la Nueva Raza]. They made it very apparent that it's important that the community—our people—begins to hear what we're doing. They liked our work with the murals: allowing the people to see the raza's history on barrio walls. They asked, "Are you doing that with poetry as well?" I hadn't thought about it in terms of literature until last summer, and I still don't know where it's going to go or how it's going to change. You still do the same sort of things.

Now vis-à-vis the community accepting the writer, that is a question of role too. It could happen as it did with the artists. See, the artists were rejected by the galleries first. No major gallery or museum wanted to exhibit Chicano art. That's where we wanted to be. It wasn't a matter of coming to the barrio or of wanting to do something for the barrio. That's where they sent us. The galleries said, "There's no room here." So much for our role in the U.S. society. So we went to exhibit in the barrio. But a lot of Movement art was not accepted by the community, or it was accepted with indifference, not with open arms. We learned that very quickly. So what we did was to use our expertise differently in the community and share our art, share the whole experience of involvement in art, with the community. In that respect it has been received—kind of. Having classes for the people, providing means for them to do art, from viejitos [old people] to little kids. It's taken a long time, but now, any time there's any kind of an art function in the community, the community knows who's putting it on and they work on it. When the RCAF has an art exhibit, the community is in on it, not only as viewers, but as participants. You have to hang the tejidos de las viejitas [knitting of the old women] and the work of the little children, which drives the people at the college up the wall. They can't understand why, now that the RCAF is being recognized nationally, we have to do it. Well, we don't *have to*: it's worth it for everybody. We have been able to get the community to see the positive function of art. It's an organizing tool.

The writers are a little behind the teatro [theatre] people and the visual artists in that respect. Efforts are being made. Holding the Floricanto in the barrio for the last few years has been very effective. Then we've started poetry readings in cantinas [bars] in Sacramento, which went over well, because there were more poets in the cantinas than we ever imagined. Everybody wanted to come and read their stuff, or not even their own, but just some poem they had memorized. "Oiga, tengo un poema muy bonito." "Pues, véngase." ["Listen, I've got a beautiful poem." "Well, come on."] Some winito would read a poem he'd memorized; but then people came with their own work. Now, if some people want to say, "I'm not going to read at the Reno any more; that viejita wasn't really Chicana; that's just a Mexico kind of thing," well then we're doing the same vanity judgment that the Anglo critics have done on us. There are ways of getting into the community, but a lot of times we'd rather be reading at universities than in a bar. But it was a mind blower. They started readings at La Peña, but the community won't go any more because it's all intellectual, and they show films on Chile and invite Latin American poets and performers. It's lost the community thing it started out with. We also worked in the prisons, but that's pretty touchy.

What is the place of Chicano literature in U.S. literature?

Well, after butting heads with this society, I don't think we should keep knocking on the door asking for a break. Maybe it's to our benefit. It's especially closed to the writers. Unless something spectacular happens I don't forsee the big publishers like Harper and Row suddenly asking for Chicano manuscripts. Their cellars are so crowded with all kinds of writers that they don't have to worry about us. The people in the English departments still don't accept our writing as legitimate. I did hear of one teacher who was going to include "El Louie" along with all those English writers. It blew me away. In the arts it's the same. They don't want to accept the existence of Chicano art, perhaps because they're incapable of understanding it. It's just wasted energy to try to change or make them see. One just keeps working and lets things take their course.

Interestingly enough, three things are happening now to the artists which affect this. The RCAF has been invited to exhibit in Denmark. Then, through Luis Valdez, Mexico wants to organize a traveling Chicano exhibit to tour Europe. They're recognizing the value of Chicano art. Rather than jumping a hurdle, go around it and save that energy. Third, La Galería de la Raza has an invitation to take a show to Rome. And there are people in Latin America and Spain who are curious about us. It's going to embarrass the U.S. later on, but if we don't fit, we'll work with what we have. Maybe it's that old thing about we'll get in, but on our own terms.

What is the relationship of Chicano literature to Mexican literature?

I have to make a real huge admission right here: I have read very little Mexican literature. I'm ashamed to admit it. There are certain people I like. Rulfo. I'd like to see some good barrio stories written by Chicanos with that same kind of rhythm that Rulfo uses, muy despacito [very slow]. Carlos Fuentes's way of writing also gets me excited, and I'd like to see a young Chicano come out with something like that. But in terms of how the two literatures relate, I don't think that too many Mexican writers want to accept or admit or deal with Chicano literature. Some of the people who have talked to Mexican writers tell me that they don't understand us either.

The Gabacho [Anglo American] aesthetic was pushed down our throat, so we had it to reject. That wasn't the case with the Mexican aesthetic. We may have to, and probably should, go back to some of the Mexican aesthetic. It might enrich and it might retard, I don't know. I don't know how important it is for the continuance of Chicano language.

Now Octavio Paz, he's another writer that I felt about in the way I said Steinbeck struck me. I had always considered Paz a sensitive person. I enjoyed reading the way he puts profundities across, because he probably writes with a bottle of sherry at his side rather than a stack of reference books. But when I read his description of the Pachuco it really—well, I heard somewhere that even he has repudiated it, or at least he's sorry he wrote it, because he really didn't know what the hell he was talking about. But I still enjoy his work.

Do you perceive yourself and your work as political?

Life, writing, everything about Chicanos, or just being Chicano is a political act. I've been accused of being apolitical or being anything but political, but that's some people's judgment, because I've made statements about the Chicano experience. I don't think I've ever set out to make a political statement in a poem or a painting. They just come out. Maybe, with tongue in cheek, in a poem [unpublished] about how the Movement has gone for its Ph.D. It pissed people off, but I thought it was funny, I mean what was happening—some of our ex–Brown Berets, revolutionary-spouting Buddhas are now attorneys with HEW; the pseudo-Marxist who came to the barrio to clean up drugs—"We got to get rid of the pushers at any cost"—and you tell him, "Your brother's pushing dope; here's a gun, go do him in." "Ah, my brother, huh? Well then quit talking that shit." A lot of frustration came out in that poem. It might have been a calculated political statement.

I think all artists can't help but be critics of everything; consequently, you criticize Movement things. It's healthy. I'd like to

see the Movement and everybody gravitate towards a society
that doesn't fear the artist. But I don't have any illusions about
what might happen to me as an artist with our own people. I see
a violent end for me because I'm an artist; and I don't care who
takes the reins, I'm going to criticize them and they're not going
to like it and they'll probably come up and tell me so. But as an
artist you have to be willing to give your life for what you believe in. I hope we can reach that state first where art and the
artist's vision, the artist's magic, don't have to be feared. I admire Castro because he's not afraid of art, though he's not afraid
to do things the artist will criticize him for doing.

Being an artist, you are constantly in danger. You see too
many things you wish you didn't. I don't know at what level or
stage we'll be able to separate politics from that. It's an interesting dilemma.

The staying power of the artists, as opposed to that of other
kinds of political things in the Movement, tells you something.
The artists are still around and succeeding, which frustrates
some radical elements who feel that artists are holding things
back. For instance, they ask, if we keep painting Huelga [Strike]
eagles and Quetzalcoatl and serpents, when will we get where
we're going? But those things have to be heard so that we can
understand our culture before we can go anywhere. There's a
frustration with a lot of people who try to infiltrate artists'
movements and don't get too far, because many of the artists'
groups are already into socialism. In the colectivas que están for-
mando los artistas [the collectives that the artists are starting],
everybody shares. Salaries go into the colectiva to keep it going.
The fact that the artist does control the means of production, his
own, is frustrating to those who are constantly expounding that
we have to control the means of production. We do. And we
have a socialist way of running the colectiva.

*Does the Chicano author have anything in common with the majority
group writers? Differences?*

The act of creation is a commonality; how we perceive it is the
difference. The majority writer sometimes considers his input as
a destructive force. Chicano artists—the ones I know—as they
assume the role of creator, they also assume willingly the responsibility that once you give life you also begin death. Maybe
the other writers haven't thought about that concept yet. But

the pain of writing, of having to write, is common to both groups.

Does Chicano literature share common ground with Black literature? Differences?

Maybe oppression is common to both.

Is there any relationship with the literature of other Spanish-speaking groups?

I wish that question didn't bother me, but it's there. I've read with Latinos;* I never saw a difference—no marked difference between Victor Cruz's poetry and my own, Roberto Vargas's and Alejandro Murillo's poetry. That's the excitement I appreciate about the San Francisco Mission District. Their Latino readings get you into a Latino frame of mind; barriers melt down in terms of origins. I share that excitement when I read with a Texas group like Nephtalí [de León], Tigre [Pérez], Abelardo [Delgado], and Ricardo Sánchez. But when the two groups come together, I sense the tension and I'm sure they also do. I don't feel it when I'm with one group or the other. I don't know what causes the hostility, friction, or animosity; it's part of something that could be worked out, and it's heading that way. It will be difficult in areas like Nuevo México, El Paso, and even Southern California. They find it hard to relate to the Mission poets because Mexico is right there, across that imaginary line. Every Latino comes from a country, a nation, either as an exile or by choice, but they have a home. Aztlán is still only a dream for Chicanos.

The Sacramento Third World Conference is very exciting. You see how Third World people deal with oppression. Blacks are still the loudest; then the Chicanos and Latinos. The Asians, aside from Janice Merikitani and Ron Tanaka, deal differently; assimilation and acculturation are, strangely enough, more apparent in much of their poetry. But then there are the Native Americans, who you would think might be madder than anyone else, and they read very patiently, simply. Totally different. In my poetry I didn't reject the union with the Native American, I

* *Latino* is used to identify people of Latin American origin living in the United States. Depending on the speaker, it may or may not include Chicanos. Here it means others of Latin American origin.

just felt that it wouldn't happen, that the two worlds were very separate. In the last few years I've come to realize that two things are necessary, and they're beginning to happen: one, we as Chicanos must assume the responsibility of our Indianness; two, the Indio must accept our Mexicanness and what it means. That's the next, most important phenomenon in the Movement. New Mexico has had the answer for a long time—communal existence adopted long ago; Indios and Mexicanos joining forces to kick ass; compadrazco [kinship] between the two. It's the next major crisis in our development.

Sometimes I find myself coming out with things that seem strong—like who am I to know—but then I think them out and they make sense. "Men to Match Our Mountains" blew me away when I wrote it. I'm going in another direction for sure. I'm probably losing a huge audience and gaining another. That's the nature of writing.

Does Chicano literature have a distinctive perspective on life? What effect does it have on the literature?

A world view is already being defined by the writers and artists. How we shake off the postulates of the other world view, the Anglo one, will determine how fast we move toward a Chicano world view, not a Mexican or Anglo, but a Chicano world view. The implications of the formation of a new world view entail tremendous upheavals in all kinds of different things. Structural anthropologists think they're finding an all-Black way of doing things, and now there will come another group with a Mexican way and rearrange things. It's coming and there's no way of stopping it. In the literature and the arts, that world view will be reflected.

Does Chicano literature improve communication between Chicanos and Anglo Americans?

It could; I'm not sure that it has. It establishes a dialogue. Whether it becomes positive depends on its reception. There's still reluctance blocking communication. A creative writing prof of mine from Berkeley is now the head of the English Department at New Mexico University. When I read there he sent a student with a note to find out if I was the same José Montoya from Berkeley. I sent one back saying, "Yes, come on over." He sent me another note saying, "Sorry, I have a class." The head of the English Department could have brought his class to the reading, but there's still that reluctance. I'm not sure they'll allow it to happen.

Does Chicano literature reevaluate, attack, or subvert the value system of the majority society? Is it a revolutionary literature? Thematically? Technically?

It helps to reevaluate it by making a statement about the Chicano experience. Whether it is revolutionary depends on how much the other culture will take before it reacts. It could create a confrontation, though I doubt it. The co-opting powers of the dominant culture are extremely wily. They may be unyielding, but they reach a point where they change tactics to practice the old adage of giving people enough rope, you know? Dealing with that co-opting maneuver will require a lot of creativity, which seems to be coming out of this newfound liberation, the discovery that we have certain talents and abilities. What we do with them is wide open. The excitement of that discovery gives us an added impetus that will propel us way over any creative endeavors being practiced by anyone now.

I talk to some of the young people in our group [RCAF], and they have no fear. There's nothing to hold them back. They see no limit to what can be accomplished. As I was saying about education, they're apprehensive about formal, academic systems, that is, education as we know it. They talk about forming our own academias, our own ways of educating our people. They're talking about some very creative concepts, concerning marriage, for instance. They excite me. I wouldn't call them frightening; they're more, ah—I can appreciate them, but not comprehend them. But I can really appreciate and feel that excitement, the enthusiasm. It's probably going to change our customs. Wild, wild trip.

What problems have you encountered in publishing? Were they racially founded?

I'm not sure you cannot attribute them to some kind of racial bias. It might have been unintentional on the part of the people doing the rejecting. Those instructors who criticized my use of Spanish and caló [slang] were sincere, well-meaning people. Their short-sightedness may have—well, it did have racial foundations. Why should bilingual expression be considered limited? Just because everyone doesn't understand Spanish? We had to learn English. But I also think the publishers had reasons other than racial ones for not accepting my writing. They had the best artists to pick from who were already established; their existence is predicated on making money, so why should they go with someone whose name they can't pronounce over someone they can print and make money off of? That was inherent in their rejections.

There were a lot of problems with getting into print; still are. That's why I was saying that it will be embarrassing when we begin to be published in other countries before we're recognized here.

Are Chicanos at a disadvantage in trying to practice the art of writing?

I don't think so. The disadvantage exists only if you think it does. The majority of our people bought the self-fulfilling prophecy about being dumb and lazy. You begin to believe it if you hear it enough times. That's the disadvantage. All this time we were led to believe that we hadn't much to contribute. Everybody sought certain proportions and ours were always less. We were the sidekicks to the hero, the worker, the peon, or just *the* Mexican. They drove things into our heads that did a fantastic amount of harm, and at times, certain ages, when we were extremely impressionable. The things that happened to us in the educational system have put us at a tremendous disadvantage. When anything that refers to your speech is criticized, it must create all kinds of turmoil within a person. To be told that you should speak English because Spanish is bad, when that's how your folks speak, puts you at odds with your folks. Even the lunches you would bring to school were not as good, but your parents ate that kind of food. Then, the contradiction about being taught Spanish in school and the Anglo students doing better than you, getting A's when you know they can't speak Spanish; or seeing the teachers going to the Mexico City Café to eat the kind of food they're putting you down for; then they ask you to eat bread and baloney instead of taquitos. All of that must have really had an impact. It's hard to survive.

But, no, I think it doesn't become a real disadvantage unless you allow terms to confuse you. I was thinking about my experience with my son, who's now twenty. He's been writing for a couple of years and I never knew it till last year. I asked why he hadn't shown me his stuff; it's very good. He answered that he wasn't sure what it is, Chicano poetry or not. I said, "Wait a minute, what does that have to do with what you're writing?" We started talking. Our life styles are different and our influences are different, but his Chicanismo is right out front. So I told him that it is Chicano poetry as far as I'm concerned. That opened up the floodgates. He's been writing more and more. I guess in a sense it became easier once that confusion was dissipated, once that vagueness was removed.

So, there is and there is not a disadvantage, you see what I mean?

What are the most outstanding qualities of Chicano literature? Weaknesses?

I don't know. Number one, the discovery of how easy it is to sing and that we have an affinity to the song. We've always wanted to do just that, but we were never allowed. Once we were allowed, everybody started singing, and we wrote some *bad* songs. But because of that quantity, also, a lot of fine songs have been produced. I used to talk about the affinity of birds and clouds and the Chicano always wanting to sing. In the *files* [fields] we always sang to each other. There were code names for the boss: "Ai viene el agua" [Here comes the water], and we knew it wasn't going to rain, so it meant something else, and you stopped singing. I always wanted to do something, and to not be allowed to was a liability. Just like a bird who has always been kept caged and suddenly they open the gate. That bird isn't going to fly right away. The first couple of times he'll stumble around, bump into a few barns, but eventually he'll hit a current and learn what to do with his wings and soar. That happened to Chicano poetry. At first, in the *Bronce* and other early underground newspapers, there was some poetry que era bien terrible [that was really terrible]. Everybody was writing. But some of the same terrible poets have trained themselves and learned.

What are the milestones so far in Chicano literature?

The first would have to be just putting the material out. In other words, for a while we didn't know how to deal with the fact that there wasn't an outlet for our writing. We just wanted to write without thinking about publication. One of the milestones is that we have finally realized that we could write forever, but if we don't have publishing houses and control them, nothing will be published. It's exciting to see Pajarito and La Causa publishing. Quinto Sol, which for a long time controlled all publishing, is now two publishing houses: Justa and Tonatiuh. There's *Caracol* in San Antonio, a fine, fine little review. In terms of the work that has come out, the timing of the appearance of these outlets, and others, makes that breakthrough a milestone. What comes from then on will be an extension.

In terms of poetry, the bilingual treatment of the written word has been a milestone. It opened up a lot of opportunities for us. I always had felt an inferiority about either of the two languages. I have certainly opened up since then.

Outstanding works? Well, talking about early milestones, most of what Alurista wrote was a milestone. I have great respect for him, as I have for the others who are on the scene. But those I would call the early vanguardia, like Abelardo—he's been writing a long time—Ricardo Sánchez and Tapón (Raúl Salinas), I have to consider milestones because at one time or another I've been very involved with them. I don't think I've run into any writers that I don't like. I get along with all of them.

What is the future of Chicano literature: distinctiveness, or the de-emphasis of the distinctive characteristics?

No bounds. Limitless. Too much. The energy and enthusiasm and brilliance of the young people that are coming out right now—I just hope that those of us who have been at this game for a while don't lay a really shitty trip on some of the visions the young people have, because they are, whew, way out in terms of what they want to say and how they're going to say it. Like a lot of us are still traditional about how the message should get across. But some of the young people are coming out with exciting novelties.

I see the future as tremendously exciting, not just in terms of materials and technique, but in the fact that there will be a place for Chicano literature. That's a mind-blowing thing to conceptualize. We're not talking about Mexican literature or Mexican American literature; we're talking about something in the whole spectrum which is Chicano literature. It can't be pushed around or sublimated; it can't be suppressed; it's going to place itself right there and that, just like all the other major influences in literature, will have an effect for all the other cultures. They're going to have to study Chicano literature not because they're Chicanos but because it will be just as important to know the Chicano poets as it is for us to know the Russian short story writers or the French novelists. It's going to be there, distinctive and whole. It's happening.

Who are the leaders among Chicano writers, and why?

That's a hard question. As I said earlier, I'm unable to dislike any of them. I consider a lot of the ones writing right now to be leaders. Louie the Foot's concrete poetry and the way he applies it to the Chicano makes him a leader. What Lorna Cervantes is doing with her poetry makes her a leader in that respect.

There are excellent Chicana writers, but it's really a sad reflection on our macho, chauvinistic thing that we haven't treated them in the way they deserved. There are probably many reasons. It may have been a protest by us, a reaction to the carnalas coming out as strong as they did when a lot of us weren't ready for it. We just closed off, which was very bad and shortsighted on our part. There's Chicanas like Dorinda Moreno, who has been writing for a long time. The young ones admire Lorna's [Cervantes] work and Bernice Zamora's. Bernice is no spring chicken; she's been around. She should have had recognition a long time ago. There were people I had faith in who let me down, too, but maybe they have their own things happening in their lives. Lupe Castellanos made a big hit at the first Floricanto, then she just stopped. There's some resentment because some poetesses use the word to throw heavy chingazos [blows, insults] at the men, which they have every right to do. They've been treated badly enough, so they have the right to get even. It's unfortunate. Chicana writers? Estela Portillo.

I don't know. What Ricardo Sánchez has done and what Tapón is doing, and Nephtalí, Pacheco, Alurista . . . I'm sure I'm missing some who will give me trouble for it, but everybody had to share the leadership anyway. That's what the RCAF has going. All we have is leaders. Nobody gets mad. How can the leaders get mad?

It's probably a cop-out, but you can't answer that question without a lot of qualifications. Like if I were to say I consider Rudy Anaya a leader, I would have to explain what that entails.

My leaders? I just have people I like.

Tomás Rivera

The Quinto Sol Prize for literature was the crowning effort of Quinto Sol Publications, the prime promoter of Chicano literature during the first years of its existence. The first prize was awarded in 1970 to Tomás Rivera for . . . *y no se lo tragó la tierra*, a novel structured as a collection of fourteen short stories and thirteen vignettes. Rivera also has published extensively in the genres of short story, poetry, and literary essay. His second novel, *La casa grande*, has not yet been released, but portions of it were read at the Floricanto II, 1975, and have appeared in journals. In addition to being one of the most admired authors, Rivera is a respected university administrator, having served as vice president of the University of Texas, both in San Antonio and in El Paso, and as the chancellor of the University of California, Riverside.

Rivera's prose style is concise, even pithy. Moreover, the vocabulary and syntax are tightly controlled, held carefully within the world of the migrant worker which Rivera has chosen as his subject. Though narrative, it is not expository, but, rather, strangely impressionistic. It is a measure of Rivera's talent that the reader thinks that s/he has read a detailed depiction of reality, so much so that many have used the book as an accurate sociological statement of the migrant's condition. What Rivera achieves is the evocation of an environment with a minimum of words, and within that environment the migratory farmworkers move with dignity, strength, and resilience.

. . . *y no se lo tragó la tierra* demonstrates a consciousness of the contemporary novel's structural freedom. The alternating stories and vignettes follow a stream-of-consciousness thread revealed only in the last story, where we find a boy hiding under a house, thinking about the events we have read in the book; apparently the narrative is held within the temporal point of the last story. What we have read, however, is not the stream itself in its amorphous flow; the texture is not at all that of an interior mono-

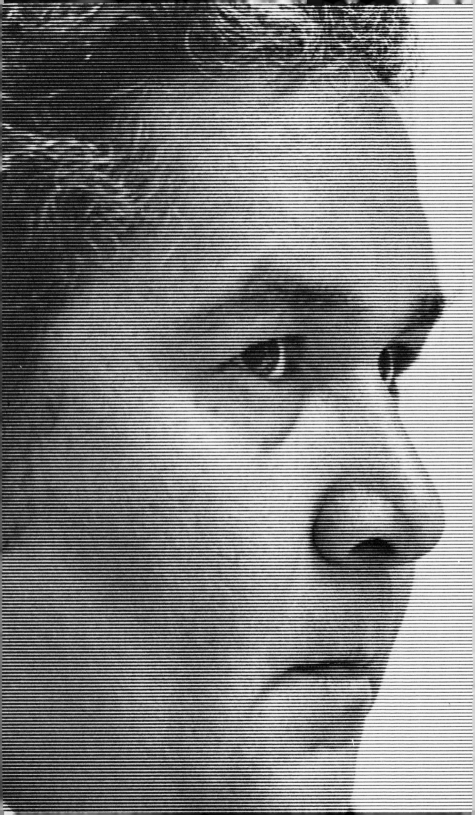

logue, but that of the written word, of the carefully structured written text. The narrative is, in the last analysis, exactly that, a text coposed by the narrator-protagonist sometime after the last story ends. As such, the last story is also the creation of the boy-narrator, who writes a novel with multiple frames in which he relates the discovery and proves the realization of his literary vocation. Rivera states his role within Chicano literature to be that of a creative documentor of the migrant workers. . . . *tierra* is the story of the epiphany revealing that role, and, at the same time, the documentation of its fulfillment.

Tomás Rivera's responses were recorded in San Antonio, Texas, in June 1977, and he reviewed the text in September 1979.

When and where were you born?

December 22, 1935, in Crystal City, Texas, which is about 120 miles southwest of here [San Antonio].

Describe your family background and your present situation.

My parents were born in Mexico, my mother in Coahuila and my father in Aguascalientes. He came to the United States at an early age, about fifteen, and wandered into El Paso, then up to the Midwest, and worked, mostly on the railroad, as a cook in different places. In 1930, on his way back to Mexico, he arrived in Crystal City, where he met my mother and they got married. My mother's family also came to the states soon after she was born, around 1920, traveling up to Dallas, then to Houston, then back to Austin for a while, until around 1930 they ended up in Crystal City.

Crystal City was at the time and is still called the Winter Garden area. In the 1920's the city became a center for truck farming, mostly for vegetables that could be grown in the winter and shipped to San Antonio. It's a fairly new town, incorporated in 1922, and it attracted many immigrants from Mexico, because it was on the route to San Antonio. So my grandparents on my mother's side settled there.

They had come first to Eagle Pass, right across the river from Piedras Negras, where my mother attended the American public school for a couple of years. She learned to read and write in a rural school in Las Minas del Seco.

My grandfather had been in mining in northern Mexico,

involved in the union organization of the minas del norte de Coahuila [mines of northern Coahuila]. During the Revolution he had been an officer. I didn't know this until just before he died he told me. As I had grown older I began to notice that he knew a lot of things, especially about the war, the war theatres, movement of troops, logistics, and so forth, and military history in general; he knew all of it very well. Before he died he had a cerebral attack which left him crippled. I was talking to him one time about the Civil War in the United States and he began to explain certain things about it; so I asked him where he had learned them, because he had no education in this country, though he had learned to read and write English when he came here. He replied, "Well, I'll tell you, I've really lived two lives, one in Mexico and another here. In Mexico I grew up as a peón in an hacienda, but I became a very close friend of the son of the hacendado [hacienda owner], and when he wanted to send his son to military school, the son refused to go unless I went along; so the hacendado sent us both al Colegio Militar de México [to the Mexico Military Academy]." There he became an officer in the Federal Army. But later he fled the Revolución when he decided he didn't want any part of it any more. I knew none of this until he was dying, because he had had another family in Mexico y luego se había venido al norte y se había casado otra vez y tenía otra familia con otra señora [and then he had come to the north and had married again and had another family with another woman]. And he said he had studied military history at the military academy. Then I understood why he knew so much about all these things. He had never revealed any of that, not even to his sons and daughters, pero a mí sí me lo reveló [but he revealed it to me]. Anyway, the family ended up in Crystal City in 1930.

My father had no formal education, nor did my mother, except for the two years in public school. My dad knew how to read and write in Spanish and he could speak English.

We were migrant workers. By the time I was born, 1935, my grandfather's younger sons and daughters were old enough to participate in the migrant stream, so they wandered all over Texas. As early as 1934 they went north to Michigan and Minnesota to the beet fields. That, more or less, is the background of the family as far as the economic base of working as farm laborers in Texas or the northern states.

My earliest recollections are of living on different farms where we worked in Minnesota. We used to go every year. The

last year I worked as a migrant was 1956, when I was already in
junior college. My parents were still working in Iowa, but I
would only work three months and then I had to return to complete the year at the college. Through high school it was different: we would leave around April 15, and return around
November 1; that was the working season. In the fall I'd finish
the year before and start the next at the same time. At the high
school level it was O.K., because it's easy to catch up, but the
junior college wouldn't allow late registration, so I had to come
home in early September. By my junior year I stopped going altogether; I had another job by then. My parents, however, were
still going out.

Now I'm married and have three children. I am the vice
president for administration at UTSA [University of Texas at
San Antonio. Since the interview, Rivera has become the Chancellor of the University of California, Riverside, after a brief
term as executive vice president at the University of Texas at El
Paso.]

When did you first begin to write?

Creative writing? About eleven or twelve years old. That's when
I first said, "I'm going to write a story and this is the title," and
all that. We had had an accident and I wanted to write about it,
so I called it "The Accident." I felt a sensation I still get when I
write. I wanted to capture something I would never forget and it
happened to be the sensation of having a wreck. I had never been
involved in a wreck before, so I thought I had to get it down,
because I felt no one had ever had a wreck like that and people
should know about it. I wrote it down and it was crummy, real
bad; but at the time I thought I had a winner: "The Accident." It
happened in Bay City, Michigan.

It turned me on and I kept writing. I guess I wanted to write
because by then I had been reading quite a bit. A voracious
reader. Then I wanted to be a sportswriter. In high school I did a
lot of writing, both essays and creative stuff, and published here
and there. But I started around eleven and I really wanted to be a
sportswriter. When people asked what I wanted to be, I'd tell
them a writer. They were surprised or indifferent. If people don't
read, what is a writer? No big thing; no one was impressed. Except my grandfather. I remember that.

My grandfather said that writing and art were the most important things, that to be a *pintor, como decía él* [painter, as he

said], was an accomplishment. I was drawing a great deal at the time, and he encouraged me, buying me many materials to use, like all types of tablets. He showed me a little about drawing techniques. He could draw very well. I still have some of the drawings from when I was seven or eight.

I kept painting for a long time, until I got married, when I stopped. The first two years of our marriage my wife and I painted together. We lived in Crystal City, and there's not much to do there, so we would spend days painting, just painting, whole weekends. It passed the time and we found it a great way to be together. But then our first child came along y ya no hay lugar [and there's no place] nor time; then the second and you kind of put it aside. Maybe someday, when our kids are grown, we'll come back to it. We found it a very enjoyable experience. It takes all your energy and time; it's exhilarating. My grandfather was more enthused about art than writing.

What kind of books did you read in your formative years?

Two types: one, the sports stories and books; two, any kind of adventure story.

In Hampton, Iowa, there was a little old lady, tennis shoes and all, who helped me out. Every day I'd walk down to pick up the mail at the post office for my parents and pass the Carnegie Library. I didn't even know what the hell it meant, CARNEGIE; they were just letters to me. I was about ten years old and it was the first time I had come in contact with a library. This lady must have noticed me passing every day, so she stopped me one day and invited me in. She opened up a lot of things to me. She took me down into the basement and showed me all the periodicals. She'd ask me, "What do you want to know about?" This or that, I'd answer, and she would take out the newspaper where we could find it. Then she'd say, "Let's go back to 1900," and she'd take out a newspaper from 1900. Amazing, discovering all these things from the past right there and being able to read about them. Then she would say, "Here, you can take these books with you. Read them. Whenever you finish, return them." I couldn't believe it. Every day she had different readings for me, one or two books she thought I'd like; lots of sports books, especially. Then she introduced me to the mystery-type books. Y así iba dándome todo eso. [And in that way she gave me all that.] Every summer we spent in Hampton, Iowa, I looked for-

ward to going back to that library where she was waiting for me
with all those books. I don't even remember her name.

My dad knew I liked to read, so he would go knocking on
doors, asking if they had any old magazines, which he then
brought home to me. We always had a lot of reading materials of
all kinds. We also used to go to the dump to collect reading materials. I found encyclopedias and different types of books. At
home I still have my dump collection gathered from the dumps
in northern towns. People threw away a lot of books.

Encyclopedias fascinated me, because you could just read
one thing after another. I find the same thing with my youngest
kid, who is eleven. I bought him an encyclopedia three years ago
and he's fascinated with it, because he can take any book, read
from page to page finding out about one item after another, continually discovering things. I did the same thing years ago with
old encyclopedias that people had thrown away.

There is one book which especially impressed me: *In
Darkest Africa* by Henry M. Stanley. I found it myself in the
dump, you see; a two-volume collection of Stanley's expedition
into Africa in search of Dr. Livingstone. Of course, I didn't know
anything about history at the time, or the exploration of Africa,
but with the books came maps of the terrain through which
Stanley had to travel. The text was a diary, a day-by-day account
of what to Stanley was the discovery of Africa, with all the details, like how much food they ate, how far they had traveled, all
those things. It fascinated me. It was better than going to a Tarzan movie. It carried over into my own life, because I started
making maps of the terrain we traveled, and my brothers and I
would explore and draw maps. It became a living thing. I haven't
read them for a long time, but that title stuck in my memory
because of the exploratory aspect. Later, when I ran into other
similar things, I was able to understand the exploration of America and Latin America because I could understand this one
man's exploration of the Dark Continent. I still have those
books at home.

That was back in 1944; I was about nine, but I could understand it pretty well. I reread that book. I would read chapters to
my mother or to my dad, and they liked it too. The Tarzan
movies came on pretty strong around then, with the serials
every Saturday, but to me they were already fake. Henry M.
Stanley was the real thing.

Another thing about those books that fascinated me was

that they had been published in the 1880's, and they were still in good shape when I found them, though they must have been fifty or so years old. I don't know what happened to the maps; maybe they fell out. See, the maps fit into pockets, so they could be spread out and you could follow the journey. I might have lost them because I carried them with me to Iowa or Minnesota. I don't know how I would react to them now, but it's the first title I remember, *In Darkest Africa*.

There were other titles, like *The Last Backboard*, and *The Last Touchdown*, or *Iron Fist*. All the stuff you read when you are eight years old. The *Wizard of Oz* fascinated me when I first read it.

Junior high school was lost; no reading that was worthwhile, pure mishmash. First of all, they didn't think you could read, *porque eras mexicano* [because you were Mexican]. They wouldn't give you good stuff and they would make us write crap like "What I Did on My Vacation," or "My Enemy," or "My Most Embarrassing Moment." We weren't allowed to read much.

In high school I got into American literature. I was really taken with the Graveyard Poets, which is natural for a fourteen-year-old; the age of reflection and all that. Steinbeck I liked very much. The movie *The Grapes of Wrath* led me to read all his novels. I got into Hemingway; read everything he had written. Walt Whitman became a very important source, not only of inspiration, but at one point he seemed like the only connection that made sense, in almost a religious way. I dropped out of the Catholic Church at about fourteen—not dropped out, really, I just didn't want to have anything to do with religion right then. By the time of high school graduation I was reading about religion and I became pretty cynical. Well, Walt Whitman was my replacement: "I sing the body electric." Powerful things like that.

After that I got more and more into American and English literature. The Spanish came later.

___

What is the extent of your studies?

I started out at Southwest Texas Junior College in Uvalde, then to Southwest Texas State University in San Marcos, planning to major in the one thing I really enjoyed doing, art. The junior college didn't have an art program, so I got my general requirements out of the way and when I went to Southwest State I was going to major in art. Also, I wanted to be a teacher, so I planned to combine the two and be an art teacher. However, at San Marcos they told me that without a background in art classes it would take me three more years to finish, so I changed my major. I had taken all the English courses I could at the junior college, so I already had a lot of credits toward an English major. I changed to English and enjoyed it very much. I didn't do much in Spanish besides a couple of courses in which we read things like *Doña Bárbara*, the traditional things.

Yet when I graduated with a degree in English, and I couldn't get a job because I was a Mexican, they said, "Why don't you teach Spanish? There's a lot of jobs open in Spanish." There were a lot of openings in English también, nomás [also, but] they wouldn't hire me. The placement office would not even give me the chance to apply and get rejected; they were very protective, más bien [more like] patronizing.

I was interested in literature, period. I began to read some Spanish novels, Pío Baroja, and I liked them. Then came Unamuno and from there into the rest of the Generation of '98. The interest built up, but before I decided to get my doctorate in Spanish, I went back to Southwest Texas State for a Master's in English and administration. Then there were a couple of National Defense Institutes. One at the University of Texas at Austin, where I studied Spanish Culture and Civilization with Blanco Aguinaga. Another was with Arizona University at Guadalajara, where the faculty included Seymour Menton, Luis Leal, Joseph Silverman, Dorothy Brown, and a fine group of people. More and more, Spanish letters interested me. A year after I left Guadalajara, I decided to study for the doctorate at Oklahoma, which I finished in 1969.

Has formal education helped or hindered you as a writer?

I think it has helped me in several ways. First of all, it allowed me to see better the context of what I write and of the literature emerging from the Chicano Movement within the whole idea of literature itself. Because of the training I have a more total picture. If a person has not had any, or has had very little training in literature, he or she could not see it in that context. I prefer to see Chicano literature within the context of all these other literatures. I can see it a lot better. Es decir, creo que hay mucho más ensimismamiento en aquellas personas que no tienen preparación [That is to say, I think that uneducated people are much more absorbed in themselves] and they think they're inventing everything under the sun. Now, maybe it's good; maybe they're more courageous that way.

Probably, I wanted to write because I had read, and the more you read, the more you want to write yourself. I think it does happen that way.

Which was the predominant language in your home as a child? Which do you speak more fluently now?

As a child, Spanish, oh yeh. Even my first two years of formal schooling were all in Spanish. In Crystal City each barrio had its own escuelita en español [little school in Spanish]. I learned to read and write Spanish when I was five and six in the escuela del barrio, a private school, before entering the regular public school. You'd send your kids to a Spanish school because they prepared them better. Allí te enseñaban a leer, a escribir, matemática, y también modales [There they taught you to read, write, mathematics, and manners], you know, how to get along with people, el respeto [respect], etc. Although these people had had no formal training themselves, they still felt that schooling was needed. You paid five cents every day and if you didn't go you didn't pay. A pay-as-you-go plan. We had to present two public funciones al año [presentations a year], dramatizations, o declamaciones [or poetry declamations]. The first poem I declaimed was "El minero" ["The Miner"]. It went something like, "Yo soy el minero. Bajo y saco el carbón" ["I am the miner. I go down and take out coal"], and I'd give gestures. You had to dress your part. Lo que quería la profesora era enseñarnos la idea del trabajo, entonces a cada uno le daba un papel, como el carpintero, el minero, el abogado, y así. Cada quien tenía que vestirse según su papel y ella le buscaba un poema. Me tocó el del minero, y mi mamá tuvo que hacerme una cachucha, y le puso una lámpara, y salí con la pica and the lantern. [What the teacher wanted to teach us was the idea of work, so she would give each of us a role, like the carpenter, the miner, the lawyer, and so on. Each one had to dress the part and she would find a poem. I got the miner, and my mother had to make me a cap, and she put a light on it, and I came out with a lantern and pick.] She was teaching us the idea of work, in a sense the idea of community, that all these people are important in your lives. That's why everyone portrayed a job. Teníamos que recitar en frente de la clase y luego en el Teatro Ideal, donde se juntaban todos los barrios a presenciar a los niños oradores. [We had to recite in front of the class and then in the Ideal Theater, where all the neighborhoods would gather to hear the children orators.] It must have been interesting for the parents to have their kids up on stage reciting. It gave a sense of pride in your child. Nuestra maestra estaba muy orientada al trabajo [Our teacher was very oriented toward work], the ideal of work, la dignidad del trabajo [the dignity of work]. Dignidad. It was also implicit in their modales también [etiquette, too], the idea that it was the way you taught respect for people. Everyone in society, no matter what he does, if he works, has dignity within the structure. Era una cosa muy importante. [That was something very important.]

Aprendí inglés cuando tenía siete años y entré a la escuela pública; para los diez u once ya podía leer bien. [I learned English when I was seven and began public school; by ten or eleven I could read well.] I didn't have much difficulty, since I could transpose from one language to the other. I already knew how to write Spanish, so learning another language wasn't hard. But it wasn't until the fifth grade that I really could understand everything. I still remember the day clearly, like a breakthrough. Estábamos allí estudiando la geografía de Colorado y la profesora empezó a explicarnos quién sabe qué [We were studying the geography of Colorado and the teacher started explaining who knows what], and at the end of the class I had understood everything. I wasn't even aware that she had been talking in English. It was a great sensation! When I was going home I thought to myself that from there on I would have an easy time in school. Me acuerdo muy bien, porque [I remember well, because] it's a breakthrough that comes when you don't even realize that you're speaking the language, and suddenly it's not a foreign language.

But if you ask me about right now, well, I haven't spoken that much Spanish in a year, so now it would be English. I have not been in the classroom for a year and all the university business is in English. Once I start, it takes me a couple of days to get back into Spanish well. Right now English interferes. If I start speaking in Spanish, entra el inglés [English comes in].

Does Chicano literature have a particular language or idiom?

No, it has to have the particular idiom of the writer, whatever that idiom is. It doesn't have to be a particular one. No, I don't think so. Let's say I hope not. I don't like any kind of dogmas, and certainly not within a creative effort of people. To say this is Chicano language and this is not, I can't take that. The fact that we only have very lukewarm dogma within the Chicano literary movement is one of the basic factors that explains why it still continues to grow and expand. If we had ever set down a dogma defining Chicano literature to enable us to know which writings are and which are not, ya se habría acabado todo el mugrero, chingao [the whole mess would have ended by now, damn]. So I'm very much opposed to any kind of dogma for creative efforts. I hope we never fall into all that. Some people advocate it, but I can't see it. If you start defining you put limitations on it, absolutely. Then you won't have anything.

How do you perceive your role as a writer vis-à-vis: (a) the Chicano community or Movement; (b) U.S. society; (c) literature itself?

(a) I'm not sure. I enjoy writing about Chicano topics, themes, feelings and so forth, but I've only written about people who existed in the migrant stream between 1945 and 1955. Right away it's a historical documentation that I want to deal with. La ocurrencia de lo que he escrito, dentro de lo que se puede llamar literatura chicana, tiene que ser aquella que le pasó a los migrant workers entre esos años. Entonces, la motivación mía, cuando escribía esto [The events of which I have written, within what can be called Chicano literature, has to be what happened to the migrant worker between those years. So, my motivation, when I wrote it] was different than the motivation of the people I write about. I have to delineate there. In . . . *tierra* and those stories, I wrote about the migrant worker in that period of ten years. During that period I became very conscious, in my own life, about the suffering and the strength and the beauty of these people. I was more conscious of their strength when I was living with them. Later, 1967–68, I'm writing. The Chicano Movement was una fuerza total ya [a complete power already] in the university and so forth. I wanted to document, somehow, the strength of those people that I had known. And I was only concerned about the migrant worker, the people I had known best. I had been a migrant worker. So I began to see that my role—if I want to call it that—would be to document that period of time, but giving it some kind of spiritual strength or spiritual history. Not just pasó esto y esto pasó, sino darle una amplitud al espíritu de la gente que existía entonces. [Not just this and this happened, but to give a spiritual dimension to the people of that time.] I see my role more as a documentor of that period of time when the migrant worker was living without any kind of protection. No había ninguna protección legal, y si no hay protección legal, no hay nada. Yo vi mucho sufrimiento y mucho aislamiento de la gente. [There was no legal protection, and without legal protection, there is nothing. I saw a lot of suffering and much isolation of the people.] Yet they lived through the whole thing, perhaps because they had no choice. I saw a lot of heroic people and I wanted to capture their feelings. That's one role, to document all this.

Sometimes, for example in San Diego, the students ask, "Why don't you write about people who are more active, more committed to the Chicano Movement?" Well, I think that's fine, but the students should write about it themselves. I mean, I can write about it myself, but it would be different. I went through that sort of thing back in 1958: querer hacer algo por la comunidad [to want to do something for the community]. La conscientización [Consciousness raising] had occurred to me ten years before the Chicano Movement. There were very few of us in the university in 1958, yet we were together. We had an organization and we wanted to do many things, but we were perhaps five or six only. There was no communication with other universities around here. But we already felt that something had to be done within the Chicano community to lighten the economic plight, specifically, and overcome the political lethargy, and find out why it was that way.

There were several of us who wanted to write, but we didn't write about Chicanos. No estábamos bastante conscientizados para creer que podíamos desarrollar personajes chicanos, o que sería interesante desarrollar a un chicano. [We weren't enlightened enough to think that we could develop Chicano characters, or that it would be interesting to develop a Chicano.] It just hadn't happened before, so how was it going to? No se nos occuría a nosotros hacerlo. [It didn't occur to us to do it.] I read, for example, Rölvaag's novels, *The Sons of the Middle Border* and so forth, about the Norwegians' and Swedes' experiences coming into Minnesota, and I thought, wow, we were doing the same thing right then. They arrived fifty years ago, worked the land, and survived. We were doing it still, working the land for them. Yet, it never went beyond that point to say, "I'm going to write a story about Chicanos up there working the land." Also, back in 1958, we thought writing should be a money-making proposition. To make money there had to be a gimmick, we thought, so we went to the people who were making it at the time, Mickey Spillane and people like that. We actually tried to imitate Spillane. We thought people would notice, that it would bring us fame and glory. We sent off the manuscripts y pues nada [and nothing]. Los chicanos que metíamos allí [The Chicanos we stuck in there] were cooks and prostitutes, very stereotyped characters, as were the Anglo ones. I don't demean cooks or prostitutes, just the fact that we would stereotype them without benefit of dignity.

Then, one day I was wandering through the library and I came across *With a Pistol in His Hand* by Américo Paredes, and I was fascinated. I didn't even know Paredes existed, though we were only thirty miles away, pero no había comunicación alguna porque no había Movimiento ni nada de eso. Saqué el libro ese. Lo que me atrajo fue el apellido *Paredes*. [. . . but there was no communication at all, because there wasn't a Movement or anything like that. I checked out that book. What attracted me was the name *Paredes*.] I was hungry to find something by a Chicano or Mexican American. It fascinated me because, one, it proved it was possible for a Chicano to publish; two, it was about a Chicano, Gregorio Cortez, y sus azañas [and his deeds]. (Y los corridos, también [And the ballads, too], I grew up with the corridos de Texas.) That book indicated to me that it was possible to talk about a Chicano as a complete figure. I went back to the old newspapers and checked the accounts for how they handled Gregorio Cortez and I found the grotesque exaggeration, as Américo says. Then I would go back to Américo's book and wonder which one was right. Was Américo lying too? Was he overdoing it también [also]? More importantly, *With a Pistol in His Hand* indicated to me a whole imaginative possibility for us to explore. Now that, also, was in 1958, and it was then I began to think, write, and reflect a hell of a lot more on those people I had known in 1945 to '55.

That's the personal trajectory of the evolution of my role as documentor. I guess that sense of it came from feeling that Américo had documented one person para siempre [forever]. It was very important. I felt that I had to document the migrant worker para siempre [forever], para que no se olvidara ese espíritu tan fuerte de resistir y continuar under the worst of conditions [so that their very strong spirit of endurance and will to go on under the worst of conditions should not be forgotten], because they were worse than slaves. El esclavo es una inversión [A slave is an investment], so you protect him to keep him working. A migrant worker? You owe him nothing. If he came to you, you gave him work and then just told him to leave. No investment. If he got sick, you got rid of him; you didn't have to take care of him. It was bad, labor camps and all that.

(b) In some respects it's the same. I haven't been doing much writing lately, so I can't see myself as a writer now. Also, what is U.S. society?

Anyway, I think of the whole American scene—both continents—and the fact that we have transplanted cultures from Europe, and the fact of the indigenous cultures still being here. I wanted to document that, but I also wanted to throw light on the spiritual strength, on the concept of justice so important for the American continents. I wanted to treat the idea of mental and intellectual liberation and where it fits into the spectrum of the Americas. Can it be achieved here, and if so, can it be done better than in Europe? Personally, I believe it can. I prefer the Americas, porque creo que aquí tenemos la capacidad y la posibilidad de una emancipación intelectual mucho más fuerte y total [because I think that here we have the capacity and possibility of a much stronger and complete intellectual emancipation]. Within those migrants I saw that strength. They may be economically deprived, politically deprived, socially deprived, but they kept moving, never staying in one place to suffer or be subdued, sino siempre buscaban trabajo [but always searching for work]. Siempre andaban buscando [They always kept searching]; that's why they were "migrant" workers. La palabra *trabajador* está muy implícita allí [The word *worker* is very implicit there]; they were travelers. If they stayed where there was no work se morían [they would die], y no se murieron [and they didn't die]. I see that same sense of movement in the Europeans who came here, and that concept of justicia espiritual también [spiritual justice, too]. It was there. And the migrant workers still have that role: to be searchers. I've written a poem called "The Searchers." Para mí era gente que buscaba [To me they were people who searched], and that's an important metaphor in the Americas. My grandfather was a searcher; my father was a searcher; I hope I can also be a searcher. That's the spirit I seek.

Now, as you commented in our conversation, Juan, this is a positive image of the migrant as opposed to the negative one of him as lost in the stream of labor. Well, that's the point: to be able to document his strength, to show that he really was not lost.

(c) As for literature itself, I don't know; it's a difficult question. Just one more voice, I guess. Minimal.

What is the place of Chicano literature within U.S. literature?

U.S. literature changes all the time. If we go by national, political lines, it is very definitely a part of American literature, U.S. American. It comes from this country, politically, no matter in what language it's written. Perhaps that's why such a literature exists, because it is within these political boundaries. What if the Southwest were still part of Mexico? Would it be Mexican literature? Would the culture be different? The literature? Probably, yes. So maybe the political boundary does have a significance; why deny it? Nationally and politically, the United States has direct implications on the literature produced in the Southwest or the Midwest or any other region. Within that context you have to say that Chicano literature is part of American literature. If you took away the boundaries it would be Mexican literature.

What is the relationship of Chicano literature to Mexican literature?

The relationship many of the writers may have with Mexican writers, and the Spanish language itself. Those people I know of who write in Spanish do have an affinity, culturally speaking, with the Mexican nation. It may be a learned affinity in some cases.

I don't really feel that I have a strong relationship with it. I used to think I did at one time, but then I realized I had taught myself that I had that strong relationship. That is different than really having it. I read the Mexican classics, became interested in Rulfo, Fuentes, Yáñez, Ramón Rubín, Lopéz y Fuentes, and the Mexican Revolution novel; read the ensayistas [essayists], like Alfonso Reyes; all that. I tried to read as much as possible from the Mexican literary scene. Once I had read it, I felt a strong affinity to it. When I visited Mexico it reinforced that feeling. Then I began to realize that I'm not a Mexican. All these things I feel are a result of learning, not of growing up in Mexico with all *its* problems, *its* history, *its* beauty and all *its* affinities. I thought, "It's not really mine. I know it as mine, now, because I've learned it. I don't actually have it, nor have I lived it." After that I had to come back and say this is reality right here.

You've said that it's an important moment for a Chicano, Juan, and yes, it is. That doesn't mean I don't like Mexico; I love its many good things, though I don't like the bad. What I am saying is superficial, I realize, but it's true. I had to ask myself if I appreciated and enjoyed Mexico because I had learned to, or if I really had a strong tie to Mexico; and what is the difference? Es como un norteamericano who studies Mexican history y luego dice que es mexicano. [It's like a North American who studies Mexican history and then says he's Mexican.] It's the same thing, the same thing. The fact is that if I had not gotten a college education I would know very little about Mexico. O.K., I could go over and buy trinkets and look at the pyramids, but reality, ours, is not there; it's here.

Do you perceive yourself and your work as political?

No, not as a writer. I don't see my work as political. But are we talking about elections, gaining seats in Congress, or economic development, or intellectual liberation? What do you mean by *political*?

I have no distinct political purpose when I write. I do not write a creative piece to prove a political point, if that is what you mean. Some people might want us to, but I don't. It's not an overwhelming desire, let's say, to put into a creative work a political discourse, or dogma, or attitude. That doesn't mean that certain characters may not be politically motivated, but it's not one of my motivations when I write. As a political writer you can do better if you write an essay, or if you become involved in the community. That's an active way of being political. And I am involved politically, but it's not through writing or literature. It's an active part of a person's life to come to be engaged in issues. In that sense I am political, but not in the writing.

I just feel that there is a separation. I want to have in literature that one point where I can really be creative and totally human, where I can really try to see things apart from any gain or loss aspects, as you must in politics. En la política ganas o pierdes. [In politics you win or lose.] En la literatura [In literature] I don't think you should have that motivation. Literature is a much more complete game than politics, which is kind of mundane and of this world, and important, very important. Perhaps more important than the literary game, you know? for our people.

Does the Chicano author have anything in common with the majority group writers? Differences?

In common? Sure! Yes.

The difference would be, basically, that we don't have the great, long tradition that the majority writers know they have, or should know they have. That makes a very distinct difference. If you or I write, we may want there to be, hope there might be a long tradition of Mexican-American or Chicano writing—there is a minimal tradition, but almost none. However, it's a very positive difference for us, because we can feel that we are beginning something and that we should write a lot to create a greater volume of our writing.

If you want to write, I think there is one common thing: you have to have a love for people; otherwise you wouldn't write. I was visiting a friend of mine's class when he was lecturing on Larry McMurtry. He was saying, "Larry McMurtry hates people." Damn, I had to sit in front of the class and tell him, "That's not true. How in the hell can you sit there and tell these students of yours that Larry McMurtry hates people?" He says, "Look at his characters; he's always stereotyping them and saying how bad they are." "He has beautiful characters," I answered, "and the guy cares enough about them to write about them." I think that's the most important thing about writing. Whether he makes fun of his characters, or makes types out of them, or whatever, the writer feels enough love for them to want to write and capture them. It's absurd for us to think that Chicano writers have more love than other writers throughout the world; my god, it's ridiculous. Yet, I have heard that statement made.

Does Chicano literature share common ground with Black literature? Differences?

I'm not that well versed in it, beyond the most common, most read Black writers. Vicariously, I can go through their works and enjoy them. They live within the same confines we live in: this country. Both of our spiritual histories are here. There is a common tradition of oppression within this political system which gives us a shared experience. However, they have had over a hundred years of intellectual development in this country. For the last 125 years they have had at least seventy colleges at any given time training their people. They have all the mechanisms of being inside the system, which they are. In those respects we're different. We have not had access to institutions. Also, for a long period they have been larger in number within the political confines. That's an implication.

At certain points there is something common in the area of moral superiority. The Black, in the 1960's, finally became an ethnic group, after one hundred years of development to get to that point. Edward Spicer says that in the '60's the Blacks realized they had a historical precedent common to all of them, they had almost a common language, and they stressed a moral superiority. We see it today with people like Andrew Young. Chicanos, also, back in the '60's came to realize that we had a common historical precedent that bound us, a common language—be it Spanish or English—and we became an ethnic group when we began to stress a moral superiority. That doesn't mean I believe that we have a moral superiority, but I do think that the only way to gain an intellectual liberation is to come to believe that we are morally superior. Some of our literature is overwrought with this moral superiority, as is Black literature. How do you portray or prove a moral superiority? By downgrading the moral attitudes of the establishment and by claiming that your value system is so much better than theirs. Well, is it? Really? We say it is and the Blacks say the same thing. It's a common element in our literature. But I don't really believe that any group of people are morally superior at any given time.

Is there any relationship with the literature of other Spanish-speaking groups?

I don't know. I don't think so. You're talking about Cubans and Puerto Ricans, ¿verdad? [aren't you?] Maybe with the urban writings I've seen. The sense of displacement. It depends on the regions. I've read the literature coming out of New York and the Midwest, but I don't know. Of course, Spanish and La His-panidad [Hispanism] are commonalities.

Does Chicano literature have a distinctive perspective on life? What effect does it have on the literature?

I'm not a culturalist, but let's say that I were, then I would say that it does have a perspective. It would only be a perspective of the oppressed, and in that case, if you would remove the oppression you wouldn't have any culture. So what does that lead us to? I think it is more than that. But I don't think Chicano litera-ture necessarily has a different perspective. If it does, it's in the area of looking at the world through the eyes of the oppressed, something like a Third World type. That would be an element of distinctiveness.

Every person has a distinctive perspective on life, based on formation, environment, people, language, etc. You go back to the formation of the writer in his age of reflection, around twelve, thirteen, or fourteen. A person doesn't lose it. By age fifteen you've come across all the questions you're ever going to ask about life; you've had some kind of answer, and that has formed your perspective. I would accept the statement only if we amend it to say that every writer has a distinctive perspective, every authentic writer. I'm not talking about imitative writers, in whose case I would say yes. If you have a whole bunch of Chicanos writing the same way, O.K., then you would have a group of people looking at the world in the same way. They're copying the hell out of each other. But we have enough of a dif-ference among Chicano writers now—which I find extremely healthy. Again, it goes back to a lukewarm dogma, if we have any. It's wide open for anyone. If you're Chicano you can write. I find that healthy. But if someone comes on and says, "Well, this is not Chicano literature, this is, this isn't," entonces ya se fregó la cosa [then it's gone down the drain].

Does Chicano literature improve communication between Chicanos and Anglo Americans?

The only thing that improves communication is economics. If it becomes economically feasible to teach Chicano literature, then it improves communications. But what comes first? I'm not trying to be sarcastic.

Yes, I think it does, from the standpoint of having an exterior, material thing that cannot be negated, that you must look at. The Gringo can no longer say there is no Chicano literature. If he is smart he'll try to see what is in there. Yes, it improves communications, both ways. It's bound to, because of its exterior nature which cannot be negated. You can always negate an interior thing.

Does Chicano literature reevaluate, attack, or subvert the value system of the majority society? Is it a revolutionary literature? Thematically? Technically?

I don't think it's revolutionary, but let me explain what *revolutionary* means to me. It is displacement of one thing by another. You revolve to the point of becoming something else. Maybe I'm looking at it only in terms of politics; I have that tendency. Well, in that sense, no. It complements, supplements American literature. The American public, in general, is much more prone to believe that it is supplementing the culture. The Mexican public doesn't give a damn about Chicano literature. Aunque los Estados Unidos tenga cosas bastantes irracionales, hay suficientes universidades que se preocupan un poco por darle una amplitud a nuestra literatura. No creo que las universidades mexicanas se interesen en nada sobre la literatura chicana. [Although in the U.S. there are many irrational things, there are plenty of universities that care a little about giving our literature attention. I don't think that Mexican universities are interested in the least.] I don't.

Now, what part of the value system are we talking about, intellectual liberation? No. That's one of the ideals of the North American intelligentsia, that we be liberated intellectually. I don't think it's subverting the great ideal of North American thought, which is exactly that: intellectual liberation. My God, we're just another supplement. I mean, the writer in America, whether stereotyping or not, has always been motivated toward the liberation of the mind. He may have downgraded the Mexican at one point, but the whole sense of their movement was that there was always one person who was supposedly intellectually liberated. I'm not talking about authors who wrote just to make money, but rather the substantive writers. We are complementary to that value. Now, we would have to go down the list point by point to talk about subverting. Subverting what, the economic system? Hell, you can't subvert it. The Chicano writer is a prime example of private enterprise. Really. When you have a desire to write and there's no one to stop you, and you start your own publishing house, refusing to take money from anyone else, and you create your own product—that is supplementing the private enterprise system, not subverting its ideal. We are complementary to it.

Again, what is technically revolutionary? Miguel Méndez comes out with a book with three languages mixed in it—which I think is kind of overdone in some places—well, that's revolutionary in some way. Linguistically there might be something revolutionary in bilingualism, texts that mix two languages. However, it's happened before with the formation of other languages, like Provençal or the Romance languages. In Spanish it existed during the reconquest: the Muwassaha.* It happens when you have two culturas fronterizas [bordering cultures]. Maybe, now, it is once again a new thing.

What problems have you encountered in publishing? Were they racially founded?

Commercially founded, and then the racism comes in. I was telling you about what we were writing in the late '50's. Well, some of those manuscripts were probably refused because they were from Chicanos. We always thought that they might have been accepted if the signature had been different. But, also, the works weren't good. Imitative. Why take on an unknown when you already have a guy writing and making money?

You know, I sent manuscripts everywhere, and I always got rejects, thousands of rejects, but I enjoyed sending them off, because some people would write back a small comment. It made me feel I had a connection, or that someone knew I was writing. It built up the expectation that someday I would be accepted. But there are so many people who write and get rejected that it

---

* Genre of Hispanoarabic poetry written during the tenth to thirteenth centuries. The main text was written in either Arabic or Hebrew, with the last strophe, the *jarya*, written in vulgar Arabic, the Spanish of the period, or a particular argot.

would be hard to say I or some of my friends were rejected because we were Mexicans.

Are Chicanos at a disadvantage in trying to practice the art of writing?

No. No, I don't consider writing a disadvantage at all. No. Hell, being born is a disadvantage; what are you going to do the rest of your life? If you happen to get into writing, it's just minor.

What are the most outstanding qualities of Chicano literature? Weaknesses?

An outstanding quality is its humanness. Then, its grotesqueness. There's something pretty about the grotesque things that have come out. I'll tell you a story about José Revueltas. I was over at Berkeley to give some talks and Revueltas was there teaching Marxism, so we had an evening together. Se puso bien borracho [He got very drunk] and we began to talk about literature. Entonces dijo, "Oye, Tomás, te voy a regalar una colección de todos los libros que he escrito. Te los traje de México y te los tengo todos dedicados." [Then he said, "Listen, Tomás, I'm going to give you a collection of all the books I've written. I brought them for you from Mexico and I've autographed them to you."] He had them all there. I felt flattered. Then he asks, "¿Sabes por qué me gustan los chicanos a mí?" Estaba bien pedo. Le digo, "¿Por qué?" "Porque ustedes son unos monstruos, hijos de su chingada madre." "¡Hijo!," dije yo. "No te enojes," dijo, "porque nosotros, los mexicanos, también somos monstruos." ["Do you know why I like Chicanos?" He was really drunk. I say, "why?" "Because you are monsters, sons of your screwed mother." "Hey!" I said. "Don't get angry," he said, "because we Mexicans are monsters, too."] He liked us because we're the same. "Unas gentes grotescas; no tienen límites. Y aunque a veces escriben como mierda, hay algo precioso allí. Se arriesgan a todo sin temor a que los humillen." ["Grotesque people; no limits. And though sometimes you write like shit, there is something beautiful there. You take every risk without fear of being humiliated."] "You go to the extremes," he said. I thought about that. He was talking about Chicano literature, and it's true. I go to teatro [theatre] presentations y hay cosas allí bien grotescas [and there are really grotesque things], and yet they're so damn human. They have substance. That's one of the qualities I find. Some critics might find it bad, and probably the works won't stand the test of time, but at one time there was one individual who thought he was saying something beautiful. The fact that he thought about it that hard, to me makes it beautiful. It's more powerful than some things that are very, very well done, because for that person it meant something. I feel that in Chicano literature.

Weaknesses? Pues, a veces se mete mucho al aspecto didáctico. [Well, sometimes it gets too didactic.] I think that would cover it. It tries to teach a lesson.

What are the milestones so far in Chicano literature?

There's one milestone: Quinto Sol Publications with *El Grito*. That was an extremely important milestone. Nick Vaca, Octavio Romano, Herminio Ríos, Andrés Ibarra, and all the other people who began it performed a tremendous service. Historically, it's the most significant thing that's happened. Now, there is one more milestone—if you want to measure milestones with prizes—Rolando Hinojosa winning the Casa de las Américas premio [prize] for the novel. But I like to think of every first book by all the writers as milestones in themselves. Those are just as important.

What is the future of Chicano literature: distinctiveness or the de-emphasis of the distinctive characteristics?

It will continue distinctive. I base my opinion simply on demographic studies. The fact that the Mexican nation is increasing in number is going to have a direct implication on the Southwest. We're beginning to feel it now in the immigration problems. La implicación es siempre a causa de cuestiones de masas críticas, y aquí nos encontramos con la situación de población. La nación mexicana sigue y seguirá creciendo. Siempre habrá un aspecto fronterizo con la cultura norteamericana y la mexicana. [The implication always arises from critical masses, and here we find the situation of population. Mexico continues and will continue to grow. There will always be the border aspect between the North American and the Mexican cultures.] That's not going to stop; it's just beginning. Las masas críticas siempre traen la cultura y los cambios. [Critical masses always bring culture and change.] Por ejemplo [For example], it wasn't until we had a critical mass of students at the university level that we had the Chicano Movement. It would have happened regardless of the Black Movement or anything else. It was going to happen. Whenever you had a large enough critical mass of Chicano students at the university it happened. It will be the same with the Mexican nation. Hay más gente y continúa el cambio. [There are more people and change goes on.]

Who are the leaders among Chicano writers, and why?

Why is it necessary to have leaders in a creative endeavor? Well, perhaps for historical purposes it's important. Let's take it by genres. In poetry, Alurista is strong and he continues to get stronger. Ricardo Sánchez; Abelardo. It doesn't mean there aren't other poets who write just as well or maybe better. We have some outstanding poets who haven't written much yet. That's why I don't like the question. To me leadership implies a structured effort, and I have a hard time conceiving of leaders in literature. In the essay there are many: Juan Gómez-Quiñones in history; Nick Vaca wrote outstanding articles, but hasn't written much lately. Novel: Rolando Hinojosa is way ahead of the field. I don't know what influence he has, though I'm sure it's positive. Miguel Méndez is writing a lot. But then, is productivity to be equated to leadership? En el teatro [In theatre], I don't know. Luis Valdez I guess. But I don't like that term *leaders*.

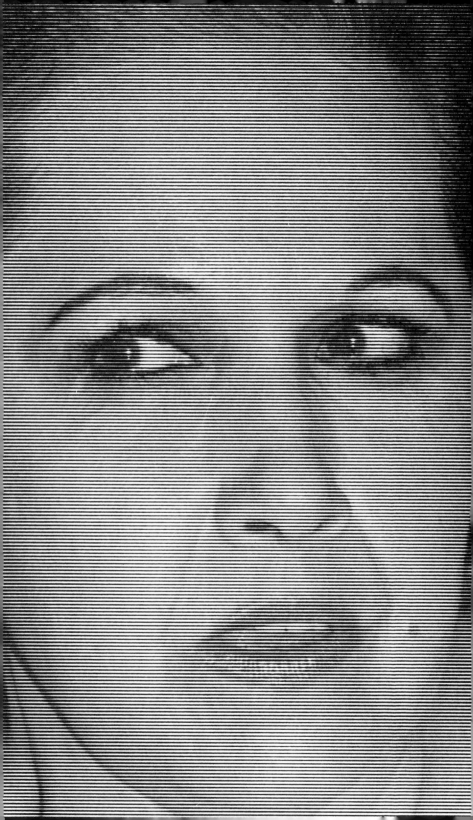

Estela Portillo

Estela Portillo has published works in two genres: drama, most notably *The Day of the Swallows* (1971) and *Sun Image* (1979), and short stories, a collection of which appeared under the title of *Rain of Scorpions and Other Writings* (1975). She also edited an issue of *El Grito* (7, no. 1, Sept. 1973) dedicated to Chicana writings, the first all-women's issue of a major Chicano journal. In 1972 she won the Quinto Sol Award for literature.

Portillo's work has a feminist strain to it. In *The Day of the Swallows*, a structurally traditional play, her main character commits suicide when her "perverse" sexual orientation is discovered. A certain Lorca note pervades Portillo's tragedy in the intensely restrained sexuality; the natural expression of lesbian love must be hidden, until circumstances unveil it and the revelation rends the social fabric. Death is the only possible ending. Yet Portillo manages to save her protagonist by turning her suicide into a mystical union with nature, a transcendence into a more tolerant realm of existence, and a victory for life and love. In the short stories, women are often portrayed as victims of their situation, used or misunderstood by men. Their self-fulfillment may necessitate the destruction of the men who oppress them, or even of those who love them; or it may lead to a radical departure from their normal life style. At other times, the woman's independence catalyzes the man's realization of his own meaning.

Two stories, "If It Weren't for the Honeysuckle" and "The Paris Gown," exemplify well Portillo's work, and specifically its feminist quality. In the first one, two women, representing successive generations, are enslaved and sexually abused by one man. To save yet another, younger woman from the painful experience the man plans to impose on her, the two older women kill him, burying the body in the garden. In a manner characteristic of her style, Portillo creates the metaphor of pruning the honeysuckle—the elimination of portions of the plant to insure the continued growth of the healthy part. As if nature were capable of gratitude and empathy, the honeysuckle seems to offer the protagonist a solution to her problem by revealing poisonous toadstools with which to kill the man. The murder, itself, is simply another necessary pruning in the general scheme of nature. The result is the preservation of a family of self-sufficient females in harmony with their environment. "The Paris Gown" offers a less violent, but certainly equally positive tale of female liberation. Besides the open attack on anachronistic machismo and the creation of a strong, interesting female protagonist, the story proposes the need to shift from a rigidly defined, intellectualized aesthetic to a fluid, sensual one, what Susan Sontag calls the move from the hermeneutics to the erotics of art, or what Portillo would call the victory of the Dionysian principle over the Apollonian. When the metaphor of aesthetics is expanded to its cosmic significance, we understand that Portillo advocates a radical social revolution. Neither story scruples to propose positively the abandonment of oppressive cultural traits in the name of self-determination and freedom. Women are forced to the extreme of perverse action to win the right to live freely. Portillo has the talent to present her women sympathetically, winning the reader over and making what some might judge to be improper action seem fitting according to the cosmic order of things.

The story "Rain of Scorpions" treats the feminist issue only tangentially, but allegorically challenges the central Chicano concept of Aztlán, the return to the mythical garden of paradise. What begins as a social-protest story becomes an adolescent adventure tale when a group of boys, inspired by a Chicano militant's call for a mass abandonment of a company town, go in search of a mythical cave, said to contain a map to a lost fertile valley. The artifacts they recover reveal that the fertile valley resides within each person; one cannot flee from reality to find peace. Meanwhile, as is fitting with Portillo's sense of natural harmony, a mud slide almost destroys the town and a mysterious rain of dead scorpions unites the Chicano community, infusing it with renewed faith and purpose through the shared experience of disaster. As are many of Portillo's works, the story is a morality play. Her particular vision of the Chicano movement may not please everyone, but, as her interview proves, she states it forcefully.

The interview was completed by recording in July 1979 in Estela Portillo's home in El Paso, Texas, and she reviewed the text in

September 1979. I am grateful to Margarita Vargas for her assistance during the interview.

Where and when were you born?

I was born in El Paso, Texas, on January 16, 1936.

Describe your family background and your present situation.

I was raised by mis abuelitos [my grandparents]. My grandfather had a tiendita en el segundo barrio [little store in the second district]. I remember sitting down against the kitchen door that led into el corral del presidio [the presidio's yard]; I would watch sunlight continuing itself on adobe walls; the silences in early afternoon had a mysterious splendor. We were poor. I am still poor, pero la pobreza nunca derriba el espíritu [but poverty never defeats the spirit]. When I was a child, poverty was a common suffering for everybody around me. A common suffering is a richness in itself. When I was twelve I went to live with my parents after the death of my grandparents. There was my father, my mother, two brothers, and a sister. My father was a diesel mechanic who really believed in the American dream. My mother gave piano lessons and was quite an expert on detective stories. She would recite from Baudelaire and would play all the songs of Agustín Lara.

I got married very young . . . just out of high school. Many times I imagined life, more than lived it. I kept house, had babies, went to college, and worked . . . an integrated time . . . Es posible que tentaba sueños y negaba realidades, y por eso lo que aspiraba fue no más un desencuentro. [Perhaps I touched dreams and denied reality, and that is why what I wanted proved a failure.] Still, there were muchos días con espacio, sin medida [many days with space, without measure] . . . I played a woman's role with great timidity and the usual illusions; always wanting much more . . . life always becomes a matter of priorities. Raising my family and working took most of my time. Once in a while I would pick up some graduate credits for a Master's degree that finally materialized in 1977.

I taught high school for many years and served as chairman of the English Department at Technical High School for six years. In 1972 I temporarily left the school system to go into mass communications.

I had a talk show over radio KIZZ here in El Paso . . . it's a country and western station now. The show was very political. At the time I was younger and had the energy. It drew a tremendous amount of flak, all kinds of calls and letters. If I backed up Castro or Tijerina! They offered me money to go to Cuba. My family was going wild. They even suspected that the FBI was tapping the phone. I was seriously thinking of getting out of the program when Herb Porras offered me a television show; he had a grant to do something cultural, nothing political. I was excited about doing something free-skating, out of politics and really involved in culture . . . I was supposed to include art, literature, dance, music, painting, etc. I was on twice a week, not in very good time slots, but I had the money to work with. Not enough! Actually I spent it mostly on getting prints from museums from all over the United States. So I had fun doing things like comparing Goya to Siqueiros in revolution in art, or a program on the Andalusian creative spirit, *duende*. After sixteen shows the money ran out and I told them I could not continue. As it was I had taken a cut in pay . . . I hate to always talk about money, but when you're poor you have to worry about groceries. But not only that, things were always happening, like the boys' choir of Mexico being refused reentry after taping a show and spending the night in my home, thirty-five children; and then there was a group of Aztec dancers. My husband was going crazy. When the money ran out, everyone sighed with relief. Porras wanted me to apply for another grant and stay on, but I thought I'd better go back to my old job. But I loved the media and being in front of a camera . . . very much an alive, organic, beautiful sense. And I wrote all the material, and in Spanish. Public Television has approached me to do it again for a grant, but it's so much work. With time, your energies just don't have the thrust. Besides, now I'm very much involved with rewriting my plays.

Another reason I didn't return to the media was because I was the resident dramatist at the community college here in El Paso, and it gave me the opportunity to stage my plays. I had written five plays and I could experiment with them. I loved it! But you know what writing and directing plays is, and being responsible for the production and the actors as well. It was another chaotic, beautiful thing. My husband said, "Why didn't I marry a nice, normal woman?" And I do feel sorry for him. So I'm not working with the community college any more. I now work with Special Services with the El Paso public schools—I am no longer involved with a classroom full of students. I love them, but it comes to the time when you cannot write and give yourself to students. I'm very jealous of my solitude. You have to have time to germinate—copulate first with ideas and then germinate. I'm content where I am right now.

California State University at Los Angeles staged *The Day of the Swallows* and invited me. In theatre they are looking for a lot of material, and since supposedly I'm the only Chicano writing traditional theatre, I had more people asking me for my material, people from Los Angeles, New York. So when I got home, I took out all this material I had never had the courage to rewrite and began to work on it.

Right now I am in the most wonderful, glorious love affair with my new play, *The Labyrinth of Love: Sor Juana Inés de la Cruz*. Right now I am Sor Juana. You know, most of the material I have done second hand, it doesn't come from my past experience that much, and when I deal with male characters it's difficult . . . for a woman it's difficult to write male characters. So I decided to write about women. People who review *Rain of Scorpions* say I am a woman's liberationist, which I didn't see; but when I look through the whole thing, well what do you know, I am.

I have a novel with an agent in New York, *Woman of the Earth*, and I started to write another one called *Luz*. I finished six chapters before getting called to Los Angeles. All of a sudden I have requests for theatre, so I came back, threw my novel in a drawer, and started working on the plays. I like the novel. It takes place in Mexico City, before it was called Cactus Rock, before language or hierarchies. It's a brand-new theory of reincarnation. I invented a reality of the first people on the earth, the Xochitl, and a sensitive girl called Luz, the last survivor in the twentieth century. I built the history behind a mythical tribe I contrived. I love to construct songs and myths and history. I will go back to it as soon as I finish Sor Juana, but right now I am Sor Juana. At this moment you are looking at Sor Juana.

When did you first begin to write?

It was during the writing for my television show that I knew what I would like to do: *be a writer*. This, however, had not been my first attempt. In high school I had worked on the school newspaper. Some years before I was working on the television show, my only son died when he was nine months old. I already had five daughters. To lessen the pain, to give my life a more palatable meaning, I went on a reading spree. I read philosophy, history, psychology: Bergson, Jung, Jaspers, Nietzsche, Huxley, the Bible, Toynbee, Aisley. I read Buddha, Lao-tzu, Kahlil Gibran, Pierre Teilhard de Chardin. Thoughts fermented for a while. An idea for a book came to mind. It was about the creation of a new kind of utopia mating Eastern philosophy to Western pragmatism. I wrote 340 pages of a book that I titled *After Hierarchy*. When I finished it, I sent it to Eastern publishers. It was rightfully refused; it was a bad, bad book. I call it my "getting rid of the measles" book. It took all of my spare time and my waking hours for three years, but it was not a wasted time, even if the book was so atrocious. The experience proved to have been a baptism. I found my own solid view-of-my-world. Although the book was extremely idealistic, it brought me back to the practical world. Little by little, going against the grain of the book, I learned to accept life "as it is." I was glad to be alive. There was much beauty in this world. I was part of that beauty. The book should have been buried in the backyard, but I . . . *I* wanted to live on. Much later, when I was writing my own television show, the writing came easier. It had an honesty.

What kind of books did you read in your formative years?

I have always read a lot. In my formative years, I was childishly addicted to novels by Stratton-Porter, Montgomery, and Kathleen Norris. I was well imbued with the protestant ethic and the romanticism of a never-never land. In college, because I was an English major, I had a sober and delightful exposure to the English and American classics. T. S. Eliot, Pound, Sartre, Genet, Balzac, the Russian writers, I picked up for my own pleasure. I always read a lot during my pregnancies. One summer I picked up Octavio Paz, and he opened the door to Vasconcelos, López Velarde, Alfonso Reyes, Pellicer, Novo, Pablo Neruda, and Asturias. I was such a reader. I wouldn't buy expensive maternity clothes I wouldn't wear later, so I would go into my room and read for the last three months. I'd start in the morning and wouldn't do any cooking or housework; I wouldn't sleep that night. It was a passion. I found myself in the glory of the written word. But I have also lost part of me in abstractions.

I am getting out of all that now, mostly because you can't

write and read. There is something about not wanting to touch anything when you're writing. What little you are, it should be you. Another thing was that my nose was so long in books that I didn't know how to relate to people, except my family. I was very selfish. It was boring. I thought their conversation was trite; I considered their habits and their ordinary things very superficial and dumb. I was going through some kind of intellectual thing which I'm glad I'm over, because at the moment I am very anti-intellectual. I am not at all Apollonian; I am very Dionysian. In the last three years I haven't done any reading. I have become an absolute nonreader. For one thing I've been so busy, writing, traveling, and trying to rearrange my life. I am relearning the use of my senses. I enjoy feeling people more than sunsets and mountains and the colors of rocks.

My second novel, *Luz*, contains everything I learned from Huxley. In his last novel, *Island*, he talked about the perfecting of man, a time before language. But, you see, this is again the English tradition.

What is the extent of your studies?

I received the Master's degree in English literature from the University of Texas, El Paso. I really wanted to apply for a doctorate, but financially, to pay for it on my own would be impossible. My paycheck pays the bills. Then, too, I had English coming out my ears; so I thought I would do something to improve my writing, thinking that it might be much more fruitful in giving me some substance, something I could point to and say, look, I can do this. I don't see why I want the doctorate anyway. So I've changed my mind. I was probably having to count my pennies when I told you, a few years back, that I wanted the degree. I still have to count them. But it's a matter of priorities also. I have to be a mother until the children can fly on their own and before I can do anything.

Has formal education helped or hindered you as a writer?

Education was never a hindrance; I don't think I was bright enough to "catch on" to its obstacles and limitations. The racism, the prejudice, the poor quality education, the denial of Mexican culture were all there. I felt it; it touched my life as it touched the lives of other Chicanos. Because of my nature and my bad habit of negating realities, I sort of "escaped" from the multifaceted rejections. In my "escape" I found time to learn "aloneness." My solitude touched upon many areas of feeling, but it also gave range to my imagination and my mind.

When my first book was rejected, someone told me to do fiction. I had just seen the movie *The Fox*, from the D. H. Lawrence story, and someone said, why don't you write something like that and make a million? I'm always thinking of a buck. So in a month and a half I wrote *The Day of the Swallows* and I put everything in. The plot is about lesbians; I knew nothing about them, but I was going to sell it. Well, it got published, it appeared in four anthologies, I get invited to talk about it, it gets analyzed to death, and it's a play I wrote in a very short time and for a terrible reason. I was just being mercenary.

When I got around to writing fiction, *Rain of Scorpions*, I had all these ideas for stories, but I knew nothing about writing fiction, never having had a creative writing course. I knew nothing about technique. So I injected all my B.S. from *After Hierarchy* into my story lines. That is a capital sin. Somebody told me about a year later that I should be writing essays. I think they have good story plot, but what I do sometimes is bore you to death by shoving all this philosophy down your throat. So, in my old age, I decided to go back to school and study creative writing and learn to write fiction. I went down to little old, humble UTEP and was surprised to find such a good creative writing department. They literally taught me how to write, the mechanics, the techniques, not my words or my stuff. I am still doing too many acrobatics. Maybe because I was an English teacher for so long, I have a hang-up about language. I like to say, whee, look at me, look at the beautiful words. It must be some kind of insecurity and I don't know why. *Women of the Earth* doesn't have any philosophy. It's fiction. I am still learning.

Which was the predominant language in your home as a child? Which do you speak more fluently now?

En la casa de mis padres hablé español siempre [In my parents' home I always spoke Spanish]; the remembrances of life with mis abuelitos [my grandparents] are always in the idiom of my emotions, el español [Spanish], the barrio dialogue. However, I learned to read in English and books became an ardent part of my life. After my marriage, I resorted to the English language all the time. I manipulate the English language better, but I also feel very much at home with Spanish. I would like to write in Spanish, but it doesn't come out. I think what happened is that I came out of the barrio too early. Oh, I go back and record people, take notes, but it's not me. I've mastered English, better than most Anglos. But in Spanish I am still groping, and if you have to grope you'll never be a good writer.

Does Chicano literature have a particular language or idiom?

Yes, Chicano literature has a particular language. I believe that the idiom of the Chicano finds its spontaneity in the natural combination of the two languages. Language reflects the human experience, and Chicanos do bridge the two cultures. It is a freedom, a flexibility and a confidence.

How do you perceive your role as a writer vis-à-vis: (a) the Chicano community or Movement; (b) U.S. society; (c) literature itself?

(a) I still am searching for my role as a writer vis-à-vis the Chicano Movement. I believe in the spirit of the Movement; La Causa has a momentum of intelligence and courage. If I were younger, perhaps, I could be more active and resourceful in contributing to its objectives: *the equality and the reality of all men.* It is part of an inevitable and historical cause. It is with the Movimiento [Movement] that the Chicano finds a sincere vitality.

Movement people read me because I'm the only woman representative, but I think they read me more as a feminist. There have been many studies of *Rain of Scorpions*, but they all deal with the stories about women, and ignore the novella "Rain of Scorpions" because it is not about women's liberation. Most male teachers of Chicano literature will look at all the men before they'll tackle me. After all, I am just a woman. I hate to say that, especially about Chicano men, but we still have our closed doors and our own way of polarizing everything between men and women. It's going to take a lot of conditioning before men say that I am a Chicano writer and that I write just as well as the men. Maybe it's because I am not as good, but in certain ways I am. In certain ways I'm better. I handle the English language better than any other Chicano writer, except Anaya in his first book. *Woman of the Earth* will be the second-best novel of the Chicanos in English.

(b) I would like to extend myself as a writer and find a U.S. audience. Not so much to be read because I am a minority writer, but because people can find themselves in what I write . . . all people. To be that kind of a writer, to go beyond the local and contemporary, to find a common denominator in unifying people, these would be the kind of imprints I would like to make in contributing to El Movimiento.

(c) I am learning to write; I experiment, I grow; I see my limitations as writer and person; I try to change to make a better, simpler offering. I think I have a long way to go before I can think of myself as a good writer; the pure lustre among good writers makes me humble. I'm going to keep on . . .

What is the place of Chicano literature within U.S. literature?

No literature has ever gone into "infinite regress." The pull of diversification in any literature leads to universality. T. S. Eliot wrote that words bend, break, and crack under pressure. The pressure within Chicano literature is a verbal miasma of sameness; it has clung too long to complaint and condemnation. There is certainly a reason for both. All literatures, in their inception, are revolutionary. It is only a phase. Chicano literature will find its own balance. Humanism, detachment, beauty, moderation measure the human condition as Art. Once these goals are achieved, Chicano literature can be well compared to the best of American literature and world literature.

What is the relationship of Chicano literature to Mexican literature?

Los siglos y la historia le han dado a la literatura mejicana una representación ordenada. Las raíces culturales están solidificadas. Por eso las perspectivas literarias toman forma precisa. Los géneros de la literatura chicana todavía pretenden fondo; los obstáculos que ha impuesto la cultura americana han causado una ambigüedad social. En Méjico, las varias culturas son separatistas, determinadas por principios económicos. Nunca ha existido una mezcla últimamente final; pero cada cultura es fija y segura. El fondo social de los chicanos todavía es innovación

ideológica. Esto se refleja en la literatura: simultáneamente existe una acción atrayente y una repulsión hacia la cultura americana. No existe esta condición totalmente entre los mejicanos-
americanos [*sic*]; pero sí alcanza a un porcentaje mayor. [The
centuries and history have given Mexican literature an ordered
image. The cultural roots are solidified. That is why the literary
perspectives assume precise form. Chicano literature's genres
are still seeking a foundation; the obstacles that American culture has presented have produced social ambiguity. In Mexico
the various cultures are separatist, determined by economic
principles. There has never existed a final mixture; but each culture is fixed and secure. The Chicanos' social base is still an
ideological innovation. This is reflected in the literature: there
exist, simultaneously, an attraction and a repulsion with respect
to American culture. This condition does not exist completely
among the Mexican Americans; but it does reach a high
percentage.]

In many ways I identify with Sor Juana, in the elements of
being a reader, a person who structures the world out of ideas
and words, rather than being part of what they call "life itself."

Do you perceive yourself and your work as political?

I consider myself, first, as an artist. I strongly believe that all
literature limits itself when its life is prolonged in political or
social-protest dialectic. Machinelike repetitiveness makes it in-
effective. En toda literatura se busca la quintaesencia de la experiencia humana; esta esencia existe fuera de lo político. [All
literature seeks the quintessence of human experience; that essence exists outside of politics.] Somehow the schizophrenic atmosphere of political rhetoric crucifies the universality that is
the end of all good art.

When I had the radio program, I wanted Chicanos to mobi-
lize to fight a revolution and blah, blah. I'm much more mellow
now. I've come to the realization that the Aztlán philosophy—
which is used in such a vague manner—is part of a great anger,
very well deserved. But to look at it realistically, philosophically,
no matter how Chicano we are, no matter how exploited we are,
there is definitely a great part of us, very inwardly, that is American: habits, school, language. Although we say we hate them,
inwardly, if we are honest enough, we want it. And those who

don't, who want to be citizens of a completely new world, well I think they are free and beautiful human beings to think it is possible; but it is highly improbable, an unreality when you look at the odds. Now you might say that that is a cop-out, that I am not really Chicano, but there are many, many viewpoints in the Chicano area, and mine fits in just as well as the ones who want isolation. We must also remember that the isolationists are young, vigorous, ready to build the fences of the mind against new words and idioms. I belong to a generation when we didn't have enough people. When I had my radio program, there was no Chicano Movement here. I was the only Chicana fighting the political cause. Not a single Chicano backed me up. The only ones who did were the Jews, Jewish political science professors from UTEP, or the Jewish Women's League. Chicanos were mobilizing, but not in El Paso. Even now we are not the most active center. Back then there was only Estela Portillo and the John Birch Society who wanted to lynch me.

The older people who are involved with the Movement are lashed to a whirlwind, but I'm isolated. I am not a professor at a university. If I were, I would be in it. But right now my thinking has changed, because I am an isolated liver. I am very Trotskyist; I can believe in eventual social evolution, but not revolution. We won't have these tremendous differences in the distribution of wealth. That is very Aztlán, but from a world perspective.

I separate politics from literature because I believe that when you inject politics into it you limit its life, as I said before. All good literature is based on the human experience which is nonpolitical. Use literature as a political tool and it becomes provincial, time bound. So I say no to any political leader who advocates political literature. They must be kept separate if you are a writer of literature. Now there are people who may use literature as a political tool, but they are politicians and this is not the end of all literature. It is a use of it, one use. But that is not literature. And there is a place for the powerful force literature can be; it's needed in our Movement to give it cohesion. But literature itself is very impersonal, nonpolitical. There is a tenacity about it, to stay alive, to believe in love, to cope, to pick ourselves up, to fly. Political literature, no matter how clever it might be, tends to make the stereotypes of the evil exploiter and the poor, innocent victim. That is not life. The exploiter is a human being too. He might be violent and selfish and greedy and mean, but down deep, despite having mutated into a Machiavellian oddity, he still is human. Once you take this away from your character in literature, you've taken away his life. Political literature assassinates characters.

They criticize me for not putting anything socio-political into my musical. I would not put anything political into it, it's a fun play! It's a time for making whoopey, and singing and dancing, and being *very Dionysian*.

So I disagree. Oh, I have a running battle with Ricardo Sánchez; he and I have almost come to blows. But it's not that I cop out. It's that I am very realistic and I think I have more of a world view on things. Say it's my age. I've mellowed out.

Does the Chicano author have anything in common with the majority group writers? Differences?

Life . . . the struggle thereof . . . the dimensions of the heart . . . the convergence of the senses toward all things beautiful and real. All writers have the need to portray the personal impression of these things with gratitude. Chicano literature is working toward a larger focus, a greater acceptance of what is.

Does Chicano literature share common ground with Black literature? Differences?

Sometimes I hear a similar tune in Black and Chicano literature; the tune of the hustler, the closed alternative of hustling or being hustled; the attack: the running down of the majority group. Both literatures have touched artistically into their own form of existentialism. Both literatures, or the people in them and of them, have the rhythms of the earth running strong in the veins. The main difference lies in the concentration of Chicano literature on myth and indigenous origins. Chicano literature has a vast and rich resource of ancestry, the "pyramid-men" ancestry. It is a larger ancestry than that of the Blacks, whose primitive origins are across an ocean. The Black is an isolate that has assimilated completely into the American mainstream. Of course, within that mainstream, the Blacks have integrated some of the cultural patterns of their origin and have created their own dialect. The Chicano will remain bicultural and bilingual because his origin is part of the Western Hemisphere.

That, perhaps, is the reason why the pace of Black literature resembles the pace of some American writings. Chicano literature has a more defined uniqueness.

Is there any relationship with the literature of other Spanish-speaking groups?

There is the common feel of the Latin nature in the sense of living. Latin American literature immobilized itself for a long time within the patrimony of nationalism. Polarization between Chicano culture and American culture could be detrimental to the growth and change of Chicano literature. There should not be a severance with the past; but national modes are not the true past; national modes are more of a passion than an essence in a reality that strives for a singular vision of Man.

I am not familiar with Puerto Rican literature, but I was reading some of those plays in the *Chicano-Riqueña* anthology [7, no. 1, Winter 1979] and I am just so jealous of all the great, sinful life in them. I've missed a lot of sin in life, let me tell you. That is a terrible thing to miss.

Does Chicano literature have a distinctive perspective on life? What effect does it have on the literature?

Part of the distinctive perspective of Chicano literature is feudal and fatalistic. It is, of course, a historical and social consequence. Time will bring about a literary solvency. Chicano literature will transform itself, as all things that are good and natural do. There is within the structure of Chicano literature a part that is revolution and another that is evolutionary; that is fitting in all good literature, and it adds to its merit. I believe the Chicano to be a bridge between the old and the new, between the primitive and the technological. The Chicano can cement tradition to changing trends; a restructuring toward universality; the new American, the cosmic man. I have written a Readers' Theatre narration around this theme, called "The Cosmic Man."

Does Chicano literature improve communication between Chicanos and Anglo Americans?

It should; it doesn't. Real literature would be communicable. It would bridge and communicate with anybody, anywhere in the

world. They would read it and say, hey, that is what they're saying, I relate to it. That is a step forward in literature. If we turn
them off, they stamp our literature as inferior. And to some degree it is, because it hasn't reached them. What makes Shakespeare Shakespeare? It's alive, it's pure flesh.

The Anglo public accepts my work, they love the words, and
the women love the women's-liberation angle, and they're so
glad they are not reading terrible books like *Fear of Flying*.
Don't I wish I could write a book like that! I got a letter saying
that my book was so far superior to that one because for once
they could sit back and read beautiful, clean words. Oh God,
what a lousy writer I must be. As I said, I haven't sinned enough
in life and I don't have the assurance of really working with sex
openly. Boy if I had! I will make one statement: I wish I had
been more sinful in my life.

---

*Does Chicano literature reevaluate, attack, or subvert the value sys-
tem of the majority society? Is it a revolutionary literature?
Thematically? Technically?*

In the natural process of its evolution, it has done so. It has attacked and subverted the value system of the majority society.
Isn't that the citadel of the written word? To attack injustice? To
verbally fight for the common man? American writers, the best
of them, constantly attack the materialistic values of the American system, for they realize the stagnant quality of such values.
There is one major difference, however. When Americans criticize themselves, they do it with a volatile honesty. Chicano
literature uses stereotypes to point out American violences.
Stereotyped situations, ideas, or characters very seldom add
strength or verity to any argument, if literature is an argument.

The positive dynamism within any literature is a balanced
reevaluation of any existing circumstances. That has the type of
sophisticated, revolutionary impact that puts the stereotyped
elements to shame. A balanced reevaluation is also dealing with
an equation of truth. I would say that, because the stereotyped
elements concentrating on attack and subversion are not as dynamic, Chicano literature tends to be pseudo-revolutionary.

The technique of "revolutionary literature" is very cut and
dried. There are patterns to follow; it's the simplest to write. But
it's not the same as the technique of good literature. The end
goal is different. The political is linear, like wearing blinders and

going in a straight line to get to the pre-established goal. When you are writing real literature you're dealing with a quantum theory. There are so many variables in the human being that it is a hundred times more difficult to write good literature than good political literature. The latter is a piece of cake. Moreover, the techniques of "revolutionary literature" are very traditional, have not changed, and will not change. It follows a method and achieves a very short-term effect. It fizzles out like a wet firecracker.

I wish I could say that I had found something revolutionary, *really revolutionary*, in Chicano literature. It is the old forms, the old words. That is why I liked Anaya's first book; it is so far superior to the second. The first has a cosmic vision and it will last, live longer than any other so far written. Of course, I haven't read everything.

What problems have you encountered in publishing? Were they racially founded?

When the Eastern publishers rejected *After Hierarchy*, they rejected a bad book. I told you some years ago that I thought quality seldom finds rejection. I still believe that, although being commercial is something else. If *Woman of the Earth* does not make it in New York, I will submit it to a Chicano publisher and admit that somehow I don't have the commercial selling appeal. I know it's better than a lot of the stuff being published.

Chicano publishers know me. They often write asking me to submit material. Quinto Sol opened the doors for me, and now I have my foot in with the university classes and everything.

Are Chicanos at a disadvantage in trying to practice the art of writing?

No writer is at a disadvantage attempting the art of writing. It is an instinctual and artistic pull. It is a love, an actualization. There are really no obstacles for one who loves life, people, ideas, words, and the glorious orgy of creation itself. There are so many rewards other than the monetary ones. The writer who senses, intuits, and knows he is a writer achieves an autonomy inconceivable of barriers.

What are the most outstanding qualities of Chicano literature?
Weaknesses?

I find myself incapable of judging simply because I think its
present weaknesses will give birth to its strengths. I would give
that last sentence an F for being vague. Seriously, it is a matter
of learning. You learn by mistakes and thinking of better ways
every time. You can never be taught how to do something without doing it; you have to learn the hard way. You actually have
to see that it is right. You have to build a hard shell to where
criticism does not destroy you. That is the hardest thing to do,
but once you get past the point of breaking to pieces over criticism, then you become self-critical of your weaknesses and you
correct them; they become the source of strengths.

The worst writer, and one that is going nowhere, is the one
who says, what I write is perfect. There is too much of that in
Chicano literature. Insecurity. Not because they are little people
or anything, but because it's a new thing for us. We have been
struggling so much for survival that the emergence of a strong
literary foundation of people secure in it is just not there. It is
something very tentative with us, so of course we are going to
feel insecure. We have to fall back on a few good writers, struggling writers, when we refer to the movement. We cannot look
at anybody except ourselves. When we are the measuring stick
of what we write, man, we know we are wearing blinders. We
become very defensive. It is not individual insecurity, but the
whole literary movement that is still not solidified.

The poetry is too political, still very defensive. Perhaps I am
going back to the old concepts of poetry writing, the use of sensibilities plus structure plus image plus contrapuntal imagery.
Now all these things are in the realm of artistry. The Chicano is
not careful enough, not enough of a craftsman. Everything is too
gut level in poetry for the Chicano. I have not heard enough of
it, but everything I read turns me off, it is so gut level. And a lot
of it is fake. Really. Poetry is the spontaneous overflow of personal and powerful feeling, and it usually comes from authenticity. A lot of Chicano poetry, because it follows the same pied
piper, tends to be contrived. Now we are not Gringo lovers when
we follow craft, we're going back to all the world literature.
Whether you are an e. e. cummings or a Robert Frost, you are
still following certain precepts. Our poetry is not intellectualized enough. I hate to say this, but outside of the fact that

poetry is the spontaneous outpouring of a powerful feeling, it is the most intellectualized of all forms of expression, the least commercial.

Which are the milestones so far in Chicano literature?

The important milestones so far in Chicano literature have been the successful establishing of publishing houses to give aspiring Chicano writers a Mecca; the volumes of reference material growing and made available in all areas to students and the public; the emergence of qualities in the literature other than those which are pseudo-revolutionary.

The last point we have covered already. This is, of course, leading to some kind of universality in the portrayal of human experience. There are so many features of the Chicano experience that are 100 percent eternal, that any people in the world can identify with. The strengths, our hopes, our family structure, our capacity to love, all the results of the closure of our society and what it has made of us. This vital and human experience could actually find readers, aside from the Americans, readers in Italy, Spain, and . . . because it is a universal one. They have all been through the same thing historically.

Bless Me, Ultima has done this. To some extent Hinojosa did in *Estampas del Valle*; he is not a novelist and in a class it would never be accepted as a novel. There is no structure, just little vignettes. But they were so real, so close to the heart, that if put together into a longer form it would be a novel. I think Hinojosa definitely has possibilities. And, oh yes, Rivera; of all of them Rivera definitely, because he is very human. The element of suffering is the most universal of them all. Suffering brings us together in a common reaction. The German *Geist*. It is there in Rivera. He has won his place in the universal. Too bad he has not written more. And, of course, Ron Arias; he is one of the best.

What is the future of Chicano literature: distinctiveness, or the de-emphasis of the distinctive characteristics?

The future of Chicano literature lies not in the de-emphasis of the distinctive characteristics, nor in its present distinctiveness. It will be the incorporation of still untapped, humanistic resources outside our barrio existentialism, its mythical font, or the romantic hold on "remembrances of things past." It lies in a convergence of truths that are universal, that places the Chicano within circumstances that focus the whole world. Always knowing what he was and what he is.

Chicano literature in the future will reflect a bicultural condition. I do not believe there will be a disintegration of either culture. Which one will be dominant? Which one will be recessive? That is hard to say. It will depend on the series of social and political changes in the world. As long as there is an expressive flow in the dynamics of each culture, as long as the flow is determined and purposive and meaningful to the Chicano, he will embrace both. The Chicano's destiny is to create a new kind of American. This will be the impetus of future Chicano literature. In the Chicano will be combined the best of both cultures. He will be equally a *homo emovere*, a man who feels, and a *homo faber*, a man who works. There will be an ascending degree of integration of the cultures . . . rather than the integration of the Chicano into one or the other.

Who are the leaders among Chicano writers, and why?

One of the reasons why we are so insecure is that we really do not have that many models. We are just solidifying. So we don't have enough to choose models from. We are all pioneers. And we are all fumbling, the best and the worst. It will take another seventy-five years before someone really solidifies the movement. It has happened to all the literatures, the English, the French, the German. Once they achieved a certain amount of security in their society, and they became writers, the mishmash of the first writings was always forgotten. It takes a long time.

For inspiration, I myself have turned to Rudy Anaya, Tomás Rivera, and Rolando Hinojosa. Their idiom is one of truth, honesty, and the undeniably real.

Rudolfo A. Anaya

In 1971, the second Quinto Sol Prize for literature brought to our attention a young New Mexican writer, Rudolfo Anaya and his enchanting character, the old curandera [shamanistic wise woman] Ultima, blessed with the magical power and cosmic vision of Carlos Castaneda's Don Juan, without the messianic pretentiousness. *Bless Me, Ultima* became the best selling of Quinto Sol's prestigious titles and still maintains its popularity. Anaya has published a second novel, *Heart of Aztlán* (1976), and his third, *Tortuga*, is in press at the time of this writing (1979).

Following as it did Tomás Rivera's award in 1970, Anaya's winning of the Quinto Sol Prize produced a contrast of Chicano fictional worlds. Whereas Rivera's subject is the migratory farmworker from Texas, Anaya portrays New Mexican families with permanent roots dating back centuries. The sense of space is diametrically opposite: though Rivera's characters wander the country, they always seem fenced in, restricted to small spaces; Anaya's characters feel the limitless expanse of themselves in a parcel of land. The same is true of language and style: while Rivera's is concise, controlled, severely limited to essentials, Anaya's is rich, expansive, profuse. Perhaps the difference can be traced to their distinct experience and the effect of the culture of the area and inhabitants each one knows. Yet close reading of *Ultima* reveals that, in spite of the surface differences and the infinite horizons of Anaya's spatial/spiritual sensibilities, the two novels and the authors share much. Anaya's expansive prose is just as carefully controlled as Rivera's within its fictional ambience. Nothing superfluous is tolerated; Anaya and Rivera—one could add Hinojosa and Arias—are their own best editors. Though at first glance it strikes one as realistic, Anaya's language is ambiguous and evocative. The imagination's power to effect change in the world is central, both thematically and structurally, in both novels. And in the final analysis, both are essentially con-

cerned with the protagonist's acquisition of the ability to see—
read—the world in its harmonious unity, beyond the superficial
divisiveness, and, then, with the need to write what is seen. In
each case the novel is the text that proves the success of the
apprenticeship.

Ultima produced expectations that *Heart of Aztlán* did not
satisfy. Not that the introduction of blatantly political topics is a
fault in and of itself—no, it is a matter of the craftsmanship, not
of the themes, and *Heart*, for whatever reason, is less polished,
less accomplished. Anaya should be admired for having the courage to explore a new space—*Heart* is set in the city—instead of
remaining within the circumference of the secure area established in *Ultima*. *Tortuga*, his third novel, promises to be yet another experiment. Anaya's readers await it with great expectations. *Bless Me, Ultima* assures him a faithful audience.

Rudy Anaya recorded and edited his responses during the
winter of 1978–1979.

When and where were you born?

I was born in Pastura, New Mexico, a small village on the llano
[plains], El Llano Estacado, which begins in those hills and set-
tles into the plains of West Texas and Kansas, the eastern plains
as we know them. It's a harsh environment. I remember most
that sense of landscape which is bleak, empty, desolate, across
which the wind blows and makes its music. My work is full of
references to the land and to the landscape; it can't help but be. I
was born in 1937.

The influence of that land was early and lasting. I have tried
to describe it in an article, "The Writer's Landscape: Epiphany in
Landscape,"* as almost a religious experience, or a religious
communication that man has with his earth when the two come
to meet at one point and the power which is in each one is ener-
gized, no longer remaining negative and positive, but fusing together. That landscape plays a major role in the literature that I
write. In the beginning, it is an empty, desolate, bare stage; then,
if one looks closely, one sees life—people gather to tell stories,
to do their work, to love, to die. In the old days the sheep and
cattle ranchers gathered in that small village, which had a train

---

Latin American Literary Review 5, no. 10 (Spring–Summer 1977): 98–102.

station, a watering station for the old coal-burning trains. It was prosperous; they were good times. Then after the visit or the business at hand is done, the people disappear back into the landscape and you're left as if alone, with the memories, dreams, stories, and whatever joys and tragedies they had brought to you.

Soon after I was born, we moved to Santa Rosa, which was on Highway 66. For me that road was the link between the East and the West. There was much life there. Santa Rosa is a geographical setting, in a sense, that I use to set the stage for *Bless Me, Ultima*. The river flows through the valley, and the highway and the railroad tracks dissect the town in another direction. And always there is the interplay of people on the stage of life with the elements of nature—and the llano itself working through the people, changing the people, finally making the people who they are. I can't think of very many things that I have written that do not have a reference to those natural forces and that earth and people which nurtured me.

Describe your family background and your present situation.

Family and roots. Everybody is into roots now, since Haley. When people ask me where my roots are, I look down at my feet and I see the roots of my soul grasping the earth. They are here, in New Mexico, in the Southwest. My family—the history I know of it—originally settled in the Río Grande Valley in Albuquerque in the old land grant, which was then called La Merced de Atrisco, the Atrisco land grant. My great-grandfather was one of the original incorporators of that land grant. From there the family moved with the first movement that went eastward into the llano of New Mexico, a recent move around the middle of the nineteenth century, after it was safe to move out into those plains. That is where you get some of those small villages along the river valleys. It was good grazing land for sheep and cattle.

My parents met in a small town by the name of Puerto de Luna, and there they married and started their family—I have many brothers and many sisters. From the time I can remember, we have always had roots here. I was fortunate to be born and raised in a small village where everyone knew each other. The families were related; there were common endeavors. People worked essentially as ranchers. We owned our own solar—our plot of land where our home was—and when we moved to Santa Rosa we also owned our own home. So we always had a firm sense of belonging instilled in us, not only by the land but, of course, by our parents. The sense of culture, of tradition, of history was always around us. People told stories when they came to visit. The elders would sit around the table playing cards or dominoes, or just talking, and we would listen to the cuentos. They always talked about the way things had been, the people who had come here, how families were related, the old people and what they had done. That filled us with a sense of pride in our own history, you might say.

I still live in New Mexico. I have traveled to many places, but have no desire to leave New Mexico. Here I can look around and have a feeling that these hills, these mountains, this river, this earth, this sky is mine. I feel good in it. For that I think I am fortunate. I'm presently teaching creative writing and some courses in Chicano literature at the University of New Mexico. I enjoy teaching. I'm always working on some project or another that has to do with writing. I've just finished a manuscript for a novel entitled *Tortuga* and I'm working on a short story. So every day I meet some collaborator, some idea, some event, some memory, some sense of the landscape, I hear something, and I start to write. That's a very healthy position for a writer to be in. I have time. I have solitude.

When did you first begin to write?

I always answer that question by saying that it was as an undergraduate student, but that's not completely true. I have always been interested in writing. I wrote when I was a child. I had good teachers who encouraged me to write. There was always a sense of mystery and awe for me in stories. But I began to write seriously as an undergraduate student. We had moved to the Barelas barrio in Albuquerque, but not many of us from Barelas were attending the university. It was in the late '50's and not too many Chicanos did, but a few of us were there and we stayed together, forming our own clique—I think we did it to survive.

We were interested in art: one of us was a painter and a couple of us were into writing. We read and discussed our early works. I wrote poetry, and I found that I probably didn't have the gift that some people are blessed with, and then changed to prose and almost immediately began to write novels. I wrote two or three novels while I was at the University of New Mexico, on my own. I didn't attend any writing classes. It was something I felt I had to do and I wanted to do and was committing time every night to it.

The first two or three novels I think I have destroyed. They were exercises in learning to write. They weren't worth keeping. Then sometime in the early '60's I began to work with characters and a story that would eventually evolve into *Bless Me, Ultima*. I began to tell the story of a family and Antonio, a young boy, and worked at it for years. It never really took shape, in terms of inspiration, until the night that Ultima came to me and appeared as a full-fledged character. She stood beside me and pointed out the things I had to do with the novel if it was going to work. She suggested that she would be an excellent character, and worked herself into the novel. From there on it clicked. It was, of course, the relationship Antonio was looking for.

Between 1963 and 1970 I did six or seven drafts of the novel —complete drafts. I was still learning to write. It has never come easy to me. I have to rewrite a lot, trying always, not only for perfection, but for some kind of balance and harmony that will exist in the work when all of the elements of fiction finally are pulled together and work well. Sometime in the very early 1970's, I was reading a copy of *El Grito* from Berkeley, being published by Herminio Ríos, Octavio Romano, Andrés Ibarra, and many Chicano students who had gathered there, and I decided I would send my manuscript to them. At that time *El Grito* was mostly full of California writers and I knew I could write every bit as well as they. So I wrote a letter to Herminio Ríos and I said, look, I've got a manuscript I think you should read. He wrote back and said, let me see it; they accepted it and eventually awarded it el Premio Quinto Sol [the Quinto Sol Prize]. Of course, I was very pleased.

What kind of books did you read in your formative years?

I read a great deal when I was a child, in grade school. I not only ran in a gang and did everything that normal, red-blooded Chicano boys do as they grow up, but I also used to spend a lot of time reading. I was the only one in the gang that used to go to the library on Saturday mornings. It was a decrepit, old building, run by one of the teachers, who volunteered to open it on Saturdays. Many Saturday mornings she and I were the only ones at the library. I sat there and read and leafed through books, and took some home. I read a lot of comic books and saw a lot of movies. I think all of that was important, in some respect, to the question of what influenced me when I was young. I also heard stories. Any time that people gathered, family or friends, they told stories, cuentos [tales], anecdotes, dichos [sayings], adivinanzas [riddles]. So I was always in a milieu of words, whether they were printed or in the oral tradition. And I think that's important to stimulate the writer's imagination; to respond to what is going on around him, to incorporate the materials and then rehash them and make fiction—to start at a point of reference which is close to one's being and then to transcend it, that's important.

Later, I read a great deal in American literature when I was at the university, and it was as formative a period for me as my childhood, because both were very full and alive with the mystery of discovery in literature.

I saw movies, all of the cowboy movies and war movies of the 1940's. The Cantinflas movies were very popular; a lot of Mexican movies were available. So there was a jumble of material there that had an influence in terms of my own writing, there was no one title or work or author that made it click.

What is the extent of your studies?

I received an M.A. from the University of New Mexico in 1968 in English. I had at the time done most of my reading in American literature, influenced, probably, by the Romantics, Whitman in particular, the Imagists, and later by the Lost Generation. I read the poets as well as the novelists. I also was influenced by the classics, Shakespeare, Milton, Pope, Dante. I read a great deal of world literature, philosophy, and religion at that time. Also, it was a very active time of the Beatnik generation. There was a lot of literary activity, new poets, new poetry, coffee shops, and I was listening to it and observing what was taking place.

Has formal education helped or hindered you as a writer?

Of course it has helped me. I was exposed to many writers, not only to American literature and contemporary writers, but world literature. I think it's very important for Chicano students,

whether or not they're going to be writers, to engage in some
kind of educational process. There are those who say that education will change who you are, how you think, destroy your culture, assimilate you—I think that's nonsense. Those are people
who are afraid of change. We cannot hide our heads in the sand
and pretend that everything that is important and good and of
value will come only out of our culture. We live in a small world
where many other cultures have a great deal to offer us. This is
very important for the writer—to read as much as he possibly
can, to learn a bit of the analytical study of literature. That's
important.

**Which was the predominant language in your home as a child? Which
do you speak more fluently now?**

It was Spanish. Both my father and my mother spoke Spanish,
and I was raised speaking Spanish in an almost completely Spanish background. I did not learn English until I started first grade.
Now I speak more fluently in English. The thrust of my education has been in English literature and I wrote in English when I
began to write, so I am more fluent and more comfortable with
English.

Those of us who were raised in a Spanish-speaking environment, knowing the language, loving it, wanting to use it as completely as English, needed help in school to keep the language
and develop the skills. We did not receive that help, so now we
are handicapped when it comes to using Spanish. It's also happening today. We are going through another generation that is
using more English than Spanish. It has a lot to do with the educational system and the little relevance that is placed on teaching the Spanish language in a bilingual setting.

Does Chicano literature have a particular language or idiom?

The only criterion for Chicano literature is that it be written by
a Chicano or Chicana. When you talk about language or idiom,
you have to remember that the Chicano—historically—is not as
tight a homogeneous group as one would imagine, especially in
language. We have writers using what we call street language;
others use language particular to the Southwest, or, for that matter, to other regions of the country. Some have a particular con-

cern with idiom and it becomes predominant in their work. I suppose you could say that the '60's had a particular idiom. I don't think that's true any more.

How do you perceive your role as a writer vis-à-vis: (a) the Chicano community or Movement; (b) U.S. society; (c) literature itself?

First of all, the role of a writer is vis-á-vis the universe itself, chaos versus patterns. I fit easily and completely into the Chicano community—that's where I was born and raised, that's where my family resides—and the Movement, because I was active in it and have seen its different areas of development. I think that in part I fit into the mainstream society, what you call U.S. society. I know it's fashionable for many Chicano writers to say that they do not belong to this society that has oppressed minorities. Nonetheless, the fact exists that we are a part of that society. I have no trouble at all relating to writers and artists in that society. There are many of its values that I abhor, stay away from, have nothing to do with. But nevertheless, there is a relationship with the creative part of that society that is very valuable for me. I meet its writers, its artists, teachers, and find that we often have a common core of views, goals, and ideas, through broad spectrums that flow from political to sociological to aesthetic.

Since I began writing, or probably since I began reading, I have been hooked into the world of literature, the world of the writer. I very often see myself as a writer first. And why not? As difficult as the endeavor is, as sullen as the craft is, still it has its rewards. It's exciting to be a writer today, to see talented young people interested in the craft and aspiring to be writers, playwrights, and poets.

What is the place of Chicano literature within U.S. literature?

I believe that Chicano literature is ultimately a part of U.S. literature. I do not believe that we have to be swallowed up by models or values or experimentation within contemporary U.S. literature. We can present our own perspective, and in such a way present to the world the workings of our imagination, filtered through a very long and rich culture. But ultimately it will be incorporated into the literature of this country. The role of the next generation will be to assure that we are not given secondary status, or the back shelves of the libraries.

What is the relationship of Chicano literature to Mexican literature?

Because of the nature of our role in this society, we are tied not only to United States literature, but obviously to Mexican literature. A great many of our writers are very familiar with it because they have studied it, as well as Latin American and Peninsular literature, and have formed a deeper relationship with Mexican literature than with that of the United States. That relationship will continue; it's natural and, I think, good.

In my case, I have not read or studied Mexican literature in an academic setting, but I have read as much Mexican and Latin American literature as possible. I have traveled a great deal in Mexico and I am more familiar with its visual arts. But in the beginning I had the U.S. American novels to work with; I didn't have the Mexican models, so I believe their influence on me as a writer was minimal. But that's only in reference to techniques— the mythology is a different story.

Do you perceive yourself and your work as political?

We can proceed from one cliché, that all work, every act of life, is political, to the other side of the board that says art exists for itself, in and of itself. Somewhere in the middle I would find my place. I have never set out to write a political work. Many Chicano critics find themselves in the Marxist-Leninist camp, where they deride and verbally abuse writers who will not cater to their personal and social needs. What such critics forget is that every man's or woman's creative, imaginative endeavor is an act of rebellion.

The artist is a person in constant rebellion. He does not take rules as they are, nor is he committed to any narrow ideology. He is in constant rebellion with the universe itself. The laws which would provide meaningful patterns to guide and some kind of harmony to exist are constantly being suffocated by chaos. It is out of this chaos that the artist would bring some order, some meaningful pattern, reinstitute some harmony. So it doesn't matter if they are the laws of God, of society, or of our own culture; we are people in revolt, constantly.

I have read some criticism by politically minded people who want to see the art of the contemporary Chicano Movement serve only a social and a political purpose. And more than that, often their own political needs. This is a danger if we are to develop artists. I have spoken against this kind of pressure everywhere. I would like to see other writers do this, writers who are influential and respected, artists—yourself included. You wrote a very interesting piece a long time ago in *La Luz* * in which you called for the freedom of expression, which Chicanos must exercise. This freedom will not be given by any political group or any other group of people. The artist will take it in his own hands and rework it as he sees fit. And it will come out in all colors, taking many different directions. There will be some political works, and there will be some that will be concerned with the smallest, most practical details of day-to-day living, concerned with love, joy, and tragedy. That is the kind of freedom we must have, that we make for ourselves as artists.

I caution young artists not to pay attention to critics, especially when those critics want to use them, to use their talents. An artist, to begin with, is a person rebelling against the status quo. He doesn't need any political mentors. An artist should be a person who is far ahead of his political mentors, or he has no business calling himself an artist.

To be quite frank and truthful, I see the effects of politics in the literature. A great deal of the poetry of the '60's was polemic in nature. I myself, when I wrote *Heart of Aztlán*, was very interested in how people take a political system in hand, one that is oppressing and using them. I'm sure Tomás Rivera thought the same when he wrote . . . *y no se lo tragó la tierra*. Perhaps he was not concerned with the system as a study. He has been berated for it. But, my God, all you have to do is look beyond the surface to see that he was addressing political and social questions. He was speaking directly about the menace of political and social oppression. So it comes in different layers, in different ways. It doesn't always have to be up front, shouting in the street. When that is needed, it will be there. That is the trust I have in the artist.

---

* Bruce-Novoa, "Freedom of Expression and the Chicano Movement," *La Luz* (September 1973): 28–29.

Does the Chicano author have anything in common with the majority group writer? Differences?

There are many writers in the country who desire to know what other regions and groups of people are doing. There is a multicultural emphasis and impetus in writing and in publishing that is very healthy. For example, I work on the board of the Coordinating Council for Literary Magazines and have served on it for five years. In that time I have seen changes. Other writers have become more interested in what Chicanos, Blacks, and women are doing, what is coming out of prisons and different regions. How do we create a truly national literature? How do we break into the literary history that will be written of the '60's and '70's? We do have a lot in common with many groups and we are beginning to work together.

In California, the Before Columbus Foundation is drawing together Black writers, Latin Americans, Chicanos, Native Americans, sponsoring book fairs, readings, interchanges, and discourse. The Turtle Island Foundation is publishing minority group writers very effectively and very enthusiastically. I see a great new generation of Asian American writers coming up in the Northwest, and California, and know some of the writers, Frank Chin, Lawson Inada, Shon Wong, to name a few, all of whom are interested in what we're doing as Chicanos. So that's a very positive development.

It's interesting to note that some of the groups here in the Southwest are exchanging works and information across cultural lines. Even in Texas one of the groups working there to promote literature is making contact with Chicano writers, probably for the first time. That is encouraging. I might add that *The American Book Review*, recently formed as an alternative to the established book reviews, which will not review our works at all, has as one of its reasons for existence to review the literature of minority group writers in different regions of the country. This movement is good, healthy, and I hope it is something we can encourage so that it will stay around.

Does Chicano literature share common ground with Black literature? Differences?

I would have to say that historically it shares many common elements. We're dealing with two minority populations at a time in their history when they both have experienced a surge or a renaissance not only in their literature but in their whole life style and perspective. They have had to deal with values of the majority group which were not their inherent values. The difficulty that both found in publishing and breaking into the publishing field has been great. Finally, the most important is the common shout of identity. I am! The Black writers, especially those who centered around the Harlem Renaissance, had to define themselves vis-à-vis the white world. We have seen that happen in Chicano literature. That, of course, can be a danger. If the literature is only one of defiance of the white world, or only a literature that has an impetus or force as long as that white model exists, then there is a danger, because we cannot define ourselves, or find ourselves, or create our literature only in defiance of that white model. We have to come out of our own experience, our own tradition, culture, roots, our own sense of language, of story, and deal with that and to hell with the white model. You see, I'm saying that we can't just push against it all the time to define ourselves. That is a weakness. We must define ourselves from our own stance. We are who we create.

Is there any relationship with the literature of other Spanish-speaking groups?

What interests me is the relationship among the Spanish-speaking groups within the United States itself. A very interesting coalition could be formed among the Puertorriqueños, the Newyoricans, the Cubanos, the Latinos, and the Chicanos to begin sharing their work.* I often find that I mention the name of Víctor Hernández Cruz to Chicano writers and very few know him. They should. He's a very important Puertorriqueño, New York writer. This relationship, that we should form in terms of readings and conferences, should be encouraged. Just recently, Alurista and Víctor Hernández Cruz and a few other Chicanos read at Columbia in New York, and there was a lot of interest, a lot of sharing. That relationship is natural, as natural as the one

---

* Newyoricans are Puerto Ricans from New York. Latinos here means people of Latin American origin other than Chicanos, Puerto Ricans, and Cubans.

with Native American writers and the Asian Americans, the Black Americans, women, and regional groups, because the tide is turning in terms of the establishment of literature in the country.

The new emphasis will be, or should be, on a multicultural, a multiethnic literature.

Does Chicano literature have a distinctive perspective on life? What effect does it have on the literature?

All literature, and certainly Chicano literature, reflects, in its more formal aspects, the mythos of the people, and the writings speak to the underlying philosophical assumptions which form the particular world view of a culture. By its more formal aspects I don't mean style, I mean the concern of particular writers for the sense of values which constitutes our world view. This has been a concern of mine as a writer. My interest is not only in the story or the plot of the story but in the presentation *of my vision* of a native American mythology which has permeated our culture with its values. In a real sense, the mythologies of the Americas are the only mythologies of all of us, whether we are newly arrived or whether we have been here for centuries. The land and the people force this mythology on us. I gladly accept it; many or most of the American newcomers have resisted it.

If we as Chicanos do have a distinctive perspective on life, I believe that perspective will be defined when we challenge the very basic questions which mankind has always asked itself: What is my relationship to the universe, the cosmos? Who am I and why am I here? If there is a Godhead, what is its nature and function? What is the nature of mankind? These are basic questions because they form the framework of our relationship with the universe and with each other, and they are questions which, I believe, we deal with on a daily basis as we progress through life. Everyone questions and the mythologies feed some of the answers; the culture acts as a prism which refracts the clear light of the questions and the answer. As our writers and artists and philosophers continue to engage in the exploration of these questions, we will arrive at a closer look at the distinctive perspective. For me, the important thing to remember is that the perspective will be a core of values molded by and guided by culture, history, language, native mythology, and all the other characteristics of the wide umbrella we usually label culture.

What we must not forget is that beneath that surface we will find the archetypes and the values and the primal symbols which we share in common with all mankind.

I understand that in the cycle of time, the present time is a time of recognition and flowering of pride, and that is a perfectly acceptable stance. History teaches us that people arrive at times in their history when they look upon themselves as a unique people with a particular role in the politics and social well-being of the world. That may be the first step in the creation of a renaissance. But times of immense hubris or orgullo [pride] can be limiting, not because pride goes before the fall—what the hell, our people have been under for so long that there isn't much room left to fall—but because the time will afford certain writers a crutch. Writers and artists who say they are different only because they speak caló [slang] or because they are brown or because they were raised in poverty (and those criteria apply to most of us) are presenting a very limiting view of the role of art in a society. In slightly different ways, 80 percent of the world fits those criteria, so it's that jump we have to make to understand not only the surface of the damaging circumstances of life but the depth. Art can be a catalyst and a force to assault ignorance and discrimination and poverty and hunger.

Does Chicano literature improve communication between Chicanos and Anglo Americans?

Yes. All art improves communication. Art is communication. I travel around the country extensively, and I have served on national literary boards, for example, the Coordinating Council of Literary Magazines board, and I find that not only are the other minority groups of this country interested in our literature, but the Anglo American who is a serious reader is beginning to read our literature. The influence of Chicano literature is spreading, no doubt. Prejudice against it and the people it represents still exists; my eyes aren't blind to that. Reviews of our work in major journals or book reviews are still nonexistent, few Chicano writers are invited to non-Chicano readings, national private and public fellowships are still denied to us, but in spite of all this there is some change in the air. There is interest in our literature, and that interest is spreading to Europe. In some cases, European universities have undertaken the study of Chicano literature more aggressively than their American counterparts.

And there's a new sense of understanding and need for the multicultural nature of this country which is reflected in the literature and art. I believe that the national character of this country will never be known until this sharing of all voices is complete.

Does Chicano literature reevaluate, attack, or subvert the value system of the majority society? Is it a revolutionary literature? Thematically? Technically?

I think I have already answered this when I spoke about my feelings of the artist as a person in rebellion. I have talked about the difficulties that the Chicano and other minority peoples have had in having their literature read and disseminated through the majority society. Is it revolutionary? I addressed that earlier in the sense that all literature is revolutionary, yes. In the sense that we are a small minority struggling for a kind of self-rule, self-independence, yes. But I have also cautioned that it is not only revolutionary literature in the political sense of the word. Its most interesting aspect, what will make it a revolutionary literature, will be whether or not the writers commit themselves to a new literature, one which will mirror or give some intimation of our world view, our values, the core values of our culture.

What problems have you encountered in publishing? Were they racially founded?

This question has probably been answered the same way by every Chicano writer who has tried to publish a manuscript. There are no publishers who are interested in Chicanos as writers. One, they don't know we exist, and two, if they do know, they keep fighting to have us remain invisible. They don't want to see us. And the most racist of them will come out and say that we can't write. I've had this said to me and told to me by other writers. So yes, the problem is there and I've encountered it. I've circulated my manuscripts. In fact, before Quinto Sol was founded and before I knew about it, I circulated *Bless Me, Ultima* and nobody was interested. I think that for a very long time our only alternative will be to publish with Chicano publishing houses. Eventually the problem with that becomes one of evaluation and one of patting ourselves on the back. I think eventually we do have to break out and try other markets.

It's important on the one hand to support and encourage our

own Chicano publishing firms because we are a very distinct literary movement, not because we have a literary manifesto. I would argue with many Chicano writers and critics about that. We are a literary movement because of a common social and cultural impetus. I would even argue that we are not a literary movement because of a defined aesthetic. Our aesthetic has been defined by our cultural roots, que son español, indio [that are Spanish, Indian], and whatever we share with the United States mainstream cultural roots. And now we share many things, the most important being language, about which I have spoken. On the other hand, in publishing it does seem relevant to begin to spread ourselves around to achieve this sort of multicultural, multiethnic idea that I talked about earlier. We can't remain in a vacuum; we can't keep reading and teaching our own works and pretend that there is no other literature around us. We have to be more closely allied with the other ethnic and regional movements that are alive in this country, and begin to send our manuscripts to other literary magazines.

Are Chicanos at a disadvantage in trying to practice the art of writing?

There are some of us who have had, at one time, a great disadvantage. We came from poor families, poor in the sense that we had no money, but we were rich with love and culture and a sense of sharing and imagination. We had to face a school system that very often told us we couldn't write. It did not teach us our own works, and we had nothing to emulate, to read of our own. So of course we were very disadvantaged in that way. For example, when I began to write I had a hard time to find those models that would click, that had a relevance to my internal being. But I kept at it, I kept at it. You can call it what you want; it's something you know you have to do, and eventually you find the rhythm and you find what you want to say and you say it and you keep practicing the skills and the elements. I don't think they become any easier, to tell you the truth. After ten or fifteen years now, I'm still in the process of learning about writing; a process that never finishes. That's exciting!

Even today Chicano children are being told they are at a disadvantage because they don't have command of the English language. The sooner you begin to tell children that, the more they begin to believe it; you build in a self-fulfilling prophecy. That is not right! We have, as I have stated before, a rich culture, rich tradition, a rich oral tradition, and we have, through part of our roots, a rich literary tradition. So we have to change that around y en vez de decir que no tenemos el talento [and instead of saying that we don't have the talent], say, "You can write! You do have talent! You can produce literature that is valuable!" We have to go out and tell the kids in high school and grade school, cuando están chiquitos [when they are little], "You can write, you can write about what you know, your experience is valuable, who you are is valuable, and how you view the world and society and the cosmos is valuable. Put it down on paper, paint a picture, make a drawing, write music!" That's the positive way to handle that.

We have to take the arts to kids in the communities and the centers where they meet, to their families. We've got to desarrollar [develop] the whole onda [scene], as the current phrasing goes, y que se acabe [and put an end to] all the negative feelings about the art of writing or the art of anything for that matter.

What are the most outstanding qualities of Chicano literature? Weaknesses?

For me the most outstanding qualities are that it's exciting and it is experimental. Every new poem, every new novel that comes out is new, is different, it has a new perspective.

Ron Arias's *The Road to Tamazunchale* is a classic. He wrote it as he saw it and it's real; it moves. Orlando Romero's *Nambé—Year One* is lyrical. Since I usually am reading or teaching fiction, I sometimes neglect to talk about the poets, but I read a lot of the new poetry and keep up with it. It's also exciting.

There is no written manifesto of Chicano literature. I'm glad no one has attempted to write one. Although some critics have attempted to define the criteria, the limits, the intra-psychology, and the sociological stance of Chicano literature, they have failed, and for that we are a healthier literature.

The weakness has been that we have had writers who are not willing to commit enough time and energy to do their work. It's a craft. When you are not dedicated and you do not take the time to get as near perfection as possible with your work, a perfector of communication, then the work will be weak. I have to continually rework my own manuscripts. *Bless Me, Ultima* was done six or seven times in complete manuscript form, and each one took a year. *Heart of Aztlán* was the same way; I wrote the entire thing three to four times. My current novel, *Tortuga*, I have rewritten three times completely. It's a process that is crucial, unless, of course, you are a genius; then you don't have to rewrite. But I haven't met too many of those.

Chicano criticism? I have been, since very early in the game, a staunch supporter of Chicano criticism. I started teaching Chicano literature some years ago and I wanted the students, in the normal process of looking at any work, to find different perspectives, different viewpoints. How are they led, as you said in one of your articles, how are they led into the work? That's what is exciting about criticism. Everybody has different ways of looking at the work that make the work grow, that make it move, that expand it and create a fuller meaning. I read as much of the criticism as I can get my hands on, and some of it is very good. I think Chicanos have gone out and trained themselves on the par with other critics.

I'm very impressed, for example, with the work Roberto Cantú did on *Bless Me, Ultima*. He wrote extensive critical papers on *Bless Me, Ultima*; whether or not I agree with him is beside the point. The point is that he is valuable for students of literature when they read that novel. There have been some who have done papers of a general nature, yourself included, that have challenged us to look at literary space or the lack thereof. There have been excellent works on individual novels. *Latin American Literary Review* just recently had a special issue that was very good. A lot of it is tough, but it is grounded upon the critics' criteria.

What are the milestones so far in Chicano literature?

I don't know how to answer that question. I think the fact that we are writing, that it is still coming is enough for me. If you mean the works as milestones, go to the people and find out what they are reading. Those are the milestones. What's filtering down to the pueblo, not just staying on the level of the study of literature at the university, but what's filtering down? Where is it being picked up? What's being read on the buses, donde está la gente trabajando [where people work]? There are many works I could name, but again I would rather not get into that. What's exciting for me is that I see the last ten or fifteen years as only the beginning of a movement and that in the next ten or fifteen years we'll see fantastic works. This time we live in is exciting.

What is the future of Chicano literature: distinctiveness, or the de-emphasis of the distinctive characteristics?

The future is bright. The de-emphasis will be on merely mirroring the cultural, in the sense of a representational or realistic mirroring of the culture, the trend is to a more personal work which will carry the culture in it, but will have a concern with experimentation, with style, and perhaps character. Maybe I'm saying this because I feel this is where my work is going. Somehow I never set out to mirror the culture, to hold the espejo [mirror] up to the culture. Many people have said this is what is in my work, but that is not a primary intention of the work. I have always thought that the background—which is the background of my own personal life—will normally fit itself into whatever my concern happens to be. In a sense I think this is repeated in the whole scene of Chicano literature.

I suppose the future will have to include many dramatic works. We have had a history of teatro, the actos. Perhaps now is the right time to experiment with more full-length dramas. Most of the dramas that have been published have been one-act plays. The other thing that I see—and I like it—is the idea of experimentation. A few people come to mind. Joe Olvera, down in El Paso, does absurdist and surrealist things with his work. I think we got a sense of that in Ron Arias. Perhaps we can even historically date it back to . . . *y no se lo tragó la tierra* and *Estampas del Valle*, where vignettes and time and points of view changed within structurally small works and helped us redefine the novel, perhaps even the short story. I see more and more being written in Spanish. I'm helping to edit, with Antonio Mares, a short collection of Chicano cuentos [stories] for the *New America* magazine at the University of New Mexico, American Studies Department. We sent out a little broadside asking for manuscripts and got a big response of stories written in Spanish. The idea of presenting the work bilingually, I think, will continue, perhaps even grow. It was an idea started very early by Quinto Sol and the Chicano writers of the '60's. Of course the form itself has a long history. When I think of myself and where I'm going, I do not want to sit still. *Heart of Aztlán* surprised many people because it was not a *Bless Me, Ultima* and that's what they expected. In fact, you yourself said as much when you wrote that dastardly review of it. No, no te creas, hombre [Don't believe it], I'm just kidding you. But you said we shouldn't have expected another *Bless Me, Ultima* from Anaya, and then you went ahead to say, well, we didn't get one [he laughs]. Well the point is that we have to be careful to allow writers to change and to move. Just as *Heart of Aztlán* was different from *Bless Me, Ultima*, the novel that I'm working on now, *Tortuga*, which has been accepted for publication and should be out by the time you get this book to press, will also be different. And people will start asking, ¿qué pasa? what's happening? What is Chicano in this new novel; is there anything Chicano in it? Change has to be there. Look at the writers who have not changed, the ones that are repeating themselves in style and in content. What do they have to say that is new? There are some writers whose poetry I read in the '60's and I read what they have published recently, and I say, pues, no cambió [nothing has changed]. It's still the same material and the same style. We should be aware of experimentation and encourage it.

Who are the leaders among Chicano writers, and why?

I don't know if I can answer this question in a short amount of time and be fair to many writers. In fact, I think I won't. It would smack too much of my own preferences, nothing else. There are too many that I like and that I admire.

Bernice Zamora

A prolific poet, Bernice Zamora had published widely in journals before the publication of *Restless Serpents* (1976), yet, as José Montoya indicates in his interview, it is a sad commentary on the male bias which predominates in the Chicano literary establishment—a mere reflection of the society—that she had not received more recognition. *Restless Serpents* now demands it.

Zamora, in many respects, can be compared to Tino Villanueva. Both are careful craftspersons who know the fundamental tools of the trade and are willing to explore the influences of other poets; their sensibilities lie more with the poetic image than with the narrative, expository style so prevalent in Chicano poetry. Zamora declares her sympathy with the Chicano Movement and carries through with committed action; her poetry reflects those sentiments, but never in the form of sloganism. There is nothing blatantly political in her poetry, but her political commitment underlies much of her world view. Her language is not precious or artificial, except when the situation demands such an effect; she demonstrates a knowledge and ability to use many codes, including the street language of our day. The latter is frankly employed in her prose.

Among Chicano writers Zamora is the practitioner supreme of Octavio Paz's concept of "homenaje y profanación" [homage and profanation]. In no way fearful of her literary influences, confident in her ability to be worthy of them without falling into subservience, she creates a series of openly intertextual relationships with such figures as Robinson Jeffers, Guillevic, Shakespeare, and Hesse, to name only the obvious. Yet her poems stand on their own merit, free of any need of the text alluded to for their existence. Like mirrors in which the masters reflect and renew themselves, her poems consciously seek out non-Chicano writers, but her mirror is bronze toned and illuminated with an unmistakably personal, albeit subtle light. Her mirror reveals on the

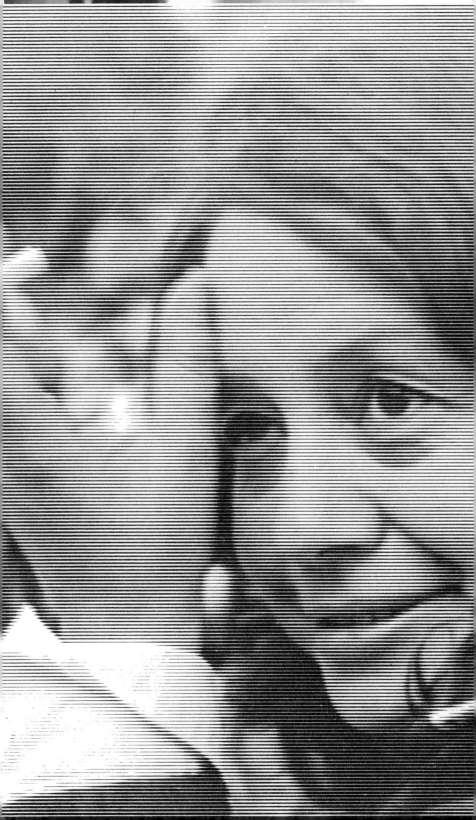

surface what many have suspected all along: Chicano literature is universal, even in its most apparently distinctive moments. Zamora often finds in non-Chicanos, like Jeffers or Guillevic, a common spirit of rebellion, outrage, and protest, and she is secure enough in and of her own ethnicity to meet them on equal grounds. In the meetings, she performs readjustments through subtle parodies, turning whatever point she and the other writer have in common to her advantage, revealing a new experience and vision. Thus, Zamora opens Chicano literature in a way few others have.

Bernice Zamora wrote the responses to the questionnaire in September 1978.

When and where were you born?

January 20, 1938, in Aguilar, Colorado. It's a small village in Southern Colorado located at the foot of the East Spanish Peak. The Spanish Peaks are volcanic conduits around which sediment has settled over the centuries and now herald a low tundra. They're the volcanoes I allude to in my poetry.

Describe your family background and your present situation.

My father was born in Aguilar, too, and reared in the surrounding areas—Mauricio's Canyon, Trujillo Creek, and Weston, Colorado, where his family for six generations farmed land acquired through the early land grants. The original deeds were lost in the rash of burnings of county court house records that plagued much of New Mexico as well. But the land is deeded today because of the shrewdness of my padrino [godfather], who had the foresight to distrust his fellow man. There is, however, government intervention with regard to the property, and ownership is once again a question for the courts.

Because the farm land was so rocky and poor, my father and the men in his family also worked in the Allan Coal Mines near Trinidad—in Segundo and in Valdez, Colorado, where we lived when I was a child. My father began working in the coal mines at the age of twelve. After we moved from Valdez to be with my mother's family in Denver, he became a car painter and worked at that until he was permanently disabled about ten years ago.

My mother was also born in Aguilar, as were her parents and her grandparents. My grandfather and his brothers were pa-

naderos [bakers] for the most part and continued that trade after
the entire family moved to Denver. A more contemporary life
style was adopted, and education and acculturation were encouraged, although my father never quite adjusted to urban life. He
moved us to Pueblo, the median point between Denver and his
beloved Aguilar. Thus, my brother, my sister, and I spent most
of our lives in Pueblo; even after my parents moved back to Denver, we remained in Pueblo to raise our families. I mention this
by way of responding to those critics who have pointed out that
my poetry is either very contemporary or very medieval. I don't
know if this piece of family background information explains
that totally, but perhaps it will be satisfactory. Specific reference, of course, has been made to the poems on *penitentes*,
though my father refuses to discuss it. My mother denies af-
filiation, but relays that as a child she watched a penitent pro-
cession which went through the streets of Aguilar, and the blood
from the whips spattered on her dress. *Penitentes* are a very devout religious group whose unknown numbers are scattered
throughout New Mexico and Colorado. One of their rituals involves flagellation in commemoration of Christ's own like
suffering, and after the fashion of the Franciscan Order in its earliest days. In 1925 the religious practice was outlawed by the
government, denounced by the Church, and so the groups went
underground to practice their religion in secret. They do so even
today. My poem "Penitents" discusses the religious accoutre-
ments, which, if you've ever seen them, are beautiful works of
art. The poem's persona is meant to be the spirit of females—
mothers, wives, sisters, daughters of *penitentes*.

My present situation is a stark contrast to my background,
which provides a vivid, but binary existence; and it's clear to me
that the Chicano Movement had a great deal to do with this
shift in my life. Currently, I am a graduate student at Stanford
University and a teacher at the University of California, Berkeley. [Since the interview, Zamora, while still a doctoral candidate at Stanford, has moved to Albuquerque, New Mexico,
where she edits *De Colores* magazine.]

When did you first begin to write?

I didn't begin to write poetry until I was thirty years old. Very
late, don't you think? But I have been writing profusely since I
can remember—letters, journals, dream diaries, travelogues. I

wrote an essay in high school on the subject of retail selling, of all things. I received a cash award in a contest given by the Retail Merchants of Pueblo. As an undergraduate I wrote—for the only time in my life—humorous essays, and my freshman English teacher liked them so much, he shared them with the other teachers, who used to congregate after class to read my latest assignment. My teacher told me this later when we became friends, but I was more astonished than flattered at the time.

The first short story I ever wrote—which was written during my graduate studies at Fort Collins—was submitted by a friend of mine to a Creative Writing Symposium. I forgot to attend the award announcement ceremony and my friend dropped by that evening to tell me I had won second place (money) and that I narrowly missed first place but for the "foul" language. That story, "Flexion" has since been published in *Caracol*. The only other short story I've ever written, "Vergüenza," was written within the same month (spring 1972). "Vergüenza" has just recently been published in *Mestizo* by Pajarito Publications.

My short stories seem to be better received than my poetry, I suspect partly because the poetry represents the curious anachronism mentioned earlier. Still I prefer to write poetry. Actually, I am compelled or driven to write it, whatever form it takes and by whatever inspiration—internal or external. If the inspiration is ignored, I fall into long periods of dissipation. The title poem of *Restless Serpents* was written out of just such an experience.

What kind of books did you read in your formative years?

Sunday missals, Catechisms, and biographies of saints occupied most of the reading I did as a child, primarily because I was attending Catholic schools. My favorite saints were St. Teresa the mystic and St. Thomas Aquinas, the latter because he was presented in the children's literature as an outcast and a dullard who, after pleading to God for guidance, became the teacher of his teachers. He thus provided me with one of my goals, ridiculous as it seems. But I am no Thomist. At one time I did aspire to be a philosopher, but rejected it as a discipline when I discovered that the field—in this country, at least—is replete with misbegotten analytical logicians. In any case, I still read Teresa and prefer Bacon to Aquinas for current reading.

What is the extent of your studies?

The extent of my studies includes a B.A. in English from Southern Colorado University; an M.A. in English from Colorado State University; and I am currently a Ph.D. candidate at Stanford University, again in English.

Has formal education helped or hindered you as a writer?

Formal education has aided and hindered my writing equally; as to what extent is yet to be determined. For example, formal education encouraged writing—not always creative writing; nevertheless, writing was stressed as a mode of communication unparalleled by any other. This diminished and discouraged maintaining an oral tradition—an equally fine mode of communication as far as I'm concerned. Necessarily one gives way to the other. I understand that. But it seems to me that the characteristics of our tradition—particularly that of rhythm—will be lost to us in our writing if we adhere to those methods fostered by formal education. In fact, I've often felt that the high attrition rate of graduate students of literature has been a result of emphasis on strict analytical exercise, rather than innovative, creative approaches to literature. The limitations of the popular critical methods have been exceeded twice over with each generation. I don't understand the persistence to go around in circles expounding on the obvious. And Chicano critics—with the exceptions of yourself and José Saldívar, whom we've yet to see in print—have yet to realize this. They just keep on imitating the imitators. That element of creative thought is what separates the true scholars who preserve the literature as opposed to those critics who, under the pretense of "enlightening" us about what's contained in the literature, merely stagnate it.

Now, how does this affect our oral tradition? The oral tradition is *pure* creativity—*renewed each time* a poem is recited, a song is sung, or a story is told. If Chicano critics insist on noncreative methodologies, they will add enormously to its obliteration. Those same critics could help preserve the oral tradition by creating innovative approaches, an approach which must be renewed with each oral traditionalist. Who among them is willing to do that? Who among them has even written on the transcribed oral qualities of Alurista, José Montoya, or Lorna Dee Cervantes?

Which was the predominant language in your home as a child? Which do you speak more fluently now?

English was and is the predominant language, and I speak it more fluently than Spanish. Most of the Spanish I know is phonetically retained from childhood experience. I remember, for example, reciting the rosary, speaking to my grandparents and older people all in Spanish. But English was considered the language of survival, and so it was encouraged, especially after it was discovered that I could read at a precocious age. I embraced that language for purposes I later determined to be harmonious coexistence, the desire to please my elders, and because of a gripping obsession to get to heaven. Silly isn't it—to believe that all one has to do in life is to do what one is told. Though I read and write Spanish, I am reluctant to criticize literature written in Spanish—too insecure, lack of confidence are the reasons I suppose. Those poems I've written in Spanish are an effort to express love—something I've not been able to do in English—but love is not yet my subject.

Does Chicano literature have a particular language or idiom?

I like to think of Caló [slang] as the language of Chicano literature, but that hasn't been established in all of our writing yet. It is evolving as a literary mode, and the writers I enjoy most for their consistency of Caló are Cecilio Camarillo, José Montoya, and Raúl Salinas.

I am particularly fond of Caló because of the usage of English phonemes with Spanish gerund or verb endings to form one word. There exist, for example, words like *eskipiando* [skipping] in conversation. In poetry, you can find lines like ". . . early mornings/Indios *pasando we watchando* . . ." [passing we watched] (from Lin Romero's *Happy Songs, Bleeding Hearts*). Caló's best usage, apart from conversation, is in poetry—without question its purest form. It's too difficult to sustain when writing a novel, although two writers I know of have tried it with labored results.

I teach Caló with the premise that it is a conflict of languages resolved. This is most effective with Chicano students who do not use it naturally. Accessibility bears its own reward, and that is my aim in using poetry, essays, and cuentos [stories] written in Caló in the courses I teach.

How do you perceive your role as a writer vis-à-vis: (a) the Chicano community or Movement; (b) U.S. society; (c) literature itself?

As a teacher of writing, I perceive my role as one of teaching; as a writer, I perceive my role as one of teaching; as a Chicana, my energies and commitment are for the Chicano Movement and our communities, but not confined solely to teaching. So I do not see my role vis-à-vis the Chicano community, but as one of direct involvement, working within and for the Movimiento. The term *vis-à-vis* is more applicable to U.S. society, particularly in light of how little recognition our literature receives within this society. My role, in this case, is one of literary critic, working for the preservation and integrity of our literature. There are, for example, critics—even Chicano critics—who insist that Chicano literature is not unique, only particular. If the uniqueness of our literature is undetected by critics, then I suspect that the terms *unique* and *particular* are ill-defined in their own minds; or—and their writings prove this to be the case— they know very little of world literature at large. As for my role as a writer vis-à-vis literature itself, well, I prefer to think of it as a role of contribution through the various kinds of writing available. Beyond that nothing comes to mind right now.

What is the place of Chicano literature within U.S. literature?

If there is a place for Chicano literature within U.S. literature, that place is unclear. Commercially, there may be a place, provided the writer is clever enough. He or she would have to be insensitive, however, to cultural traditions, or exploit his cultural knowledge to reinforce the stereotypes attributed to us. Academically, the interest in our literature is limited to folklore. Contemporary Chicano themes are a reality few academicians care to deal with. I suppose the place for our literature is within the larger framework of Third World literatures in the U.S. We have, after all, certain affinities and respect for one another's traditions which we acquired in those places where we have all been "lumped together" such as classrooms, factories, and prisons. An oral tradition is one important affinity we share with Native Americans and Blacks; another is our penchant for integrating our religious and spiritual symbols with our arts; and most important is our similar experience of resistance to cultural suppression. Yes, the place for Chicano literature is to be found among Blacks and Native Americans within the U.S.

What is the relationship of Chicano literature to Mexican literature?

I'm not sure what the relationship of Chicano literature to Mexican literature is, since I've read very little concerning such relationships. The Mexican articles I've read on Chicano literature have been from an external point of view, one of curiosity, or sensationalism. And those Chicanos writing on the subject (myself included) fall short of moving from one to the other. The reason is that, though culturally our backgrounds may be similar, once the border between the two countries is crossed, the Mexican experience on this side becomes an experience of engulfing, an experience of cultural shock, if I can use a newly trite phrase; and a struggle to retain Mexican traditions ensues. Chicano literature is about that struggle for the most part. There may be some relationship between the literatures of the *llanos* [plains], but I'm not sure.

Do you perceive yourself and your work as political?

Yes, of course; it's political in the sense that I write about the use and abuse of freedom and justice that affect Chicanos politically, socially, and personally. Whatever political decisions are made and whatever social actions are taken, they affect each of us personally even to the last breath of intimacy.

Pressures? You mean political pressures? Well, I don't know if tapped telephones and opened mail can be construed as political pressures to write with a particular bent. That relates more to my activities as a supporter for human rights rather than to my writing, I should think. Besides, the writing is not that politically effective anyway. But I have received admonishment from Chicano critics who call themselves "dialecticians" in search of synthesis. This is an admirable goal, to be sure, whose means, however, I question, at least with regard to Chicano literature. I question the use and exploitation of Chicanos and, by extension, Chicano literature, to promote any particular ideology. The Chicano experience is so vast that it merits more attention than what either/or concepts can provide. But Chicano critics seem to

have realized this, if judgment can be made on the recent sum-
mary of their meeting in Corpus. It's clear they are still floun-
dering as to what to do or which direction to follow, but at least
they are questioning.

*Does the Chicano author have anything in common with the majority
group writers? Differences?*

There are some Chicano authors who have things in common
with the majority group writers in technique, in approach to
subject matter, and in some cases even similar themes. Tino
Villanueva acknowledges the influence of Dylan Thomas, and
there is strong internal evidence in his poetry for Imagist and
Confessional inclinations of thought and theme. Raúl Salinas's
early poetry contains many characteristics of the Beat poets. My
own poetry, too, is replete with similar influences. I think this is
true of most Chicanos who are introduced to poetry as late in
our lives as we were by institutional thought. Chicanos writing
under such influences contribute a new and interesting dimension to American poetry, but very little to Chicano literature.
The early poetry written in Caló—poetry of the Chicano Movement of Villanueva and Salinas—was their best contribution to
Chicano literature.

It is interesting that José Villarreal maintains that because
he, a Chicano, has written about his experience, that alone does
not make him a Chicano writer. And, in fact, he insists that he
is an American writer, not a Chicano writer. At first I was disturbed by that notion, but as I've studied the evolution of our
literature so far, I'm inclined to accept his stance. Just as a person should be allowed to work in a country other than that of
his birth, so, too, should writers be allowed to express themselves in other idioms, techniques, and forms than those of their
birth.

The difference? Well, Chicano literature developed out of a
communal tradition—an oral one. Most Chicano writers have
tried to maintain that tradition in writing against enormous
odds. José Montoya is most successful because he consistently
writes to, for, and about Chicanos. Granted, he names Whitman
as an influence, but it is more an influence of what Whitman
said rather than how or in what form he wrote. Whitman not
only sang of himself (*of* himself, not *to* himself) but he sang of
workers, housewives, children, leaders, thieves, prostitutes, etc.,

and he insisted that poetry should be in the language of the people. That is what Montoya does; it does not go against his inherited tradition.

Does Chicano literature share common ground with Black literature?
Differences?

The common ground we have with Blacks is, of course, our respective oral traditions and our heavy reliance on internal rhythms for expression. We may write in English, but we rarely write in iambic pentameter. Our sense of time and timing is internally different.

One interesting manifestation in our literature, as with our speech, was pointed out to me by Ethridge Knight, on the topic of rhythmic sounds: people of oral cultures tend to use labial sounds when referring to something in a derogatory way. For example, the word which refers to white man by Afro-Americans is *tobo*. Chicanos use *gabacho*. There are enough consistent incidents of this to merit some further study.

Another interesting commonality we share with Black literature is found among the writings of women of both races: the recurring theme and lamentation of the loss of their men to the white woman. The long-range implication—the disappearance of the race—is taken seriously by both Black women and Chicana writers. The burden of responsibility and foresight is more and more apparent in their poetry, as well as in their lives, for women of color have resisted assimilation to a larger extent than the men have. In this country assimilation is synonymous with "success" and "progress," and the more ambitious men of both races respond accordingly. Intermarriage is one method of display. Compare the portrayals of white women with those of Black women and Chicanas in the literature of the men of both races, and an interesting phenomenon reveals itself.

The women writers of both cultures have an enormous task both as women and as writers to offset and decry the one-dimensional stereotypes the dominant culture favors. In the case of the Black women, there prevails the cruel and misleading notion of her as matriarch. When there is a concentrated effort of over two hundred years' duration to mutilate, degrade, and obliterate the Black man, the Black woman in trying to keep her family together lives in a vicious and violent state of oppression, not one of matriarchy.

In the case of Chicanas, the prevailing stereotypes defy logic. We are portrayed in the literature as silent and passive, childlike creatures. If these are true accounts, the adages that *silence is golden*, that *in silence there is strength*, or that *silence is wisdom* seem not to apply to us, presumably because we are (1) women and (2) Chicanos—uneducated and ill-bred. (That we are receptive women seems not to have occurred to anyone.) Revolutionary activities, community organizing, union labor actions should demonstrate that we are active, not passive women. If we are childlike—well, what child is silent or passive? But this is the portrayal. When Chicanos write about us as women of strength—and I'm thinking of Ultima—we are sexless, saintly, and sterile. When Chicanos think about us at all, they perpetuate the stereotypes. Gabacho depiction of us as emotionally unchecked, sultry women lusting after pale bodies is just an extension of the fantasy they have about all women. Such dishonest portrayals are why Chicanas are "breaking the silence," as Rita Sánchez calls it.

It would be a mistake, however, to call us feminist writers. To be purely a feminist writer is to ignore the issue of race—racial discrimination, division, and deprivation—these are entirely overlooked by the feminists. They, like the "dialecticians," have yet to address the racial issues to the satisfaction of Third World women writers. Besides, our relationship with our men is far different than that of the feminist with her man. These are the affinities we share with Blacks as I have discussed them with those Black writers I know.

Is there any relationship with the literature of other Spanish-speaking groups?

Apart from the political themes of revolution, I know of no other tangible relationship. In noting relationships or making comparisons with other Spanish-speaking groups, we should not forget that contemporary Chicano writers—with few exceptions—are the first generation of our culture to receive formal education, unlike the other Spanish-speaking groups of writers flourishing in their respective countries. And if we make observations on academic terms from long-standing literary traditions, we may contribute to the distortion already in existence with regard to our writers and their work. You're right, though, we do have common experiences with Puerto Ricans in this country and so, of course, they are reflected in the literature. Overall, Puerto Ricans have a more strident sense of rhythm in their literature.

Does Chicano literature have a distinctive perspective on life? What effect does it have on the literature?

The perspectives on life are as diverse as the writers themselves. One prevailing perspective that is somewhat disturbing, even in my own writing, is viewing the Chicano experience in retrospect. I'm not sure why we do this. Maybe we're Chicanos only in retrospect; or, as you suggest, maybe we are recuperating traditions lost, abandoned, or misunderstood. We could be trying to fill gaps in our history, too. Changes in our lifestyle, though, are beginning to find their way in the literature. As the precipice widens, the writers watch.

Does Chicano literature improve communication between Chicanos and Anglo Americans?

This question implies that there is already communication between Chicanos and Anglo Americans. It could be. Chicano literature improves communication between Chicanos and other Chicanos. At this stage, what more could we ask for?

Does Chicano literature reevaluate, attack, or subvert the value system of the majority society? Is it a revolutionary literature? Thematically? Technically?

Yes, Chicano literature reevaluates the value system of U.S. society, particularly the interpretations of that value system. Now, I'm interpreting "value system" to mean those ideals contained in the Constitution: freedom, equality, pursuit of happiness, etc. Much of our literature questions—not the ideals themselves— but the monetary reward-and-punishment means and methods of upholding those ideals. Oftentimes such interpretations by the perpetrators are confused with the ideals, and it is the writer—particularly the poet—who constantly strives to avoid and/or perpetuate the confusion. Our literature reflects an admirable stance and clarity of thought in the writings on the subject of the value system. For example, you'll note that few of our writings espouse "equality" or "pursuit of happiness," because, as terms, these ideals have become synonymous with a monetary interpretation. But *justice* and *freedom* are important themes with us; and it is especially for the freedom to reinterpret this value system that Chicano writers continue to struggle. In this sense, it can be said that our literature is "thematically revolutionary," and it is extended "technically" as revolutionary insofar as a new language—Chicano Caló—evolves.

What problems have you encountered in publishing? Were they racially founded?

Chicano publishers have been graciously receptive to my work. Most notable are *Caracol*, Pajarito Publications, *Mango*, *El Fuego de Aztlán*, and, of course, *Diseños*. I've had no problems with these publications/publishers, or, in general, with other Third World presses. About ten years ago, before I even knew Third World presses existed, I submitted work for publication to small presses, university-affiliated and independent ones. From the very first, my work was accepted; but it wasn't until 1973 that a culturally related poem was ever accepted for publication, although those poems were consistently submitted along with the others. After it occurred to me what was happening, I submitted to those magazines whose editorial staff included at least one Chicano. And now as a matter of policy, I prefer to publish with Chicano or Third World presses.

Are Chicanos at a disadvantage in trying to practice the art of writing?

Not at all. We may lack confidence in ourselves, but that's to be expected, considering the long-imposed silence we've endured. Last winter I had the privilege of teaching Creative Writing for Chicanos at Stanford. Few of the students had ever written a poem. By the end of the quarter they were bringing three and four submissions even though they were only required to turn in one poem per week. The variety (English, Spanish, Bilingual, Caló—even corridos) and the quality (the students' works are published in the Spring 1978 issue of *Miquiztli*) are a stabilizing assurance to anyone who had any doubts about the future of Chicano literature. I used to feel lucky to have just one student who was highly motivated, energetic, and creative. To have an entire class—*privilege*—that's the only word to describe the experience.

What are the most outstanding qualities of Chicano literature? Weaknesses?

The outstanding qualities I enjoy are the rhythmic expressions in poetry, the humor and poignancy in our cuentos, and the experimentation and extension of our oral tradition in the novel.

The weaknesses lie in our critical writings. We have yet to learn to separate the cultural qualities from the societal and academic ones in order to restructure a balanced approach. As yet, we have no methodological models that apply to our literature. Those of us in the field are acutely aware of this, and are working toward a methodology of our own. One positive step taken in that direction among writers of oral culture is to declare ourselves "affirmers of art" rather than to call ourselves "critics" in the traditional literary sense. This step is basic and necessary for the sake of more positive interaction between writer and affirmer in collaborative efforts toward discovering that methodology.

The search for new methodology must begin with the literature—Chicano literature. It makes no sense to go outside the literature to explain, analyze, or evaluate what's contained in it. Donaldo Urioste and Francisco Lomelí ask an important question: "How do we chicanalizar la literatura [Chicanalyze the literature]?" When we find the answer to that, we will be on the threshold of our own methodology, and we will be better prepared to provide accessibility.

Which are the milestones so far in Chicano literature?

Yo soy Joaquin / I Am Joaquin was the first important milestone in Chicano literature because it gave to Chicanos a significant place in the world, politically, sociologically, historically, and literarily. It united us as a people unlike any other piece of Chicano literature before or since its appearance.

What is the future of Chicano literature: distinctiveness, or the de-emphasis of the distinctive characteristics?

That's an academic concern, isn't it? Chicano literature is not a contrived literature; it's an organic one. It's a reaching out for clarity in the midst of confusion. That's what oppression does to us—keeps us in a state of confusion. And the future of Chicano literature will come out of a *natural* expressive response to whatever the social and political situations elicit.

Who are the leaders among Chicano writers, and why?

Perhaps the question is best left to the future, since those of us who have published or have been published are the first generation to do so, and that makes leaders of us all, doesn't it? Still I don't want to risk predicting the future.

If you are asking "Whom can we look toward as models of writing?" then I recommend José Montoya for poetry, Ron Arias for prose, and Olivia Castellano for critical analysis. There are other equally fine models, but I've already mentioned too many people. It's very difficult for me to think in terms of "leaders," "best," or even "model" with regard to writing, since I don't believe any one person, culture, or nation has the last word on what good writing is, or who the best writers are. My own preference has always been those writers from whom I can learn the most.

No more comments. (I've said enough, don't you think?)

Ricardo Sánchez

Ricardo Sánchez converts his writing into the manifestation of blatant resentment, anger, and passion. As is clearly seen in the interview, he is impatient with any type of structure dictated to him, usually taking it only as a point of departure for his highly creative flow of consciousness and conscience. His creative works, *Canto y grito mi liberación* (1971), *HechizoSpells* (1976), and *Milhuas Blues and Gritos Norteños* (1978), are a hybrid genre of epistle-diary-essay-poetry (similar to that practiced by Abelardo Delgado), whose main character is Ricardo Sánchez. They should not be read as absolute truth in the sense of factual information, but they are absolutely true in the sense of fiction and subjective sincerity. Sánchez is one of Chicano literature's most talented creators of poetic narrative. His apparent goal is to write the literary autobiography of Ricardo Sánchez, poet-militant, writer engagé. However, though he insists on social relevance, stark reality, political involvement, he is the epitome of the artist: a person incapable of living anything without raising it into an aesthetic experience, expressed in whatever media are immediately available, and eventually transposed into the written word. In other words, Sánchez makes living an art. And he lives to the extreme—a deluge of writings, only a fraction of which has been published to date. His language is equally extreme, unfettered, juxtaposing vocabulary from the most academically esoteric to the legendary Pachuco or pinto [prison] slangs, the two latter in themselves forms of esoteric language. But what here may sound like utter chaos must be experienced in its direct, dynamic manifestation, preferably at a Sánchez recitation, to feel its power, its brilliance, its Gargantuan scope, to begin to sense the difficult coherence of the total work. Everything about Sánchez is extreme, including his capacity for empathy, love, and gentleness, expressed in some of his best moments, though the dominant key is indignation and protest. Of course, as an extremist he suffers at

times from overkill, especially with respect to certain persons within the Chicano Movement whom he repeatedly attacks. Sánchez demands our attention, and perhaps only by giving it to him to an extreme to match his own will we begin to understand better his significance.

Ricardo Sánchez wrote his response to the questionnaire in June 1975. The arbitrary use of capitalization, etc., is his and should be read as part of his style.

When and where were you born?

Yo, Ricardo Sánchez, nací el 29 de Marzo, 1941, en el coro del Segundo Barrio, El Paso, Tejas, en lo que seriamente y sin sonrisas nombramos "the spiritual nation of aztlán," pero lo que en cábula es "the de-spirited notion of Aslum . . ." [I, Ricardo Sánchez, was born on March 29, 1941, in the heart of the Second Barrio, El Paso, Texas, in what we seriously and straightfacedly call "the spiritual nation of aztlán," but which in slang is "the de-spirited notion of a slum . . ."]

Describe your family background and your present situation.

Soy un manito por herencia y un pachuco por experiencia [I am a native New Mexican by heritage and a pachuco by experience] . . . my parents migrated south from New Mexico back then when, and i was born number 13, the first one in the family to be born outside of New Mexico and Colorado since somewhere en el siglo 16 [in the sixteenth century] . . . soy mestizo [I'm a mestizo], scion to the beautiful and turbulent reality of indo-hispano concatenation, ay, mi abuela materna [my maternal grandmother] was born in the tewa pueblo of san juan, there between taos and española, and my family tree bespeaks a historicity encumbrando los nombres de [including names like] gurulé, lucero, martínez, gallegos, baca, sánchez, y otros que fueron principiantes [and other pioneers] in the settling and mestizo-making de un mundo ni español ni indigena: ay, mundo de policolores [of a world neither spanish nor indian: ay, world of poly-colors] when mindsouls se ponen a reconfigurar [start to restructure] new horizons . . . due to political embroilments and economic needs, mis padres [my parents] became sojourners throughout the southwest, working in fields and mines, seeking another place to settle and they inadvertently chose El Paso—

ese lugar donde nació el pachuquismo [where pachuquismo was born], that fabled city of cábula [word play] nicknamed El Pachuco or El Chuco or El Pasiente . . . i grew up in the stench-filled llanura del Barrio del Diablo [plain of the Devil's Barrio] (el D.D.T./Del Diablo Territorio) within the insanity of gangwars, anomie, alienation, and the onslaughts of racism . . . i yearly visited the homeland of my parents—northern new mexico, acquiring the values of tierra [land]—allí donde la tierra curte mentes y acaricia almas [where land strengthens minds and caresses souls]—while during school time i spent desultory moments seeking the means to create my own personal cantogrito (songshout), hectically in need of being real and realizing that tejas had consigned me to become another school drop out statistic . . . i was finally pushed out, for school had ceased to mean anything to me . . . told that messicans can't write and i should aspire to that which should be within my means, menial labor, by racist teachers, i withdrew from school and its insanity . . . "no, you pachuco dressing, pachuco speaking trouble-maker, you may not—cannot—write for the Jefferson High School *Branding Iron* (their tabloid)," became another realization of what school meant . . . dropped out/pushed out, dropped in into another demoralizing institution: US ARMY . . . could not reconcile self to their damn orders . . . deaths in the family became forces which made me react with anger, for life should be a festivity—yet all i had seen had been a rancid smelling barrio (the county sewerage disposal plant was located in the very heart, nay, the entrails, of the DDT) . . . years of prison followed, from Chino to Soledad, CTF-North, in California . . . years of idiocy and riots, penury, home, hunger, hate, and dejection . . . paroled in 1963, i sought out means to publish . . . wanted to go to college (for i acquired a G.E.D. while in the army) . . . yet the parole officer would not hear of it . . . he felt that parolees should work only and not think of education . . . he wanted me to do menial labor for meager wages . . . i worked for Farah Mfg, but it was too much like Soledad Prison—the same kind of rules and regulations, the very same dynamics for mass control existed in both places . . . whistles, p.a. systems, individual numbers, patrolling guards/foremen, etc., and the same system of rewards/punishment . . . so i quit and went to work for colliers, selling encyclopedias and became very adept until i started earning too much and the parole people made me quit . . . telling me i should work at a more stable and dependable job, one that did

not require my constantly traveling all over the city . . . they had
me fired, and then they demanded that i find another job . . .
numerous jobs later and after much conflict with the authorities, and by that time married (having been out 22 months with
only 8 months to go for a parole discharge), the parole officer—in
his infernal need to speak to employers—visited the Plaza Motor
Hotel, spoke with the manager about my being a felon and had
me fired . . . my son was on the way, i was busted and unable to
come up with the money for doctor's, hospital, and other bills
. . . and i picked up a gun hoping to assure by one way or another
that our child would be born in a hospital, that Teresa—my
wife—would not have to go to a butcher shop like the county
general hospital or any of the ones which proliferated in the
southside which are notorious for taking people's money for neg-
ligible health care in unsanitary conditions . . . robé con arma y
por consecuencias de mis actos fui arrestado (I committed armed
robbery and consequently I was arrested) . . . tried and convicted,
i was sentenced to serve twelve years in the department of deformation at the texas prison system . . . along with my new sentence came a parole violation and the resumption of a one to
twenty-five year california sentence . . . híjola, but una eternidad
y media me esperaban detras las rejas [oh! but an eternity and a
half awaited me behind the bars] . . . my son, Rikard-Sergei, was
born, a lively and beautiful child i felt i would never hold nor
caress—for life was seemingly to be but a sure death in the hor-
ror show which is texas prisons . . . picking cotton, harvesting,
planting, back to cotton picking, et al, with guards on horseback,
gun on hip, rifles, and whips . . . whipped, isolation, near pto-
maine food, verbal atrocities—"giton, yo' mangy ass,"—hung by
handcuffed wrists from the bars, arbitrarily whipped, kicked,
punched, and ever hated—DAMN, but we prayed to yahweh,
jessie [jesus], quetzalcoatl, or nature to kill us and get it over
with . . . death would be preferable . . . a steady diet of denigra-
tion . . . still most of us survived and did manage to get out . . .
in 1966 my father died, ay, mi jefito [my father] (the only man
hombre bastante para que yo llame JEFE [man enough for me to
call him BOSS]), Pedro Lucero Sánchez . . . i could not attend his
funeral . . . and it hurt . . . i played the game of being rehabili-
tated in order to get out and hit back . . . i heard, while in prison,
of the efforts of three Chicano giants: César Chávez, Abelardo B.
Delgado (now my compadre), and Reies López Tijerina . . . i plot-
ted means and manners to get out to work with them and to

struggle with them in a cause that would see us liberated, see us as a people of dignity. California dropped its hold on me and texas paroled me in 1969 . . . i started working with VISTA-MMP, a Chicano group in el segundo barrio, but the parole people became uptight when i began questioning the local and vocal poverty pimps, while also organizing to take over programs which allegedly were to be in the hands of the people . . . about to have my parole violated, pete duarte secured a Ford Frederick Douglass Fellowship in Journalism for me with the Richmond (Virginia) Afro-American and the Virginia Council on Human Relations . . . in my mind i became an expatriate from my homeland . . . i had to spend, along with Teresa and Rik-Ser, close to two years in the South, New England, Colorado, the migrant stream, and the tragic valley of south texas, seeking the means to return home . . . i had been run out by both the authorities and others . . . in the process i finished the fellowship and went to work for the School of Education, University of Massachusetts at Amherst, as a staff writer/research assistant/instructor . . . then i left for the Colorado Migrant Council, Denver, to direct the Itinerant Migrant Health Project, a several hundred thousand dollar program . . . in the interim period i had become a fairly recognized poet/lecturer, having read at such places as harvard, yale, northwestern, washington state univ. at pullman, univ. of colorado, unm, and places in between . . . i returned to el chuco to build and create, dreaming of setting up a publishing company (which we did: Mictla Publications), but the parole people grounded me from going out on speaking engagements . . . seems that program raza [chicano] people were conferring with the gendarmes about my being a radical and dangerous element to all kinds of community . . . not having a job (for the programs in el paso were afraid of political repercussions), my parole was going to be violated . . . i had made contact with some batos about getting a couple of guns, having decided that i would rather be killed than be sent back to prison, and had ready access to the guns . . . meanwhile, Tomás Atencio and the other carnales [brothers] from La Academia de la Nueva Raza [The Academy of the New Race]—people i had never met—heard about my plight and out of their much needed funds (for their own programming needs) gave me a $500 a month stipend allegedly for doing research for them, which i never did . . . but they had told me to use the funds to support my family and to

tell the law that i did have a job with La Academia, etc., a ruse
which worked . . . the stipend lasted for over seven months, until their funds ran out, but it gave me the time needed to consol-
idate resources and to make the kinds of contacts which could
countermand the pinche [goddamn] parole people . . . about this
time, i met un gavacho, Dr. Randell Ackley, who respected what
i was doing . . . he kept after me to apply for a ford graduate
fellowship and to apply to Union Graduate School for admit-
tance as a doctoral candidate . . . seeing my growing family—we
now had another child, Libertad-Yvonne, who had been born in
Northampton, Massachusetts—a funny birthplace for a Chicana—and realizing that i wanted to seriously work with youths
within a pedagogic framework, i applied to UGS [Union Graduate School] and ford [foundation] . . . in the meantime i helped
develop the counseling component for the Trinity OIC of El Paso
and then went on to work at New Mexico State University in
Las Cruces where Tony Lujan and i tried to make the social welfare teaching center responsive to Chicano needs . . . it was a
time of reflection and writing, but not having credentials limited
my efforts in cracking their cracker uni-scar-city . . . UGS and
Ford processed my applications and i was granted both, and i left
NMSU to begin doctoral studies in August of 1973 . . . a process
which took me to numerous cities and regions, culminating in
my passing my terminal exams in December of 1974 . . . i had
jumped from a G.E.D. to a Ph.D. in about 15 months of study,
intensive reading, multifaceted symposia, travel, dialogue, and
writing . . . the dissertation was entitled CUNA: the Barrio and
the Poetics of Revolution . . . a book manuscript of poetry, vignettes, stories, etc., dealing with critical theory, language, literature, and Chicanismo . . . I was recently awarded a National
Endowment of the Arts poet/writer in residency grant to be utilized for the purpose of teaching and writing at the El Paso Community College for the coming year . . . it is a happy occasion,
yet the recent loss of our third child kind of mars the moment
. . . los meses se han bañado con fragmentos y pedazos vitales,
aun quebrando la realidad con verdades dolientes [the months
have been washed with fragments and living pieces, still braking
reality with painful truths] . . . death, in its inexplicable manner,
claimed the beauteous fragility of our Pedrito-Cuahtemoc within
two weeks of his birth in january, leaving scattered memories to
sort themselves out in the chiaroscuro of timespace and idea-

tion/feeling . . . congenital heart anomalies with severe visceral
congestion . . . a poem cut short by naturaleza's arbitrary exigen-
cies . . . thus the quick lived joy and exuberance of a doctoral
terminar and expectancies for a brighter morrow now question
the madness of being, yet that piercing and joyful fetal son of life
keeps creating newer dimensions to all that prances before sight,
hearing, taste, and feeling—distilling desperate thoughts into
a vital gelatine . . . one lives in order to create meaning out
of life's chaoticness, striving to dignify socialization with real
and pungent words of human passion, ay, cantando, gritando,
bailando, festejando, y obrando una liberación humanizante
[singing, shouting, dancing, celebrating, and creating a humanizing liberation] . . . fragments of our humanity shredded by a
quasi-coolness, our social pretentions, into una vida hecha de
puros compartments . . . el alma aquí, la mente allí y el cuerpo
enloquecidamente buscando formas de encapsular una totalidad
hechizada por miedos a inseguridades [a life only consisting of
compartments . . . the soul here, the mind there, and the body
crazily seeking ways to encapsulate a totality cursed by fear and
insecurity] . . . still, life is beautiful, and there can exist creativity—a projecting toward dignity and meaning as liberation is
culled from our experientiality . . . living is a struggle, yet all
struggles must have a greater sense of meaning other than just
being efforts to just survive, even if on a near starvation level . . .
a new book shall be out soon, HechizoSpells, Aztlán Publications, Chicano Studies, Univ. of Calif, LA, 405 Hilgard Ave.,
L.A., Calif 90024 . . . yes, i sense my new book about to hit some
stores, y ay, que lo poético quiebre otras cadenas, que la música
suele emanar como lo sabroso de la vida, dejando en
el almamente huellas enbellecedoras, ay, notas poetizantes
bailando sobre las cuerdas, elevándose hacia lo más glorioso de
la experiencia . . . ay, lo cultural es un sueño gruñendo en lo más
cabal del pensarsentir . . . lo del presente, ay, pero esta situacion
es buena y cabal [and ay, that the poetic break other chains, that
music usually emanate like the tastiness of life, leaving in the
soulmind beautifying traces, ay, poeticizing notes dancing on the
strings, rising to the most glorious level of experience . . . ay,
culture is a dream growling in the heart of thoughtfeeling . . . Of
the present, ay, but this situation is good and full], i live life-
times in the space of moments, seemingly able to penetrate all
areas of thoughtfeeling con gusto [with joy] . . . desahogado en
mi existir [freed in my existence] . . . writing and poeticizing.

[Since the interview, Sánchez has moved from El Paso, Texas, to Salt Lake City, Utah, where he teaches at the University of Utah. He has ventured lately into experimental cinema with his screenplay *Entelequia*; he starred in the short film as well.]

When did you first begin to write?

Empece muchas veces [I began many times] . . . firstly, in the lower grades, composing poems for different events . . . xmas poems, birthday poems, and other works . . . ever discouraged by those who could not understand the passion(s) i felt toward writing, telling me that it was not a practical undertaking . . . teachers and others who spoofed my hopes as being also de locos [a crazy thing]—y ahora hasta soy loco con papeles y credenciales [and now I'm crazy with papers and degrees]. i wrote while in the service, did a few minor small magazine things in san francisco in 1959, later wrote in soledad and the texas prison system . . . also in between both prison stints used to write . . . even attended meetings of the El Paso Writers' League, with tennis-shoed, aged whites chattering niceties and witty phrases . . . angered by their lack of commitment to art as a means of redefining the world and freeing self . . . exasperated, gauchely quit the league, laughing at limited rewards and mushy sentiments . . . my real commitment came with realizing that we did not truly exist in the social/cultural schemata of this nation . . . searching like a maniac for us in book after book, and then hearing about a galvanizing social movement led me to look at our historicity, at the proceso del pachuco como un levantamiento social con raíces políticas [process of the pachuco as a social uprising with political roots], and knowing that we would have to be the ones to write our history on the pages of timespace, pues [well] i began to write at the Ramsey I Prison Farm, Texas Department of Deformation: La PINTA! [Prison] 1965 . . . ay, pero [but] then was the flame really lit . . . published in the prison newspaper, the Echo, and began to prepare for my eventual release when i declared that i would publish a major work within five years of my release—it took two years to publish *Canto y grito mi liberación* after my release in 1969 . . . i began to write when my mind first read and understood the implications of language, its beauty and configurations . . . publishing was another matter.

What kind of books did you read in your formative years?

Books read in my formative years were varied—from poetry to
fiction to anything i could pick up wherever i happened to be . . .
i used to read everything that was printed, from ads to comics to
newspapers to magazines to technical materials, etc. . . . more
important than the type of books was the fact that language existed, that it could be written and reconfigured to create other
realities than those one had read . . . more than literature was its
process, the curvatures, so to speak, of language, its tones and
ritmos [rhythms], its pirouettes and slides, peaks and valleys . . .
poetry was the harshness of one sound as it collided with the
exquisite tenderness of another sound, ay, that swirling synthesis which inundated mindsoul with the exequies of reso-
nance . . . i write more for the graphic and aural and audio
juxtapositions and configurations of words than for the sake of
arcane literary pretentions . . . words are to language what contours can be to anatomy, and in the gelatin of language are the
forms, contours, textures of beauty which in other arts become a
plastique shaded and/or highlighted . . . i still tend to read anything i can pick up—from highly literary materials to utterly
pornographic trash, for the contents do not matter as much as
the tatters or intricacy of the words, the nuances, tones, and ac-
cidents of language . . .

What is the extent of your studies?

i formally have a high school equivalency (GED) and a Ph.D.; no
bachelor's and no master's . . .

Has formal education helped or hindered you as a writer?

Formal education has neither hindered nor aided my writing, for
i write as a street's poet would haciendo de la realidad [making
from reality] the kind of structure that the words i use will
create . . .

**Which was the predominant language in your home as a child? Which
do you speak more fluently now?**

Español and English were used extensively in my home . . . i
have an equal or near equal facility with both . . . in the streets
did i pick up on calo [slang] and jive, with which i also have
facility of expression . . . churros, loco, pero soy un chavo de bastante arranque para toriquear, como chuco u cristiano u como
un arracliento al estilo americano, si pues y que-te-cles, nichis,
monchis, chiclosín [sure, crazy, but I'm a guy with lots of talent
for talking, like a pachuco or a christian or loose American
style . . .].

Does Chicano literature have a particular language or idiom?

All literatures have their particularized idiom, while at the same
time having a universal sensibility to being-ness . . . in Chicano
Literature, we find confluent language(s) charting and re-chart-
ing patterns of thought and feeling. New dimensions to being
within a tertiary process—the synthesizing of thought and feeling by the formation of newer symbols, the creating of new sen-
sitivities to the existential quagmires of our multifaceted
survival and socialization. Chicano literature is a political statement which derives its essence from socio-politico-economic realities vying with cultural and historical affirmations, and in so
doing a language of engagement and confrontation takes form
. . . the affirmation of a mindset predicated on the merging of
dual language and dual culture configurations and the attesting
that the process is valid unto itself as all other linguistic and
cultural phenomena have been cantagrita su realidad [singing-
shouting its reality] and it adamantly confirms our rightness as
the unique human beings that we can be and are. The manner in
which we speak and use English is definitely Chicano in terms
of nuance, just as we use Español in a very Chicano way—our
language merging is uniquely ours, just as our calo [slang] is . . .

**How do you perceive your role as a writer vis-à-vis: (a) the Chicano
community or Movement; (b) U.S. society; (c) literature itself?**

(a) My role as a writer as regards la raza is one of striving to help
create a liberatingly humanizing process wherein we, as Chicanos and Chicanas, can do more than share in decision-mak-
ing—rather, one that can be said to be free and vitalistically
affirming. I realize my existential responsibility to respond polit-

ically to being-ness, to share in a common cause hacia nuestra liberación humanizante [toward our humanizing liberation] on terms bespeaking our culture, language, and uniqueness. Words must be real, just as weapons are real—my writing, I strongly feel, must be a driving wedge and force, una arma que se pueda usar para enfrentar lo social y crear más que consciencia [a weapon which can be used to confront the social and create more than consciousness], ay, a commitment must exist within the writer/artist which agglutinates vision with the historical struggles of the oppressed to seek freedom. Art must deal with living and theory in order to serve the need for humaniza-tion/liberation of all; thus the writer should also be willing and able to respond with action akin to the ideas he/she espouses. Como Chicano, pinto, y oprimido, pues tengo que coyuntarme con la causa del mero pueblo para así todos obrar hacia una liber-ación popular y humanizante. [As a Chicano, ex-con, and op-pressed person, well I have to join the cause of the real people so everyone will work toward political and humanizing liberation.]

(b) I hold no allegiance to US society as such, for all so-cieties seem to be predicated on the subjugation of humankind. As a writer, I must relate the implicit role of society, which is to colonize people, to the real needs of people to free themselves from any form of oppression. As a human being, I acknowledge my obligation to wage struggle against barbarism and to strive toward any humanization at whatever the cost, to fight my own fears and to affirm my commitment to liberation. People have historically created societal monstrosities which have ever ma-nipulated people—if there is to be an allegiance, I espouse one toward my humanity and the humanity of all people to live in dignity, justice, freedom, and commitment to creative ideals, rather than kow-tow to the technocratic systemization of the US or any other societal construct.

(c) Literature is one of our most basic means of capturing a slice of timespace, molding it, and projecting it into other mo-ments . . . as Chicanos, we must create out of our social chaos a realization of our past/present/future, imprinting our historicity and morality on the pages of humankind's journey through being-ness, and in that way share our meaning, while assuring the survival of our people as a unique entity . . . we must delve into our language, culture, and history without fear . . . creating out of our truth and striving to affirm our history without dis-torting or controlling our people . . . we must present a strong and real imagery of ourselves, not a pseudopyramided idiocy peopled by facile, docile, and benign plastic indígenas [native Indians] . . . too often have we relied on the de-gutted pendejismos [idiocies] of los aztlanecas, nalgahuados, and florindoflori-cantistas [aztlanites, softbutts, and flowery-flower-and-song-singers] for a distorted sense of self . . . ay, carnal [brother], we can create out of a truthful sense of historicity an understanding of our ontology, and we can stop accommodating academia and pleading for pittances . . . we must learn to stand on our own merits and speak a truth which we can defend—but only if we dare commit ourselves to our humanization. Just as humanization implies cultural/linguistic diversity, so does it affirm liberation . . . if we are to have an aesthetic, then must we also have integrity and ethics, for all three are part and parcel of one another . . . Literature should not be a fling for convienencierros [opportunists], but a process of concienciación y liberación [consciousness-raising and liberation]. As critics and writers, we should be willing to deal with the instant Chicano writers out for a fast buck—esos bofos [those rascals] seeking to capitalize on chicanismo. Stuff like what Vásquez, Villaseñor, and others of their ilk write should be seen for what it is. Chicano writers must begin using language creatively, movingly, and truthfully. Much of what passes for Chicano literature is dead imagery and boring symbols and rhetoric. If our writers lose their fear of language(s) and ideas, then will our literature flourish and inspire.

[At this point in the interview, Ricardo Sánchez broke with the question-by-question format and, in his own, highly individual style, proceeded to discuss the remaining questions en masse.]

Though our literature (as Chicanos) is relatively young, it is the literature of a people seething with the idea of becoming a sovereign and free people, able to make decisions, questioning the foundations of society and its decrees, and marking real time-space demarcations in the world of art: territorial imperatives a la aesthetic . . . all literatures are universal yet particularistic, so that we share certain realities with blacks, whites, indios [Indians], asians, yet we express our vitalism in our own terms and nuances. I sense a cantogrito [songshout] in art—the breaking of chains and the declaring of our human rights to create our own visions and live them. Lloramos Nuestra realidad y también la festejamos, ay, dando al momento nuestra desgracia [We cry

Our reality and also celebrate it, ay, giving the moment our beauty and our misfortune]—from the canto jondo [gypsy song] to the grito enloquecido [crazed shout] somos lo que somos [we are what we are] and in that realization we can conclude que no habido dios que es neta y que nadie se la meta, de modos que vivimos lo inseguro vital, chamusquiando y desafiando vida y muerte [that no god is just, so don't get screwed, therefore we live the vital insecurity, beating and challenging life and death]. Whether we improve communications with anglos is not as important as whether we come to basic understandings of each other as a people in order that we might liberate ourselves—that is if liberation is important to us. Our very integrity hangs on a limb, viewing as we do the genocidic policies of this human shredding nation. I feel that the survival of our raza is indeed important; thus I sense that only a politicizing poetics can be of value. What need we of prissy historical distortions and wispy hopes? Strong writers like Tigre, Raúl R. Salinas, Lalo Delgado, José Montoya, Tomás Atencio, Carmen Tafolla, Irene B. Gutiérrez, Len Avila, Nephtalí de León, Rudy Anaya, José Armas, Javier Pacheco, Raúl Valdez, and others are helping create a real sense of liberation. They do not pretend to be other than what they are: gente neta [real people]. Yet, we find ourselves inundated by prissy types with pseudo and facile crap, such as the pyramid builders and their so-called jive of actionless indígenas [native Indians], roseated indios, and their perpetuation of quasimystical idiocies adumbrates our youth even more. Too much praise has also been given to our demagogues and their I AM JOKING phantasmagoria. If Corky [Rodolfo Corky Gonzales] is indeed a poet, writer, and playwright, where are his obras [works]? It takes more than one poem to make a poet—does it not? As of now, those writers and Poets I respect have more than one obra [work]—and they continually write and write, striving to create salient statements and armed literature.

Hopefully, raza shall realize that our literature belongs to all of us and that real literature shall emanate from the minds and pens of all kinds of Chicanos and Chicanas . . . we have a great need for writers from all our social strata, to create imagery of what it feels like to be pobre [poor], middle class, and powerless or powerful—if possible. The middleclass raza has been manipulated también [too]—where is their story? From the pinto [convict] to the academic must come a testament as to the real experience of our people—for within our mindsouls see the turbulence, hurt, and beauty/joy. If we are part indian, then let us affirm all nuances of our indian-ness, not just pollyana indian-ness which never existed nor pyramided jive and distortion. Let us also affirm lo español y gitano [the spanish and gypsy] of our reality . . . if urista [Alurista] was really so hot on indigenismo, he should have attended the s.w. poets' conference on the navajo reservation/nation . . . he was sent tickets to attend and he didn't . . . maybe he feared coming into contact with indians who live because they were born of blood and fetal flesh, eat, defecate, piss, fuck, and die . . . they also drink, fight, and are not angelic nor prissy. No, there are no pyramids nor fancy ideas at the navajo nation, just as our barrios are not beautiful nor edifying . . . there is a great stench enveloping the societal world—death of human integrity, soul, and mind . . . ours is the chance to denounce sordidness and create with integrity an aesthetic bespeaking humanization and liberation.

Along with our need for a stronger literature, we also need real criticism. Most critics play at popularizing themselves and securing good jobs. Integrity lacks and fantasy swells. The nicety of our academics is blight. Our fear of offending each mother's son of us must cease. Conferences on literature and criticism appear to be but jockeying for position and jobs, ay, societal insurance. There appears to be no academic freedom to intellectual vigor. Our ethics? Our commitment? Our creativity? Art must confront regimentation—but our critics affirm a horrid accommodationist trajectory which putrefies our art. In the main, our ph.d. enunciators are fearful of rocking the boat—pues [well], only those willing to fight can become free . . . cowards neither love nor live, they merely are there occupying space and gorging on the leavings of those willing to wage a humanizing struggle. That is why I quit writing for la pus [the pus], I mean *la luz* [magazine]! Life must be memorable, festive, not a static and uneventful charade. Too many damn treatises on meaninglessness and objectification. If we are to disappear from this earth as an integral people, it shall be due to our moral and social cowardice, not because of our oppressors. I do not want to see our literature boxed in, yet I sense the urgency for strong criticism and historical awareness. Our critics seem to be much more fearful of j. a. prufrock and his peachy prissiness, our wasteland is our pretention, and our holocaust our accommodation . . .

Those of us in the movement who publish, we do so at great

personal expense—for we can seldom get our best material published . . . too radical or real so say editors . . . even Ortago did a hell of a lot of editing on my material . . .

Much more exists which I want to say, but time is scarce . . . let us communicate, carnal . . .

Hacia la liberación popular . . .

Ron Arias

The Road to Tamazunchale (1975) made its author, Ron Arias, an instant candidate for best Chicano novelist. A journalist by profession, Arias had years of solid training and writing experience before he began to publish fiction. At first he was known as an able short story writer, winning the University of California at Irvine literary contest with a story that later proved to be a chapter of his novel. Since the publication of *Tamazunchale* he has published more stories in the leading journals and continued his freelance commercial writing. Among his credits he counts episodes for major television series, like *Quincy*.

Tamazunchale narrates an old man's fanciful creation of an active death to substitute for the passive one imposed on him by failing health. The story is highly literary, full of allusions to and parodies of other novels, short stories, and even movies. Considering that the dying man is a book salesman with a good sense of humor, the literary playfulness is quite in character. On his death bed, Fausto, the protagonist, calls upon his experiences—read or lived, no difference—as the only source of material available for his invention of a death more fitting his active life. The character is brilliantly created, rivaling Anaya's Ultima as the most memorable in Chicano literature.

Stylistically, the novel is the Chicano work that most resembles the current Latin American literary production. Its disregard for the conventional frontier between reality and fantasy relates it to the trend loosely known as "magical realism." Yet, more importantly, Arias is a skilled, patient craftsman, with a healthy sense of irony about himself and the world. If one is to relate him to the Latin Americans, it would be more fruitful to note that he shares the current—we could say modern—sense of literature as one enormous text, interrelated and consciously self-referential. To fix his quality or his significance in what amounts to the style he chose for one book is to limit his true scope. His future pub-

lications may well disappoint the devotees of magical realism, but one doubts that they will lessen his standing as a master technician of the written word.

Precisely for its similarity to magical realist literature, *Tamazunchale* has become the center of controversy in Chicano literary circles. Those who advocate a political or social (socialist) realism line call it irrelevant, reactionary, commercial; the aestheticians welcome it with the highest praise, utilizing it to implicitly denigrate other Chicano works by contrast. The dispute over this slim volume accurately reflects the Chicano literary scene's unfortunate split into two extreme camps, with a more tolerant third attempting to bridge the gap and often getting caught in the crossfire. Meanwhile, *Tamazunchale* goes into new editions, increasing in popularity with the Chicano as well as the non-Chicano reading public, standing on its own merits.

The first draft of the interview was published in *The Journal of Ethnic Studies* 3, no. 4 (Winter 1976), Western Washington University, Bellingham, WA 98225. The completely revised and much extended version that appears here dates from the winter of 1978–1979.

When and where were you born?

November 30, 1941, in Los Angeles, California.

Describe your family background and your present situation.

I was raised traveling. If it wasn't from one part of Los Angeles to another, it was from one part of the U.S. to another, with a few stops in Europe added. My stepfather was in the Army as a career and we traveled from one assignment to another, especially after the Korean War. I loved it—Texas, Louisiana, Kansas, Oklahoma, Colorado, New York, Germany, Italy, Spain. I got a taste of a lot of places very early. I suppose I identified with both my real father (from Juárez) and my stepfather (from Nogales): one was an orphan and the other had left home at sixteen—they were pícaros in the original sense of the word, traveling, hustling all kinds of jobs. Very soon in my life I was trying to do the same, enjoying the adventure of changing places and jobs since I was about nine. The strangest work I've ever done—and that lasted one night under a full moon—was to artificially inseminate female turkeys. It requires two persons working in tandem;

one to operate the semen "gun" and the other to grab and hold the thirty-pound animals, one after another all night while they are still in heat. Of course I had the hard part; it was backbreaking and I don't think I lasted more than three or four hours.

As for traveling on my own, as soon as I could I left home for the summers and started hitchhiking. About all my mom (from El Paso) could do was give me blessings and wait for postcards. One summer when I was seventeen I spent a few nights sharing a basement of a Sisters of Charity building with two cot-rows of winos, thieves, and other kinds of vagos [vagrants]. That was in Pamplona, Spain, and I remember thinking one morning that the sun *always* rises for the poor and have-nots. Some of those people in that basement had just stepped out of *Lazarillo de Tormes*. Before I left Pamplona I was lucky enough to meet Ernest Hemingway sitting at a table in the plaza drinking wine. I asked for an autograph on a bullfighting program, and he ended up asking me to sit down and have a glass of wine with him. That was in 1959 when he was following Ordóñez around the corrida tour for *Life*, I believe. I'm still not a big fan of his writing—except for some stories—but I'll always remember his kindness, his curiosity about my situation, and his gentle manner. I also remember that he was sad about Pamplona having become crowded and modernized since his early writing days in the twenties.

About my present situation: I'm married to a remarkable woman—a college teacher, an author and lover of books. She's also attractive, very smart, and is perhaps the most honest person I've ever met. We have a young son named Michael who does a lot of stage acting and wants to be a film-maker. Besides teaching writing and literature courses, I also earn money writing freelance magazine articles on all kinds of subjects, from comedians and medicine to politics and mixed drinks. I'm also working on TV and film scripts.

When did you first begin to write?

I began to write when I was nine in the maternity ward of Camp Pendleton Marine Base. For some reason there was no more room in the children's ward, and since I was there to have my tonsils out, and I also looked like an inconspicuous six- or seven-year-old—they put me with all these very pregnant women. I got quite an eyeful every time I went to the restroom, which had no doors on the stalls. My mother brought me a pen and note-book after my operation and told me to write down everything I saw. I did. And that was my first consistent writing effort. Un-fortunately I must have lost the notebook because I never could find it—or else my mother hid what she probably thought was pornography.

Later, I continued writing for high school and college news-papers, then went on to write for city dailies in Los Angeles, Buenos Aires, and Caracas and for wire services like the Associ-ated Press. I was about twenty or twenty-one, ducking tank fire and tear gas while covering yet another golpe [coup] argentino, or interviewing the neo-Nazis who were carving swastikas on Jewish girls. Or watching campesino squatters near Cuzco being shot down by machinegun fire, police at the trigger. I wrote a lot of human interest features, business profiles, travelogues, inter-viewed people like Indira Gandhi or famous moviemakers, ath-letes, and entertainers who passed through the city. In other words, I was a sponge for experience. Now and then I look at some of those pieces that I saved, and realize that I must have worked very hard at putting some of those things together. Once in Buenos Aires, I remember trying to put something together for, I believe, the *Christian Science Monitor*. I was living in a cheap, walkup partitioned room—one of many in the pensión run by a parental pair of Gallegos. I was next to the kitchen with the only bathroom also nearby. Lots of noise, a naked bulb above, suffocated by a sweltering Buenos Aires summer, a tiny Olivetti portable between my legs on the bed, and a pile of notes. And me in shorts, if that—me, twenty green-years-old, ace foreign correspondent! A ridiculous scene, and I only see the humor in it now. Then, I was very serious, hurting, existential. But of course I was working hard at writing.

Years later I went on to editing work in Washington, D.C., then to teaching in a junior college. It was only when I was past thirty that I started to write fiction seriously, along with some drama. I published a few stories and even attended a week-long writers' workshop. Peter Beagle, one of the visiting professionals, liked a story of mine called "Fausto" and suggested I do more with this old man character. I did and it became my novelita [novelette] *The Road to Tamazunchale*. Today I really don't need the kind of experience and encouragement I once had. Most everything I'll ever invent will be some combination of thoughts already in my head. I've also got stacks of half-finished or unpolished works. I suppose I have a mine of material—years of rich observation—but my main hangup now is that I'm trying to find the best, most solid vein of ore. Or maybe I suffer from Rulfismo—I won't write anything or have it published until I have something unique to say and a unique way of saying it. Juan Rulfo got plenty of mileage out of two books, so who knows?

What kind of books did you read in your formative years?

Comic books, of course, in my earliest years. Sure, Classics [Illustrated] Comics too! But what most affected me were historical novels and histories: a lot of Charles Lamb (the first author I ever wrote to, to tell him how much I liked his Alexander the Great book) and things like *Anthony Adverse* or H. G. Wells' *World History*. Later, in high school I learned to hate Silas Marner and respect the usual writers anthologized for English and American lit courses. Actually I was never that turned on to so-called great writers until they fulfilled an emotional need, or should I say, a craving or intense curiosity that I often still feel today. As an example, I remember one of the most idyllic, most restful weeks of my life. It was spent in San Juan, Argentina, in the home of a friend who spoiled me with good food and wine. And all I did was read, take walks, and enjoy the man's quiet patio. And most fortunate of all, I had the perfect companion for reading: it was a Henry Miller book about a time of intense reflection on some Greek island. Probably because San Juan is so hot and white and wine-like, Miller's book was the perfect complement for my thoughts at the time. In other words, I think I would have had an almost *physical* need of such a book if it hadn't been around. About every day, if I have the time, I have that kind of reading need. And for the weirdest things, and I don't know where the curiosity comes from. It might be for books on sailing, or a book on Marx, Fraser, or Darwin, or a history of Chinese science or of Moslems in the Sudan. It's all crazy but very exciting. Occasionally I like to spend a half day in a large university library, pick a section and make myself at home. I guess I'm still traveling the way I did when I was younger. In fact I have a story written (but not too polished) about a guy who loses himself in a library and his family and police search for him everywhere until the trail leads through several books to a diary or autobiography written by the missing person who simply relates in the final pages that he is lost somewhere in a library. A bit like Borges, I suppose, even though I've read very little by him—odd because he was even my teacher in a medieval English class I once took at the University of Buenos Aires in 1962. As with Hemingway, I was taken more with the real man than the man's literary works; he was erudite, curious, aristocratic, and in love with all things British.

What is the extent of your studies?

I have a B.A. in Spanish and an M.A. in journalism, both degrees from the University of California (Berkeley and Los Angeles). But, as I've suggested, my true education—at least where writing is concerned—took place in travel, work, and in all kinds of books I picked up here and there. For example, every time I'm faced with a long journalistic or TV piece, I must research the subject. I've taken a lot of self-directed "mini-courses" that way. A typical research trail was one that led me from certain imported vegetable insecticides—very toxic to humans—to the most poisonous animal venom known in the world, a skin secretion from a pea-size, rare Colombian tree frog. That bit of work was necessary before I could write a *Quincy* script for TV.

By the way, I might say that I studied Spanish and Hispanic literature, again mostly because I had to know more about my own past, my historical past. I'm fascinated by how people have become what they are. An ability with Spanish helped the process of discovery—and I've also come to love the language, whether it's spoken in Tarija, Bolivia, or Arecibo, Puerto Rico.

Has formal education helped or hindered you as a writer?

I can say that my first year was exciting, but the remaining years, during which I dropped out many times for years or months at a time, were a frustrating, boring series of one novocained professor after another. There were a few exceptions. The two finest instructors I can remember were not only enlightened, enthusiastic persons about life and knowledge but also happened to teach two subjects I had only recently discovered—one was geology and geography taught by Carl Sauer at Berkeley and the other was anthropology taught by Johannes Wilbert at UCLA. And one more, a Quixote course given by Richard Andrews. Who knows, maybe these three profs made my "formal" education worthwhile. As for my major in Spanish literature, certainly I read the required works, but I was familiar with most of the authors since I had already lived in Latin America a number of years. Back around 1962, before the so-called "boom" began, I was reading people like Arreola, Borges, Cortázar, Juárroz, Huidobro, Ciro Alegría, Quiroga, Donoso, and many others. But I also remember hanging out in the American and British libraries, thirsty for works in English or English translation—Golding, Suzuki, Babel, on and on.

Which was the predominant language in your home as a child? Which do you speak more fluently now?

With my parents, especially after I started school, it was mostly English. My mother was very intent on our (my two brothers and I) learning correct English. She was a busy reader, for example, and our home library was almost entirely of English works, which were a lot of romantic and popular novels, along with a good *Encyclopedia Britannica* set. I suppose it was through her inspiration that we all managed a good hold on English and made a game try at college courses. I should add that my mother never lost her Mexican Spanish accent, but in her way she pushed us to lose ours.

I also spent several years of my childhood in El Paso with my grandmother, and there I spoke Spanish almost exclusively. I was even put with the "Mexican-only" first-grade class at Ascarate grammar school at one time, and later when I returned to L.A., I remember getting off the train at Union Station and not being able to speak English. Today, I'm much more fluent in English than in Spanish, which is typical for most Chicanos. English is also a more "comfortable" language for me to write in—probably because I've had so much professional practice with it. And as I said, when I wasn't with my grandmother or my great-aunts in El Paso, my young ear heard mostly English at home. Also, everyone from my parents' generation on spoke primarily English. In the forties, that was obviously the practical language of esteem, and my parents had all the right middle-class pretensions. I don't think they consciously disparaged Spanish—it just wasn't practical. Strange, once I started taking Spanish courses in college, I refused to speak with them in Spanish until I felt comfortable—and that only came about after three years in Latin America, and by then I could do pretty good imitations of a porteño Buenos Aires accent or sibilant Andino speech. I could even wow them with some Quechua and Brazilian Portuguese. In fact, I think getting an "educated" mastery over Spanish and having lived in Latin America helped me in overcoming any lingering feelings of cultural or ethnic inferiority I might have felt previously. It's a common Chicano experience; that's why I tell students to travel and see the rest of the world, get some perspective on who they are.

I should say that my childhood "Spanish" experience with my grandmother was an emotional one and had little to do with language. It was the substance, *what* was related between us, that mattered and not the medium we used. Unfortunately she wasn't a storyteller—no one in my family really was. I'd have to pry information out of them and sometimes make up the rest.

Does Chicano literature have a particular language or idiom?

A while back I would have answered "maybe." Now, I don't think so. Speaking of my own writing, I don't think it matters too much whether a page is read in English, Spanish, or Greek. Sure, some nuances are lost, but ultimately I'd like to think that the content is what mattered most to the reader. The other night on the Dick Cavett show I. B. Singer was saying that what's wrong with American literature these days is that there aren't many real storytellers around; everyone's too busy experimenting. I'd add that that probably holds true for the strong Chicano emphasis on the importance of language. I'd like to think that the story itself is what matters most. Recently I translated parts of *Tamazunchale*, and I doubt if it loses much to the Spanish reader. Actually, it's the reader's cultural background or reference points that determine his or her response as a member of a particular community. For instance, I remember riding a crowded bus one day in Caracas, and two women who looked like secretaries on their lunch break were laughing over certain episodes they'd read in *Cien años de soledad*. I joined in; then it seemed half the bus did. This was in 1969 and it was the year's best seller. Everyone who had read it was bringing up his or her favorite character or episode, and we were all howling together. The book as a whole had struck a common chord with us all, since historically we had all once come from a Macondo or Aracataca, we all had a tío [uncle] or two in a revolution, and I'm sure there were people in our lives chasing more than butterflies. I saw the same kind of "bus passenger" reaction in Portugal, where everyone it seemed was talking about *Gabriela, Cravo e Canela*, the current TV series based on the Jorge Amado novel. The story is what mattered most—not the medium or language that conveys the story. Sometimes, either for political or very esoteric, even trivial, reasons—we make too much of the importance of language. And because "bilingualism" has become such a political issue among Chicanos, many of us approach imaginative writing—novels and stories, let's say—as potential weapons to be used in the fight. Too bad, because I think it takes a lot of the "jugo" [juice] out of some good works. I would like to think that literature is so much more pliable and not as brittle and hard as some would like it to be.

How do you perceive your role as a writer vis-à-vis: (a) the Chicano community or Movement; (b) U.S. society; (c) literature itself?

(a) All I can say is that I hope Chicanos like what I write. After all, they were my original and main inspiration to write fiction—I would like to think we have a common language and ambiente [environment]. I would also like to think my work brings a bit of pride to other Chicanos in our own achievements. For instance, personally I may not care for Luis Valdez's early trips into mysticism, but I feel great for him and for us all when I read that his *Zoot Suit* has broken box office records at L.A.'s Music Center—and that a lot of Chicanos who've never gotten near an established downtown theatre are now making headlines.

(b) Sure, it would be nice if recognition spread beyond the Chicano community. But money or quality or both are the keys to success in this country. If a commercial publisher sees a book I write as a potential moneymaker, that book could easily be in every Pickwick Bookstore in a few weeks. It's all so capricious, depending on the popular tastes of the times, promotion, and publicity. These things should be the writer's last consideration. To put it another way, ultimately I have an ideal reader I write for—it's me, myself. And I've been around long enough to know that I share important sensibilities and experiences with a lot of people—and they're not all Latinos or Chicanos or neighbors or relatives. When I write, I must trust these sensibilities, trust myself, or I'd never get beyond the first word, the first sentence.

(c) What can I say? I hope that I, like Don Cacahuate [Mr. Peanut], can add my two bits.

What is the place of Chicano literature within U.S. literature?

It's really too soon to say. When you say "place," it sounds as if you're talking about a corpse, something dead that should be shelved or stuck in a chapter of some criticism book. However, I do believe we're as "American" as Twain, Malamud, Ellison, or anonymous Native American tales. In other words, I think the distinction or label "American" is absurd. Not for political reasons, but simply for a humanistic one. What I write is for anyone, really, and I refuse to start slicing people and their creations into categories. I hated that in those awful undergraduate lit courses I once had to take, and I feel the same today. Thinking of literature as a mass of categories is for me simply a memory device and is pitifully uncreative.

What is the relationship of Chicano literature to Mexican literature?

Again, I have to put any body of good creative work into categories. At any rate, I suppose most Chicano authors have read Mexico's major works—and probably in Spanish. To some degree whatever favorite pieces that we read have to affect what we write, but really why any more than what has deeply affected us by a Faulkner, a Dostoevski, or a García-Márquez? Some of B. Traven has as much pleasure and fascination for me as some of what Carlos Fuentes has written; in this sense "The Night Visitor" is very similar to "Chac Mool." And I don't care if Traven was born in Wisconsin or Minnesota and wrote first in English or German. Again, it's the feeling and the story that count, not the language or national origin of the writer. Yes, of course, I like everything Rulfo has published; I learned a lot from his stories—terseness, pace, time structure, on and on. He's a master of narrative form. And I also like pieces by Arreola, I like the anecdotes of Martín Luis Guzmán, I like the lyricism of some Nahua poetry, and I like the detail, adventure and sense of wonder of many sixteenth- and seventeenth-century cronistas [chroniclers] and travelers, some of whom—like Thomas Gage—wrote in English. But these works are only a part of what has affected my style and substance.

Do you perceive yourself and your work as political?

Stendhal once said that bringing politics into art is like "shooting a real gun during an opera. It's too strong for the medium." I'd say that politics is too weak for a literature (including film) that purports to be more than essays in narrative form. Human lives are richer than ideology, even if I might call myself a Marxist or Socialist or Humanist. Those are labels politicians, sociologists, and dogmatists use. Journalism, commentary, caricature, farce, and argument are more appropriate forms for political statements. I have done quite a few journalistic pieces for just such purposes. The other night, for example, I had dinner with a forty-eight-year-old man from Uruapan, Michoacán—a bitter, overworked, and obviously exploited cement worker. I won't go into his whole story because I doubt if I could ever do it justice as anything more than a simple anecdote. And it's my nature to want to make what deeply affects me something "literary"—something powerfully, emotionally affective. Instead, as I've done so often, I turn to reporting, noting, arguing, more journalism; it's an established, predictable form for factual accuracy. Also, "fixing" the story up in this case would be unnecessary; it seemed quite strong at the time of its telling.

In other words, I try to confine my overt political thoughts and actions to more appropriate and, in the end, more effective arenas: the classroom, newspapers, magazines, picket lines, and bumper stickers. If political persuasion is a product of some of my imaginary writing, I only hope that the writing is expressed with great subtlety and is not shrill and simplistic. And if someone interprets a piece as pure escapism, maybe it is—for a sentence or two. Am I writing *The Hobbit* or *Lord of the Rings*?

Does the Chicano author have anything in common with the majority group writers? Differences?

Like all writers, we claim certain places in the mind; our work appeals to certain people at particular times—our works may even become fads. In this respect, we are like public persons everywhere—we come and we go. Regarding differences with so-called "mainstream" authors, I would say our uniqueness springs from our cultural background, which of course involves those thousands of common behavior patterns and attitudes that determine who we are as Chicanos. Also, our body of work is very small when compared to that of other ethnic or racial groups. Although our literary tradition is actually centuries long (if we include our Hispanic and Indian past), the growth of those creations with strong Anglo-American influences—especially stylistic influences—is a recent phenomenon. Not only do we increasingly express ourselves in English (or with a dominance of English syntax)—some of us have also adopted narrative devices popularized by Hemingway, Salinger, McCullers, Faulkner, or a thousand others, at school, on billboards, in magazines, on television, at work, and certainly in bed. That is, the living language around us more and more has become English. It is a language that we as Chicanos have only begun to explore and use well. By the way, in saying this, I'm not implying we "give up" our Spanish—that's a matter of personal choice and circumstances. I might add that for me, learning to speak and write Spanish well was a matter of personal pride and practicality. Cada uno por su cuenta. [To each his own.]

Does Chicano literature share common ground with Black literature?
Differences?

Thematically, I assume it does, but I haven't read that much by Black authors to give an answer I trust. The themes I'm thinking of are human misery, oppression, the "outsider's" or "invisible man's" view of white society, racism, identity loss, sacrifice, bondage. That is, some Chicanos also write a lot about the pisca [picking], poverty, the fields, boys growing to manhood (as in *Bless Me, Ultima,* . . . *y no se lo tragó la tierra,* and *Pocho*). And as for *sounding* like Blacks, just listen to Alurista do his Black shtick. The poets, I would think, are especially influenced by Black music and rhythms.

As for important differences, I think it's mainly in our humor, which can reveal so much about a people's general attitudes toward the usual problems of living. Unfortunately, there aren't too many Chicano authors that I know of who handle humor, satire, irony, and mockery well. Rivera in his story "El Pete Fonseca" or Chapo Meneses in his "Chavalo Encanicado" or the standup stage routines by José Montoya and Jesús Negrete— these are some of my favorites. I think they get to the essence of Chicano humor, which of course often has slightly different points and ways of expression than a lot of popular Mexican humor. Moreover, these guys frequently reach a wider, non-Chicano audience with almost the same impact they have on Chicanos. But what's most sad and yet hopeful at the same time is that some of the best, most incisive most humanly appealing humor I've *heard* is from women—but this is always in kitchens, classrooms, bailes [dances], or in stores. Not much in writing—so far.

Is there any relationship with the literature of other Spanish-speaking groups?

I can only speak for myself, and I would say yes, there is some connection and it has to do with a not-too-studied preference for the style, the atmosphere, you might say, the living, emotionally affecting depth of this atmosphere. It's in the gloomy forebodings of Horacio Quiroga's jungle stories, the broad compassion of Ciro Alegría's *El mundo es ancho y ajeno*, the urban solitude I feel when I read Mario Benedetti's stories, or the ominous, slightly mysterious movement of detail I feel in some pieces by José Donoso or something like "The Third Bank of the River" by João Guimarães Rosa. Or the perfect selection of metaphor, of essence of human conflicts in Juan Rulfo's stories. And for an explosion of sheer inventiveness, I'll always remember my sense of pleasure and wonder when I first discovered, page-by-careful-page, *Cien años de soledad*. That was in 1969, when I was in Venezuela. For me, García-Márquez transformed, *deepened* reality in so many of its aspects—tragic, humorous, adventurous, wondrous. The work was alive, entertaining at every word. There was nothing sloppy, facile, overly clever, belabored, preachy—all the things I detest in literature. I'm only talking about *Cien años*, because that's all of his writing I've really read and absorbed carefully. For me, it's a matter of *immediately* liking a story ambiente, direction, and voice; I felt that from the first line in *Cien años* about the boy who discovers ice. It's the same kind of wonder and fascination I feel when I read, or shall I say "share," discovery with the European cronistas of the exploration centuries. For instance, a few years ago I remember reading the Penguin edition of Richard Hakluyt's *Voyages and Discoveries* with the same pleasure and interest I experienced with the "discoveries and voyages" in human nature contained in *Cien años*. Oviedo, Cabeza de Vaca, Sahagún, Durán, Garcilaso de la Vega, the Portuguese cronistas, they are all storehouses of life—full of commentary, science, ignorance, brutality, eroticism, comedy, on and on. I suppose such time-and-place trips help give me a wider perspective on the present, and of course it's bound to effect my own fictional work.

Getting back to contemporary writers, I'd like to say I don't care too much for a lot written by Mario Vargas Llosa, Carlos Fuentes, José Lezama Lima, José Donoso—mostly because I find certain works too cerebral, propped by artifice, too "planned," sometimes too dense. But I'm sure my own limitations prevent me from liking a particular novel or story. Much of a story's successful effect on me also depends on my present circumstances and state of mind. Years ago when I read Peter Mathiesen's *At Play in the Fields of the Lord*, it struck me as strongly as *Cien años* or Faulkner's *Wild Palms* or *Light in August*—yet I tried reading it the other day and nothing happened. In fact, I wanted to edit the long, dense sentences. On the other hand, I've tried reading work by Rosario Castellanos without much success, yet I know that someday *Oficio de tinieblas*, for example, will have its strong effect on me.

As for other Latinos in the U.S., I liked Piri Thomas's first book, *Down These Mean Streets*, and a few Puerto Rican poets, on the continent and on the green island. There's also a lot I'm not aware of that I might like.

Does Chicano literature have a distinctive perspective on life? What effect does it have on the literature?

Crazy questions. I would think so. I would also hope this "distinctive perspective" would be evident in our best work.

Does Chicano literature improve communication between Chicanos and Anglo Americans?

If by "communication" you mean discussion, yes, I think our work does do that. However, I haven't seen much evidence that it improves understanding between Chicanos and Anglos. Right now, our better stories, novels, and poems are not much more than curiosities to the "mainstream" literary folks in this country (I mean critics, publishers, teachers, reviewers, and readers). With few exceptions, I still think it's generally true that only Chicanos are interested in what Chicanos write. That is, for the most part we're talking to ourselves. The causes of this situation

have to do with the attitudinal barriers of the country's magazine and book-publishing conglomerates, literary agents, literature teachers, commercial book distributors, and bookstore
managers. Some Chicanos call it racism. I'd call it ignorance and
the fear of losing money or trying something new.

*Does Chicano literature reevaluate, attack, or subvert the value sys-
tem of the majority society? Is it a revolutionary literature?
Thematically? Technically?*

As I said, we're mostly writing to ourselves, so what effect can
our work have on readers outside our community? I've seen
cases of tremendous momentary effect on mixed audiences by
Chicano poets. But lasting or deep impressions left by written
works—who knows? I mean, take a writer like Kafka, or better
yet, Traven. Forty years ago nobody but John Huston and the
Treasure of the Sierra Madre film crew had ever heard of him.
Now he's popularized for all sorts of reasons—profits, politics,
aesthetics. So who's to say right now what some Chicano's literary output will be used for in the future, ten or forty years from
now—regardless of what the author might have intended in the
first place. Whether or not some of us "subvert the majority
value system" or pose as revolutionary or angry writers, certainly some Chicano writers attempt this. The intentions are obvious. As for effects, if any, I think it's too soon to say. Personally, when someone says they liked *Tamazunchale*, if the
person is a writer too, I'd like to think that what the book does
thematically or technically would inspire him or her to explore
this or that new avenue of literary experience and skill.

Perhaps our major contribution so far has been one of character and location. Our characters have rarely been seen in the
stories of American mainstream literature (usually in a derogatory or simplistic portrayal); the locations we depict also have
seldom been seen and expressed from an "insider's" perspective.
Lastly, the humor I mentioned before—of some writers and especially some teatros [theatre troupes]—is unique.

*What problems have you encountered in publishing? Were they ra-
cially founded?*

I don't have much trouble getting my pieces published in Chicano or small-press magazines. Beyond that—the commercial

houses—I have the same problems every new writer has. I just try to keep writing and not think about the notion that writing must be salable before it can be good.

Are Chicanos at a disadvantage in trying to practice the art of writing?

In a sense, yes—because it's so easy to pigeonhole us. In this country every artist is inevitably reduced to an epithet. This may be deserved, but I would like to think a novelita like *Tamazunchale* transcended the labels ethnic, Chicano, magical realist, or fantasist.

What are the most outstanding qualities of Chicano literature? Weaknesses?

I realize you're trying to get at the essence of Chicano expression. All I can provide is opinion, even though I believe it's much too soon to answer your question. Actually the outstanding qualities you mention are the same ones found in good writing everywhere—surprise, invention, insight, on and on. The same is true for the so-called weaknesses. Concerning specific Chicano works, I tend to like works that entertain and provoke, and I have my favorites—just as there are a lot of things I drop after the first sentence. This is probably a journalist's habit of scanning newspaper leads, and if the first sentence grabs me, I stay with the story. If not, I skim on. In fact, I operate in my own writing as well as my reading with a lot of little habits or "rules." Some I wish I could follow. Steinbeck said you ought to be able to tell your story in one sentence before you even begin your novel. Faulkner said "take a chance." Things like that—they all get thrown out the window when I'm hot into the flow of something. Myself, I could never pass on any serious advice to any other writer. Maybe that's why I don't like to read criticism; it usually turns out to be prescriptive. A lot of Marxist pieces do this, which only tells me those persons know very little about the creative process. Their remarks are very similar to the hustling producers of commercial TV or the publishers who scour the land for still another potboiler novel. And if they don't find the moneymaking script or book, they simply hire a writer to crank one out. A lot of critics, also, would like to prescribe and dispense.

What are the milestones so far in Chicano literature?

I would say Tomás Rivera is a tremendously careful and perceptive writer with a wonderful touch for humor. His . . . *tierra* is certainly a milestone for fine Chicano writing. Villarreal's *Pocho* is of course important historically and for its strong sense of place and character movement. Likewise—as with *Pocho*—Anaya's *Bless Me, Ultima* has set records for popularity. These two books each tell a rich, appealing story with characters that readers come to know and discuss and seldom forget. Also, Rolando Hinojosa's *Klail City* deserves mention, especially since its winning of the Casa de Américas prize. And Luis Valdez and the Teatro Campesino are still erecting milestones, the last one with the superlative *Zoot Suit*. Of the Chicano poets I've read or heard, Gary Soto—of those who write exclusively in English—recently has made a few literary waves by winning several highly competitive prizes for his work.

What is the future of Chicano literature: distinctiveness, or the de-emphasis of the distinctive characteristics?

I can't answer this, and I'd be very interested to know who of your other interviewees can.

Who are the leaders among Chicano writers, and why?

With only a few dozen writers who've published books to date, I think that's a premature question. Besides, it sounds too competitive, as if we were digits in the daily Dow Jones quotes. I'd rather think of us all writing, creating in some sort of giant, unorganized collective effort, all of us adding our very best talents to an entire, diverse body of Chicano expression.

Tino Villanueva

In 1972 a small volume of poetry was published in New York: *Hay otra voz Poems*. Since then its author, Tino Villanueva, has steadily grown in the admiration of the critics, his fellow poets, and the readers. He has been included in the major anthologies and appeared in literary journals in this country and Spain and Mexico. He is a respected critic and a promising short story writer. Less prolific than his peers, Villanueva is a consistent, but careful and patient writer, in no rush to publish a poem until he has reworked it to his satisfaction.

Hay otra voz shows him to be an exacting taskmaster of language. Often he employs in a key position a word which contains possible connotations which ironically undermine and complicate what at first glance might seem obvious and simple. There is a constant irony underlying his words. His central images represent time, death, and silence; his central preoccupation is the disappearance of living beings (or a culture) without having really lived at all, or at least without having left us a record of passage. The structure of *Hay otra voz* allows us to read it as an extended *ars poetica* in which Villanueva relates and documents his poetic development: in Part I, the aspiring writer experiments with literary techniques, learning his craft, while pondering existential questions; in Part II, declaring himself a poet, he questions his function in the world and, finally, decides in favor of social relevance; Part III, titled "Mi Raza," contains poems in which the poet applies the skill learned earlier to themes relevant to Chicanos.* Yet, though he calls his work social realism, he anchors his poetry in imagery, never forgetting lessons gleaned from the contemporary poets he admires, especially Dylan Thomas, to

---

* See Bruce-Novoa, "The Other Voice of Silence: Tino Villaneuva," in *Modern Chicano Writers*, ed. Joseph Sommers and T. Ybarra-Frausto (Englewood Cliffs, N.J.: Prentice-Hall, 1979).

Tino Villanueva 255

whom he pays tribute in several poems. Villanueva is the faithful voice of his people, but he continues true to his particular influences.

Like Bernice Zamora, Villanueva does not fear open reference to the poets who most impress him. He allows them to reverberate in his poetry, confident that his Chicanismo will surface on its own when not expressly evoked. As we could expect, this has brought charges that he is not always writing as a Chicano. Villanueva, however, has a number of "committed" works, including a broadside poem, "Speak Up, Chicano," which one can read seriously, or, as I suspect, as a tongue-in-cheek response to those who call for a literature accessible to the masses. Irony is his forte.

Tino Villanueva responded to the questionnaire in writing in the spring of 1975, and chose to make only minor revisions when he reviewed the translation in 1978. The translation was done by Margarita Vargas.

When and where were you born?

I was born December 11, 1941, in the small town of San Marcos, in the state of Texas.

Describe your family background and your present situation.

Well, there is a lot to say and, frankly, I don't know where to start. I'll tell you that my father, although he tried to learn English, worked the rugged fields of the towns that surrounded my home town; and my mother helped him. From there they settled down in San Marcos, where I was born later. My father became a laborer and my mother stayed at home, except when she worked as a seamstress during World War II. That was not enough for them to be able to meet the economic demands, and since there really was no industry in my little town, well, traveling was the order. And in this way, my family joined the endless wave of migrant workers who traveled all through Texas, and to Colorado, Michigan, Illinois, North Dakota, etc., following the harvests.

My father now works in a hotel in San Antonio, although he has also worked in a civil service job with the post office; and my mother has worked for fifteen years as a clerk in a clothing store in San Marcos.

I am an only child. Two other boys died shortly after birth. My childhood was like that of any other kid in the barrio. We went to school; only, sooner or later, in complete frustration they dropped out.

I remember that wherever we found room, whether in our yards or on the gravel streets (which were really extensions of our yards), we played a lot of football and marbles; but we mainly played baseball. There were several of us who aspired to one day be baseball players, like our heroes in the big leagues. It was an ardent fantasy to overcome our immediate economic misery. Whenever it was possible we got jobs here and there, wherever we could, selling newspapers on the street, washing dishes in restaurants, working in gas stations, mowing the Anglos' grass, and things like that. But this didn't pay much, of course. Therefore, most of us were forced to go with our families to work harvesting; to weed, to pick cotton, tomatoes, potatoes, onions, cucumbers, beans, etc., all over the United States, as I told you before. But this didn't last more than six months altogether, time during which we went to school if our parents insisted we go.

In high school I excelled a little in sports: baseball and track. I can't say the same for my academic life. But I had no trouble graduating from high school in 1960, and after that I started working in my home town in a furniture factory, which providentially had transferred from San Antonio. It didn't pay much, but it offered a secure job, in contrast to the instability of having to work the crops. I worked there for three years before I was drafted into the army, which sent me for two years (1964–1966) to the Panama Canal Zone. And it was there that I took two history courses from Florida State University [by extension]; the credits were accepted later at Southwest Texas State University [in San Marcos], from which I graduated in 1969 with a Bachelor of Arts degree. I got my M.A. at the University of Buffalo in 1971. Now I am a doctoral candidate at Boston University and teach at Wellesley College.

When did you first begin to write?

I started writing my first year in college at Southwest Texas State University. At the beginning my poetry came out in exaggerated rhymes, dripping with feigned sentimentalism and a self-evoked nostalgia. I still have them put away somewhere, though.

A little later I was recommended to read Dylan Thomas, Ferlinghetti, Ginsberg, Corso, Eliot, and Cummings. It was in them that I discovered the imagery of the poetic language of the twentieth century.

What kind of books did you read in your formative years?

So I bought a book by each one of the poets I just mentioned. Of all of them, Thomas began to fascinate me: his rhythms and very resonant verbal magic attracted me very much. Much later, and on my own, I read Lorca and Vallejo. Darío I studied in class.

What is the extent of your studies?

As I just told you, I graduated from high school in 1960, received my Bachelor of Arts in 1969, and my M.A. in 1971.

Has formal education helped or hindered you as a writer?

I can tell you that the instruction that I have received has made me understand and appreciate literature. I don't always agree with my professors, but they have made me see the delights of literature. All of this literary consciousness-raising continues pushing me to write with the same vigor as my favorite authors.

Which was the predominant language in your home as a child? Which do you speak more fluently now?

Look, in my home Spanish was always heard more than English and it was the language that I first suckled on, as we say. When I entered kindergarten and in the following grades, I quickly learned English equally well as Spanish. Now I harbor the fantasy of being a completely bilingual person with the goal of improving in both languages.

Does Chicano literature have a particular language or idiom?

Well, not a "language" per se, but a particularly alive and vibrant dialect, like the one we would hear in Castile, Peru, Mexico, or the Caribbean. I am referring to a Chicano dialect which corresponds to a Mexican Spanish (without forgetting and excluding the extremely rich linguistic contribution of the Pachuco and

the expressive neologisms of English origin). Of course, not
every author resorts to the Chicano dialect and there's no reason
why they should. A Floyd Salas or a John Rechy would say it in
English; a Miguel Méndez in standard Spanish; an Alurista or a
Ricardo Sánchez would say it in Chicano, so to speak. But this,
of course, doesn't exhaust all the possibilities. My "Que hay otra
voz" (I'm referring to the poem) is a fusion of Chicano dialect
with standard English and Spanish.

---

*How do you perceive your role as a writer vis-à-vis: (a) the Chicano
community or Movement; (b) U.S. society; (c) literature itself?*

With respect to the Chicano community and the Movement, I
feel that my role is to display, as literally as possible, our situation as I see it. Our reality of the barrio (of all the barrios, because there are many) has to come to light so that everyone,
including Chicanos, can know about it. It must be understood
that we are not a homogeneous but a heterogeneous group, composed of different ways of living and thinking; from different socioeconomic levels. Our situation in the Texas Río Grande
Valley is very different from that of Albuquerque or Chicago; our
concerns in Iowa City are not the same as those of Billings,
Montana; and our situation in San Antonio is not the same as
Denver's or Delano's. Therefore, my role is to contribute what I
know best; what I have lived and what I am living so that everyone, including my Raza, will know me, and thus all of us arrive
at a knowledge/understanding in the spirit of fraternity, of Car-
nalismo [brotherhood], as we like to say.

Regarding United States society my role is to try to make
them see that there are other American experiences, other pages,
another voice equally as valid as that of any other "American"
writer: Whitman, Saul Bellow, James T. Farrell, Langston
Hughes, Truman Capote, John Dos Passos.

Regarding literature, I only wish to be faithful to It. I hope
that my writing is literature and not reportage in verse. But of
course, we would have to determine what is literature; but this
is somebody else's job.

What is the place of Chicano literature within U.S. literature?

Well, its place is to be among many others, another page, previously forgotten, but very much a part of the "American experi-

ence." Until recently United States literature was an exclusionary literature, and in a certain sense it still is, but I believe that with the Chicano Renaissance we have made ourselves felt. We still have a long way to go, though.

What is the relationship of Chicano literature to Mexican literature?

I wouldn't be able to tell you because I haven't read that much Chicano and Mexican literature. From what I have seen, there are themes that relate to each other: that of the Indian, for example; of oppression, in other words, the social. And then there are those who write "traditional" and "vanguard" poetry.

Do you perceive yourself and your work as political?

As I see it, I write from two aesthetics. On one side my poetry expresses something which could be called generically "historical realism"; and on the other side I have a lot of poems which deal with time, death, love, beauty, and other intimist themes.

Does the Chicano author have anything in common with the majority group writers? Differences?

I wouldn't be able to tell you what other writers think. I can only limit myself to what I have attempted to do. I have several poems, among them "My Certain Burn towards Pale Ash," "Cycle Bound," and "This the Place," which in addition to the themes, pick up certain rhythms, cadences, and resonances from Dylan Thomas. It was a mimetism on my part. I have other poems which echo Ferlinghetti, César Vallejo, and others.

The differences are obvious, that as Chicano (bilingual) writers we have three ways of writing: in standard English; in standard Spanish; and in our dialect, if we want. And then there are the multiple combinations which can be taken from there.

The themes, especially that of the Indian (that Indian who makes up half of us) are also different. In American literature, the author is more of a spectator with respect to the theme of the Indian, and not a participant in it like many of the Chicano writers.

Does Chicano literature share common ground with Black literature? Differences?

Yes, in the use of themes and myths as well as in the levels of language. I'm referring to the social themes; to the use of African myths, while there are Chicano writers who resort to Aztec myths; and to the use of the dialect which corresponds to each one: the Blacks use the "Black idiom," and we make use of our only dialect, the Chicano dialect.

As far as differences go, it strikes me that the Blacks have their "gospels" and we don't, while we have the "corrido" and they don't. I can't think of any other differences at the moment, although I confess that I have never given it much thought.

Is there any relationship with the literature of other Spanish-speaking groups?

Maybe it resembles more that of the Puerto Ricans. The spirit of social commitment is the same. I see this in Víctor Hernández Cruz, Pedro Pietri, and Piri Thomas.

Does Chicano literature have a distinctive perspective on life? What effect does it have on the literature?

If you mean different from American literature, I would say yes. But we would have to distinguish between white Anglo Saxon American literature, Jewish American literature, and Black American literature. I don't like to classify literature in that way, but it is undeniable that these two groups come from different cultures. Each one has its own concerns. And I would say at this point that these two ethnic groups harbor the same concerns as the Chicano Renaissance literature. In this sense there is a close relationship. The other literature, not the Black or the Jewish, seems more egocentric, more confessional, and thus less humanistic, the exception being the latest wave of feminist literature. I understand that this is a very general and facile way of perceiving our American literature, but this, in generic terms, is what I see.

As far as the perspective on Chicano literature nowadays, I can say that it is "the word in time," as Machado said; it is a humanized literature in which the collectivity of a group reveals itself through its passions and frustrations, its energies and weaknesses, its fantasies and nightmares. But I once again insist that there is, with equal rigor, that vein of traditional and vanguard orientation.

Does Chicano literature improve communication between Chicanos and Anglo Americans?

As I was saying a moment ago, what we write should be literature. Therefore, if we're going to write literature, then without a doubt we're going to break the linguistic/racial/cultural barriers, and will thus improve communication between us and the rest of the world. And this should be one of our goals: to write literature. Communication and human ties will logically come later.

Does Chicano literature reevaluate, attack, or subvert the value system of the majority society? Is it a revolutionary literature? Thematically? Technically?

Well, yes. Socially oriented literature reevaluates, attacks, and subverts (and confronts and denounces) that system of values. There's no need to go any further than to mention *Yo soy Joaquín*, which does all of this: which questions the entire United States society and attacks the most pernicious part of the puritan ethic, which is the most sacred value of that culture. Not all of our literature being written today makes this clear, but it is in a certain sense a literature "in time" and of confrontation. And sometimes revolutionary when it encourages a certain (our) Cause. (There come to mind the Teatro Campesino and the infinite number of "corridos" of social tone, both of which spring from the very fertile popular soil and which are obviously two revolutionary expressions.)

With regard to technique, what strikes me first is its aesthetics, which are revolutionary: the practice of utilizing two languages in the same flow of a poem—Spanish and English. Philip Ortego calls this the "binary phenomenon." This is nothing new if one thinks of Eliot and Pound, who use Greek as well as French and other languages in their poetry so much. But they did not do it as often (and there is no reason why they should have), and besides, it is an "artificial" composition, or at least artificious, although certainly intellectually valid. I say "artificial" because although they may have been bilingual they were not bicultural; they did not live from day to day two cultures, two languages.

On the contrary, notice how the majority of Chicano authors express themselves more naturally, because it's the way they talk (and here I am referring more to poetry). Thus, they offer us two worlds, two resonances, and two linguistic spaces, sometimes in harmony, sometimes in tension. And those who know Nahuatl even write in three languages. That is unheard of in the rest of American literature.

What problems have you encountered in publishing? Were they racially founded?

Well, yes, I have had some problems. Frankly, I don't know if on previous occasions what hindered my first attempts to publish were racial questions or not. Each publishing house has its own literary criteria. Besides, it should be taken into account that, as I didn't have a well-known name, the publishers weren't going to risk a lot of money to publish me.

Are Chicanos at a disadvantage in trying to practice the art of writing?

Well, I said that American literature has been, and in part continues to be, an exclusive literature. Nowadays, even though we've published a few things here and there, we still have not appeared in the prestigious anthologies which are the ones used in public schools and universities. And even though there are a lot of anthologies of Chicano literature, what we need is for publishing houses to start publishing more manuscripts of individual authors: poetry, novels, collections of short stories, etc. During these last few years we have begun to take giant strides forward but still have not reached the territory of what is literarily acceptable according to the publishing houses most preferred by the educational institutions. Our progress is still in movement.

What are the most outstanding qualities of Chicano literature? Weaknesses?

First, the "binary phenomenon." I think that this part of our literature (specifically, our poetry), is doubly forceful when written in two languages. When two languages are utilized, what's expressed reveals more nuances and, therefore, it is richer, it is dynamic. And this should not be called "Spanglish" as the sterilizing linguists usually do. More than anything it is an aesthetic not only viable but linguistically and poetically invigorating.

(But we should remember that this literature is generally for the bilingual reader, specifically for Chicanos, the majority of whom are bilingual/bicultural. It can be said, then, that this portion of our literature is intended for a relatively limited group.) Weaknesses? Well, sometimes I think we put forth a shrill voice too much and this bothers me. And I believe that even I have done it in perhaps "Non-Ode to the Texas Rangers" and in "I Too Have Walked My Barrio Streets." Although I could defend these two poems, since they are based on an elaborated imagery; besides, literature is a cathartic act as well, isn't it true?

What I want to point out in answering your question is that we lament our misery a lot, too much. What bothers me the most is that it stays lamentation and doesn't necessarily become literature. We have to go beyond lamentation for this expression to endure. We have to transcend. Sometimes we spend too much time saying, "Oh, poor us, look at how we've been treated!" I feel that there are other ways to say the same thing—and communicate a deep and sincere emotion—without always bewailing.

What are the milestones so far in Chicano literature?

The founding of Quinto Sol Publications has undoubtedly been one of the most important happenings for Chicano literature. And later, the rest of the publishing houses which also began to work in favor of our Renaissance letters.

And from there, the key works: *Pocho* by Villareal; *Actos* by Luis Valdez; . . . *y no se lo tragó la tierra* by Rivera; *Yo soy Joaquín* by Corky; and a thick bunch of poems by Alurista, Montoya, Ricardo Sánchez, Raúl Salinas, and others. In addition, a few isolated short stories which have, for some reason or another, been overlooked by the critics. I'm referring to "One Week in the Life of Manuel Hernández" by Nick Vaca, "Waiting for Zamora" by Philip Ortego, and "Un hijo del sol" by Genaro Gonzales.

And, finally, the symposiums in which the critics, with their presentations, have put forward observations and doubts about our literature. Also add to this the festivals which have been celebrated in Aztlán and the Midwest, but with singular importance those of Floricanto so fervently urged on by Alurista.

What is the future of Chicano literature: distinctiveness, or the de-emphasis of the distinctive characteristics?

Look, I frankly don't know. Each artist will have to analyze and later determine his own condition as far as his creative work goes. Whatever happens, our literature cannot but join the great literature of the world, and let it be made clear that it has already been doing it. What we need is more objective as well as sensitive critics, and translators who will translate our work.

And I don't think we're ever going to lose the flavor and the knowledge of our culture, that is, our two cultures.

Who are the leaders among Chicano writers, and why?

At the moment, the following: Alurista, for having shown us the vigor of the "binary phenomenon"; Montoya, for his verbal concentration; Rivera, for his faithful and moving portraits of our meager infrahistory; Raúl Salinas, for having taken us on his two semi-epic trips (in reality it's all one: "A Trip through the Mind Jail" and "Journey II"); Ricardo Sánchez, for his incessant and disturbing flow of words (consciousness); and Corky, for having put our situation in perspective. But remember, please, that I have not read everything, and besides, there are works which I would like to reread before putting forth my opinions.

Alurista

Alurista is consistently referred to by critics as the Chicano poet who has made the most significant contributions and innovations, and by the majority of his peers as the most influential among them. He has published three collections of poetry—*Floricanto en Aztlán* (1971), *Nationchild Plumaroja* (1972), and *Timespace Huracán* (1976)—appears in every major Chicano anthology, and has also published essays and theatre.

Thematically, he is the originator and main exponent of the Amerindian ideology of Aztlán, which synthesizes a Chicano identity, drawing from the Mexican indigenous heritage and the actual realities of barrio living in the United States. With Aztlán, Alurista gives a mytho-spiritual dimension to Chicano nationalism. Although in the earliest poems the indigenous presence was mainly Nahuatl-Mayan—a fact decried by his detractors for its supposed irrelevance to Chicano reality—he later evolved toward a Third World emphasis on one hand, and the inclusion of indigenous peoples more geographically related to the U.S. Southwest on the other. To appreciate the totality of his vision and avoid erroneous impressions of him as an exoticist, one should read Alurista's books in toto and in order. They are like programmed instruction manuals. He begins *Floricanto* with messianic assurance, asking "when raza," intimating that he already knows our destiny and wants us to catch up to him. What follows, in *Floricanto* and the other books, is his program for salvation through a mytho-historical ethnic affirmation, not devoid of political implications.

Stylistically, Alurista popularized and legitimated the interlingual text, combining Spanish and English in one poem, producing new tensions at all the linguistic levels of language. He was the first to utilize language as many Chicanos speak it in everyday conversation; at least, apparently he did, for we lack a thor-

ough linguistic analysis of his work or, for that matter, of any Chicano's work.

Another of Alurista's roles was highly significant: he organized the annual Festival Floricanto, the major event on the Chicano literary calendar, which for several years brought together writers—critical and creative, established and unknown—to share their work not only with each other, but also with the Chicano community. Although the festival has degenerated in the last few years and has now been eclipsed by the Canto al Pueblo festival of arts, Alurista deserves recognition for his pioneering effort.

Our estimate of Alurista's work may change in the future, but it is indisputable that during the first decade of Chicano literature he has been a vital, significant force in shaping events, toning our sensibilities, expanding our imagery lexicon, and catalyzing our literary production; to many he is the poet laureate of Aztlán.

Alurista recorded the answers to the questionnaire in March 1975 in Austin, Texas. True to his interlingual style, he responded to the questions in a mixture of English and Spanish. Unlike most of the others who mix the languages, Alurista's mixture consisted in much more than an occasional Spanish phrase. Simple parenthetical translation was ruled out in favor of translating the Spanish directly; the former would have almost doubled the length of the text. To convey some sense of the original mixture, the translated portions have been italicized. Translation was done by Isabel Barraza. The final version was edited by Alurista in September 1979.

When and where were you born?

I was born in the womb of my mother. *I emerged from the belly of my mother.* As to when, it was after nine months, like everybody else. I don't like to get into date and place of birth; *it identifies one in a manner which to me seems unreal.* What really counts is the experience and the creativity that one is able to derive from it, *don't you think?*

Describe your family background and your present situation.

Well, my mother was born in Veracruz and her mother in Yucatán. On my father's side, well he was born in Linares, Nuevo

León, *and he is a northerner. How my father and mother
united, who knows? They say, God creates them and they
unite; well, God created them and they united.* Let's go into
where I was born, *which has no real importance,* though keep
this to yourself, because I really don't think it's that relevant. *I
was born in the Lake of Texcoco in* what is known today as
*Mexico City, in '47, on the 8th of August, and grew up in the
states of Morelos and Guerrero.* I came to California *when I was
twelve or thirteen* and I've been there ever since; until I got here
to Austin, in August of 1974.

*I am married. My wife's name is Irene. I have two children,
a five-year-old boy named Tizoc and a girl named Maoxiim.*

[Since the interview, Alurista has returned to California,
where he is a doctoral candidate in Latin American literature at
the University of California, San Diego. He divorced his first
wife and has since remarried. He and his second wife, the poet
Xelina, edit the literary magazine *Maize.* Xelina and Alurista
have two children of their own: Zamna and Zahi.]

___

When did you first begin to write?

I think I first began to write very early in my days. I remember
having picked up the pen to write poetry in the second grade. By
the third grade I was already *reciting for the school and writing
poetry for Mother's Day, and all of that.* So I started writing very
early. Of course when I started, I began to discover very quickly
the power of the word. *The word is truly a very flexible instrument and very powerful, very creative. I immediately became
aware of* many things one could do with the word. More often
than not I realized *that he who had the word, could move,
could do this or that, etc.* Communication became a very important thing to me in my early days. So I've been writing from the
second or third grade. *We could say that I began at eight or
nine. Of course, in those days I was playing or experimenting
with the word. It is a discovery about which even to this day I
am happy.* I continued writing and it was not really until 1966–
67 *that I realized the necessity of taking my poetry seriously
and it was at that time that I began to develop poetry so that it
could be published. And it was also at that time that I realized
that I no longer spoke solely for myself;* anything that I put
down would reflect in one way or another on our people, our
Chicano people. Since then I have taken my writing very se-

riously and I consider it not an inspirational situation—even though in my early days in the sixth grade I used to think that I needed to have inspiration to write. Now it's more like hard work. *One has to work very hard to develop what one wishes to develop. And no matter how hard one works*—and that is the paradox of the poet—*one never feels that one has said what one wanted,* and to that degree our work is never done, it's never really finished. We put it out for publication because we simply don't want to work on it any longer, *but* we could work on a poem the rest of our lives and yet never feel that the poem was complete or that it says everything we want to say.

What kind of books did you read in your formative years?

Well, I went to seminary school for about three months—that's all I lasted—and I was going to be a priest; hence, my reading in those days was very much religious. *I would read a lot of catechism, the Bible, etc.,* but upon becoming disillusioned with the Catholic Church, I turned to the study of other religions *within Christianity*—Protestantism. I started reading *Luther, Calvin; all of those people.* I quickly discovered that Christianity was not the only religion in the world, so I got into reading Buddhism, Hinduism, Taoism, Zoroastrianism, Islam. I was interested in finding myself. I thought I had an easy answer by going into the *seminary, but I quickly realized that that was no answer, truly, because the Church was a big business.* They wanted to train me for something I didn't intend. In my early days—junior high days—I was reading about religions.

In high school I felt a little alienated, *because I began to read philosophy: Plato, Socrates, Plotinus, Descartes, all of the traditional philosophers, classics of the western tradition.* That alienated me from my *companions* in high school, *because everyone was in the* rah-rah trip of football games, and I was not into that at all. As I followed my own path, I started reading eastern philosophers.

There are numerous people that I can say have affected my life deeply. However, I don't think any *one* of them can be given absolute credit. I think it was a conglomeration of many, because *I like to read. There was a period, when I was in* high school and the first two or three years of college, *when I would read a book per week—now I don't do it. They were books on philosophy, on religion, metaphysics. Then I got a little into sci-*

ence, trying to tie up the spiritual world and the material world. *A little bit of chemistry, biology, mathematics.* This was over and above those responsibilities which the educational institutions outlined for me.

What is the extent of your studies?

I got a Bachelor's degree in psychology. Psychology became an enthralling subject for me, because *after having studied philosophy, religion, metaphysics, and a little science* on my own, I was very interested in understanding the soul of man and woman, their inner life. For that reason I graduated in psychology. When I first went to college, I started studying business administration; in about a month I realized it wasn't my bag. From business administration I jumped to religion. I couldn't follow that up because people were *very dogmatic.* The same was true in philosophy. I jumped into sociology. I couldn't even take that. *Then* social welfare, *because within myself had awoken a need to channel my energies in a manner which would aid in the well-being of the rest. I wanted to change things. I wanted to help my brothers and my sisters.* I quickly realized that a social worker was not what I wanted to be. Finally I stumbled into psychology. While I was finishing my Bachelor's, I painted for about two or three years, which helped me keep my sanity. During those years, between painting and writing, my reading dropped from one book a week to one a month. Now I read one book every two months, *a book which interests me.* Now I try to learn more from people, from what I observe, more than from books.

Has formal education helped or hindered you as a writer?

I never found that schooling gave me any education. If anything, *it only certified the educational process; but in reality, my education was self-directed. I've learned more through my own direction than through my "teachers." I've also learned a great deal from life;* I like to observe. A writer has to be very observant. *One has to pay attention to things if one wants to learn.* Starting from the age of thirteen or fourteen, when I first came to California, *I became aware that* something was going on in the U.S. that was not particularly palatable. I experienced cultural shock, but it didn't really hit me until my first few years of college—1965, '66, '67. It was in those days that I became committed to my writing.

Formal education has attempted, if you will, to hinder my education. Schooling is where you are trained to follow directions, and as a poet, as a writer, as a creative person that is the last thing I wanted. I don't want to follow anyone else's structures, *no path that anyone would mark for me.* So in that way they didn't help me very much. Anything that has been accomplished has been in spite of formal schooling.

Which was the predominant language in your home as a child? Which do you speak more fluently now?

In my parents' house, *well, it was Spanish. English was not spoken, because although my father and my mother understood it, they hated it.* They will not speak English to any of us; even when they go to the store, *they only speak when they have to.* They say that it's a very dry, cold language, only suited for business transactions and things like that. As for my own *family, in my house Spanish and English are spoken.* I speak bilingually and I do it very deliberately when I speak to my son, who can now understand me. *I speak to him in English and in Spanish; I speak to him in Chicano Spanish* and Mexican Spanish; *I speak to him in Yankee English and sometimes I even throw him a little Black English, so that he'll get into it.* He's got to be hip; he's got to know what's happening. I want him to get a full view of what language is all about. Let him learn whatever language he wants to learn. As far as I'm concerned, he ought to know at least one form of Spanish and one form of English well, so he can communicate with anyone; that is, with Chicanos and Chicanas, as well as non-Spanish speakers.

Which more fluently? Now that will be hard to judge. I have deliberately exerted myself to become proficient in both languages, so that *it seems to me that both languages are natural to me, one the same as the other, truly. Even when it comes to the question of writing. I write and read in English and Spanish, and I do it very deliberately. I try to read a book in Spanish and one in English. I write bilingually.*

I don't want to brag, but I believe that I was the first modern Chicano writer who dared send bilingual work to an editor. I remember the reaction of one editor when I first gave him my poetry. *He said, "Listen, this is a pochismo. Why can't you write either in Spanish or in English?"* Or, "This doesn't look very good, and what's all this Black English you put in here? You ought to use correct English. *And all of these vatosisms or chicanoisms; that doesn't sound good; it's the decadence of our Spanish language." I told him, "Look, I am a writer and a poet. If you like it, publish it; and if not, don't fuck with me, leave me in peace."* He said he wouldn't publish trash like that when I first talked to him. However, *a week later he called me on the telephone and said, "Send me your work because it's going to be a hit."* So I sent him the work he wanted. I sent him about thirty pieces, out of which he published ten. After that, if I'm not mistaken, many Chicano and Chicana writers began to publish bilingually. And that was only a natural thing. I knew that this would happen; *that all that was needed was for someone to get the nerve and through sheer balls to say* this is the way I think, the way I write, *this is the way the people write and think, this is how they speak.* One of the responsibilities of the writer is to use the popular language. *In such a way that once that work was published I knew* that more people would begin to contribute at that level. That's exactly what happened. So my relationship to both languages is equally good.

Does Chicano literature have a particular language or idiom?

What truly makes chicano literature so rich and fertile is the fact that we can and do in fact write in Black English and Yankee English, in *Mexican Spanish and Chicano Spanish.* Many of us are beginning to restore, or bring to life, *some of the indigenous languages,* such as *Mayan and Nahuatl.* I try to do this in most of my work, at least the work published to date. *I use six languages:* Black English, Anglo English, Mexican Spanish, Chicano Spanish, Nahuatl, and Maya. So I really don't think there is a particular language in Chicano literature. We cover this full range in Chicano literature, the full range of colors, the full rainbow. *All of the sarape. It is one great sauce and that makes it all the tastier, don't you think?* That shows our versatility and multidimensional view of the world. That makes us stronger, a broadly based, more universal people. And as writers, that puts us in a completely different category in the history of world literature.

How do you perceive your role as a writer vis-à-vis: (a) the Chicano community or Movement; (b) U.S. society; (c) literature itself?

In regard to the Chicano community, or the Chicano Movement, as I said before, it was not until '66 or '67 that I realized the need to take my writing seriously. *I noticed immediately that in 1965, Mr. César Chávez, with his farmworkers' strike* throughout the nation, had started the Chicano civil rights movement. When that happened—between '65 and '67—I made my decision about using my writing skills, my *literature, as a means of communication.* I'm convinced that my *poetry reflects,* or at least I try deliberately to reflect the experience of our people. *I am not the author of my poetry, I am not the author of my words, my images or metaphors.* I am the weaver of these things. The people are the authors of the language; the people are the authors of the imagery, of the symbols. All I do is weave them together in such a way that our people can reflect themselves in them, can see themselves in them. *It seems to me that one of the functions of my poetry is to reflect popular experience. Another is to criticize the Movement, because the Chicano Movement if by far without fault.* There are many errors being committed, there are areas that call for improvement, and it is my responsibility as a poet to be critical of that development. I don't consider myself a writer that isolates himself and hides away from life to write his work. *Quite the contrary. I like being in the thick of it, being involved.* If there is going to be a protest, I'll be out there. I want to be right in the middle of it. I want to feel it, I don't just want to read about it. Thus, I have found myself involved more often than not as an organizer at various levels. I worked with the Brown Berets, Mexican American Associations, MECHA [Movimiento Estudiantil Chicano de Aztlán—Chicano Student Movement of Aztlán]. I helped develop Chicano Studies and *Chicano Studies Centers, cultural centers.* My participation is not as a withdrawn observer, but as a fully involved, immersed *writer. It seems that in that way my poetry is more real, more honest, much clearer. It better reflects the reality of our community which finds itself in the struggle.*

With respect to U.S. society, of course I'm very critical of the United States of North America. I consider this country to be an empire. I am convinced that one of our responsibilities is to be very, very critical of North American society. Expose *the*

farces, political, economic, and social, which exist in this country.
As to literature in general, I consider myself a revolutionary writer, on two levels. On the first level, my literature is revolutionary because it advocates a revolution, which does not mean, in my terms, a violent revolution. I am convinced that you cannot put out fire with fire. *That is why if these imperialist Yankees have succeeded in controlling through the use of violence and their gold, we are going to have to beat them in another fashion. We have to beat them with peace and not with violence, rather with the will of the people.* Second, it engages in revolutionizing the poetic form. I try to develop *new forms of expressing our thoughts, our emotions.* And I try to do it in such a way that we can afford ourselves the widest, the largest possible range of experience. I like to see many levels in my poetry. I deliberately try to develop a multidimensional reality.

What is the place of Chicano literature within U.S. literature?

There is a great argument going on today as to where Chicano lit belongs. The people in the Spanish departments and the people in the English departments are the traditional departments that engage in this kind of discussion. Both of them invariably consider our literature as subculture literature, as minority literature. I think they're wrong. I don't think Chicano literature can be properly classified as Spanish or English literature, or North American literature. We use both languages. It's a little bit of both and it's neither. It's something in itself. *It has its own existence and gives its own flower. It has its own root, and its root, without doubt, from my point of view, is indigenous.* Poetry is the traditional means of philosophical, theological, and scientific expression in the Indian world. *The Indians wrote in poetry, not because they did not write prose, but simply because they thought that poetry was more realistic, more dialectic, more dynamic. In prose* we have a linear construction of the universe. *It has its beginning and it has its end, its subject and predicate.* In poetry we find reality depicted in its dynamic sense. Everything moves, changes in the world. Everything is experiencing constant transformation. Nothing is static. We are constantly dying and constantly being reborn. This applies to our material world, our psychological world as well as our spiritual world. *Our thoughts spin. Some die, others are born. Our cells die and are born. Therefore everything is in constant motion.* Hence, *poetry is the best medium for reflecting this objective reality, subjective and concrete, and abstract also. I don't think that one can separate these terms.* I do believe that poetry is the best means to communicate reality, its dynamism, the changing nature of reality, its moving nature, *because poetry neither begins nor ends, and it always changes, rises, transforms itself. It always has more levels than even the author, when he writes it,* intends to put in it. I find that when I read my poetry, *I discover levels which I had not consciously thought about, but there they are.* That is the beauty of *poetry.* The continuum, the process is what is important in poetry. It gives us a glimpse of what reality is all about. Reality in motion.

What is the relationship of Chicano literature to Mexican literature?

I don't think Chicano literature is the northern extension of Mexican literature either. If we were to place our literature in some context, it would be better to place it in the context of Latin America, including, but not exclusively, Mexico. We're talking about Central and Latin American literature. It best fits within that context, *above all because Latin American writers today are in the vanguard in the literary world.* They are producing the most creative works in world literature today. Chicano literature is part of that historical time-space, *but our literature promises more than any of the literatures of Central or South America.* We are the belt between Anglo America and Indohispanic America. Descriptions of reality can come out of hearts that cannot come from any Latin American writers, simply because they are out there. They talk about colonialism and imperialism, *but we are inside of the shark.* That gives us a different perspective. We look at it from the inside and the outside, because although we're inside we know that we don't belong, or at least they don't let us belong. We have a dual view. *Our position in historical time-space is a missionary one,* whether we want it or not. We can either choose to assign ourselves that task and recognize our historical role, or the development of history *is going to move us into that position.* There is no way we can go unnoticed. All the eyes of the world will be on us. Our time is about to come; it's not that far away. *The socio-political and economic farce of the United States of North America of Yankee imperialism will give us an opportunity to come out a*

*winner, to grow and give fruit. Now we are preparing ourselves
for that.*

Do you perceive yourself and your work as political?

Of course my work is political. To be political is to be concerned
with the welfare of the many. I am. But I don't think my work
can be defined only as political, because *it's political, it's scientific, it's psychological, it's spiritual, it's cultural.* It's a lot of
things, all at once. Some people say my poetry is protest poetry.
No. It's also about reconstructing. To reconstruct ourselves, *because being colonized people,* the self that we possess, the view
that we have, is colored by the colonization that we suffered, by
the schooling that we have been subjected to. *We have to expel
the Yankees from our heart.* We have to give ourselves the responsibility of constructing a vision of the world that is truly
ours, not a colonized vision of the world. An independent, liberated view of reality. If we paint a more humanistic world to live
in, we will construct that world. If we paint a nightmare, we'll
live in a nightmare. Therefore my poetry is not only political,
it's *psychological, it's spiritual.* It is multidimensional. I don't
think it can be called just protest poetry. I'm also trying to nur-
ture, to cultivate my heart as well as the heart of my people, so
that we can reconstruct our selves. So that we can restore faith
in ourselves, *because that is the beginning of things, as the
Mayans said in one word: Men.* In it they synthesize the creative process. It meant, simultaneously, believing, creating, doing, being, in an endless cycle. To be creators, which all human
beings are. *We are gods because we are creators, but we have
to awaken that capacity, that creative impetus in our people.
To do it we have to restore faith in ourselves. Believe-to-create-
to-build-to-be.* Yes, my work is political, but it is many other
things. I'm a cultivator. I consider myself *a farmer of the heart. I
cultivate hearts, thoughts, feelings.* And I'm not the only one.

**Does the Chicano author have anything in common with the majority
group writers? Differences?**

If you mean writers in the world or in North America, of course.
We are using language and we're using at times established languages that are recorded in dictionaries. We differ in that sometimes we use *languages that are not in dictionaries.* Chicano

Spanish or Black English. *These languages are very metaphoric.*
They do not allow themselves to be defined in a denotative
manner. The meaning of Chicano words is largely connotative
and depends on the context. So there are *also* differences. All
writers are creators, and they stimulate others to become creators themselves. That we have in common. But as I said before,
we have a mission directly related to the welfare and restoration
of our people to their rightful place in the world. *Our emphasis*
is to work with our people. I imagine that other writers also
work with their people. Maybe they consider themselves universal, and that would make us regional, but *we are not regional,*
because any human being is universal. The world is not sepa-
rated. The Mayans had one word: in lak'ech which means "you
are my other self." And this applies to everything. To tree people, to fish people, four-legged, two-legged, fire, wind, water,
earth. All things are living because all things are in motion.
Even if something appears to be static, like this table, science
tells us, *as the Mayans told us, no, this table is in full motion.*
Electrons moving around nuclei. Everything is in motion. *Every-*
thing is alive and is part of the whole. We are one with the
world. There is no distance between ourselves and anything
else. We are truly one. It is only our rational mind that for practical purposes distinguishes us, separates us, establishes dis-
tances between us and the things that surround us, between the
subject and the object. *But truly, distance does not exist be-*
tween the subject and the object. There is no distance. It is a
question of perception. We have to accept intuition as a source
of knowledge as much as we accept reason as such. Reason and
intuition go together. The conscious and unconscious worlds go
together. The dream world is just as real as the world of wakeful-
ness. We have to do away with all these divisions. Unify. In that
sense maybe we differ greatly from writers in the world, and
North Americans particularly. I don't perceive any distance between me and any other living thing. I am made of earth, wind,
fire, and water. My earth is my flesh and bones. My water is my
blood and body fluids. My wind is my breath; my fire, thought.
We are made of the same elements of which all are made. My
body functions are regulated by the same laws that regulate everything that moves in the universe. *The name of God among*
the Mayans was Hunab Ku. Hunab Ku was not a metaphysical
god, or a metaphysical idea which had to be accepted solely
through faith, but rather the only giver of measure and move-

ment. Hunab Ku was a mathematical equation. Or, rather, religion was science and science, religion. In this manner I consider my poetry to be mathematics, and mathematics to be poetry. I don't know if this establishes any differences or similarities with other writers. I think most Chicano writers are committed, *committed to the humanization of our people as they are to the humanization of this country, of this continent and this* earth. We do believe that part of our responsibility, *as creators, is to humanize, and this is to live in harmony with all the other beings who are our brothers.* Human beings are not superior to plants. Human beings are not superior to animals. People say, "Hey, how can you say that? Human beings are rational, we can theorize, hypothesize, analyze, synthesize, and no plant can do that." Granted, but we cannot photosynthesize. There are differences between all beings, but that doesn't mean that they are superior or inferior. We are equal, though different. This applies to races, to everything; we are all related, all relevant. That's where I'm coming from. That's the philosophical, the cosmological, the theological, the spiritual motivating source of my creativity.

Does Chicano literature share common ground with Black literature? Differences?

Of course, because among Black writers there are also many committed people, so we have lots of things in common. As to what differences, there are many, especially linguistic. We are willing to use many languages. They are not. *Although on certain occasions I have encountered Black writers, especially Africans, who write in various languages.* I couldn't go into specifics on how we differ or how we are alike. I'm more concerned with how effective we are.

Is there any relationship with the literature of other Spanish-speaking groups?

Again the relationship would be quickly established on a linguistic basis. At least some of the same language that we use, they use. We don't limit ourselves to the one they use, the Spanish they use. We are willing to use indigenous languages. They usually are not. Spanish writers would not use English that much, even though you find some English in Neruda, and some others. *And also, the emotional capacity or the Hispanic emotivity is very similar to ours.* Of course, they would be lacking the indigenous counterparts. There is some level of relationship.

Does Chicano literature have a distinctive perspective on life? What effect does it have on the literature?

I have a distinct perspective on life. I think most writers are in the process of developing this perspective, *but to me it seems too early to affirm* as to one distinct perspective on life. I think we can discover trends right now, identify *avenues*, but it's too early to finalize. I do know that our literature is going to take on mythological proportions. *We are realists.* We write about reality as viewed by other people, *but* mythology is just as real. It happens within and without oneself. I find three levels of time-space, within which anybody lives and functions. The historical time-space, which is the collective time-space, one that describes reality as accorded by a consensus of people. There is a personal time-space that is very individual, psychological. It belongs to the individual and not to the collective group. And a third level, the mythological time-space that unifies the personal and historical time-spaces. When we write we can readily identify one or two or, at times three time-spaces in any of our writers, poets, novelists, playwrights. All of us are using one level and, more often than not, at least two: historical and personal are the most common. But we're coming of age where we will use mythological time-space. I think I've already addressed myself to whether I have a distinctive perspective on life.

And the effect? Obviously, the way we view the world is the way we will accord our description of it. It is important to realize that the way we view, intuit, describe, and record our observations of the world has a lot to do with how the world is going to be when that printed word gets to the point where it can affect the hearts and minds of our people, as well as of other people. We really have dreamt up the psychological world in which we live. If we live in a nightmare, it is because we have been dreaming nightmares. *If we want to live in a dream and not in a nightmare, we have to paint a more humane, more loving vision of the world.* Our responsibility comes back. Not only do we have to reflect the people's experience, to criticize the people's movement, *but also,* I think that part of what literature can do, or at least what I'm trying to do, is make it a healing art, not only a reflective art. It is also a surgical tool. On the one hand it is a machine gun, but it's also a guitar, *a doctor's scalpel. We can extract the tumors from the people. We can close the wounds, and cure the diseases. We can see our creation as a* source of healing. That is very much a part of my perspective. I realized early how metaphors and images and words shape the way I see the world, shape the way I behave in the world. By now I'm convinced that, given the power to describe reality, we can construct a more human reality beginning with a more human description.

Does Chicano literature improve communication between Chicanos and Anglo Americans?

Yes and no. *Sometimes not understanding what we write really irritates them.* They still think we're talking about them. But you know, they're right, we are talking about them. But we don't write in Spanish so they won't understand, but so that they will be forced to recognize the need to learn Spanish as well. *We learned English; why can't they learn Spanish?* It's just as difficult to learn one language as the other. Of course, for the Yankee mentality this is unthinkable. They expect the shoeshine boy to speak English. They're so centered on themselves, so egocentric that they can't see themselves as having to share in someone else's culture and language. *That's their problem, not ours.*

Does Chicano literature reevaluate, attack, or subvert the value system of the majority society? Is it a revolutionary literature? Thematically? Technically?

Subvert? Attack? I think I've answered that. Revolutionary? *Of course.* Both thematically and technically. Thematically, because the themes we deal with are revolutionary. We are talking about humanizing the social and economic order of earth. But technically we are creating new forms, because we are developing new levels of perception. We are describing the world in a multidimensional fashion. Reality is a multidimensional experience. A one-dimensional perspective is very narrow, linear, and it's deadly, almost suicidal. We are engaged in revolutionizing literature technically and thematically. We talked about this before.

What problems have you encountered in publishing? Were they racially founded?

A lot of them. In my own experience—because until now I've written bilingually—there was no market for bilingual poetry. Poetry, *as a creative genre, generally has no market. Poets generally die of hunger if they try to live off their poetry.* So I've encountered lots of problems.

I don't think they are racially based. I think they're culturally based. The value systems that we predicate, that we advocate, are not the value systems which Yankee society would like to see printed. What sells in North America is what the market is willing to buy. People of this country are racist and egocentric and sexist and capitalistic, and those people are interested in reflecting themselves and seeing themselves in the things they read. So if we are not writing capitalistic, sexist, egocentric, and racist stuff, well maybe people won't buy it. In that sense publishing houses—well it's a business. *They are not trying to humanize the world or any of the like. They are trying to sell books and make money. That is what they are about.* This is a real problem for the author today. Do I sell myself out; do I produce what sells, or do I produce what I believe has to be produced? Do I say what I believe has to be said, though it may never sell, it may never be printed, or do I produce what I know will sell? In my own personal choice I have decided for the former. I would like to see my work printed, distributed, and read, but if that means compromising my work, I'm not going to do it. I'm not going to capitalize; I'm not going to capitulate to the business enterprise of North America. Both of my collections have been printed with small Chicano publishing houses. I had an offer from a couple of North American publishers to reprint *Floricanto en Aztlán,* after they realized that all the copies that were printed were sold out. They realized there is a market. They wanted the book. Of course they wanted me to make all kinds of concessions, to give them a translation of every poem. *Well, I sent them* through a tube. You print my stuff the way it is or forget it. I have faith that what I'm doing is worth its salt. So they can go find another author *who will be willing to sell himself.* For that reason I have not written in English. I'm fully aware that if I wrote *totally in English, I could sell many more books, right? But first, for me, my responsibility is to communi-*

cate with my people; that is what interests me the most, what is most important to me. Perhaps with time, let's say, when I'm happy about, and more or less satisfied with, my communication, with the rapport I can establish with our people, *then, perhaps,* I will write something in English, perhaps a novel or short stories. I really don't know at this point. As a matter of fact, now that I find myself in Texas, *I'm going in the other direction.* I'm writing solely in Spanish. I am interested in communicating first with our people, second with our Central and Latin American brothers and sisters, and third, and last of all, with the North American crowd, with the English-speaking crowd. My first priority is our people, Chicano people; second, Central and Latin American people, which I'm moving on now. My third collection of poetry [*Timespace Huracán*], as I mentioned, is totally in Spanish. I intend to continue that. I have another work in progress which is bilingual again. I don't know if I'll get it printed. *As I was telling you, poetry does not have much of a market. Thank God that I don't make my living from it, or I'd really be screwed over.* My bread and butter is teaching, and I'm glad it is; that way I don't have to compromise my principles or the things that I view as real and meaningful.

Are Chicanos at a disadvantage in trying to practice the art of writing?

Does that mean that we are at a disadvantage because our schooling has been bad? I don't know. I think that people ought to write the way they speak. Anybody who speaks can write. If you don't know how to write, *grab a tape recorder and start making your poetry,* and have someone else be your scribe. I don't feel that schooling is necessary to become a good writer. What is necessary to become a good writer is to write. One can read, one can be instructed, but until one writes and writes and writes and writes, etc., one does not know how to write. It's hard work. *It's not something that comes—inspiration is not reliable.* Maybe that's the way writers begin; I did. I had a need to be inspired to communicate. But now it's just hard work. *As the master Rolando Hinojosa says, until you get hemorrhoids.* You have to write a lot. You don't need to "know" how to write, as I said before. You need to know how to talk and listen. I think it's very important for a writer to know how to listen and observe.

What are the most outstanding qualities of Chicano literature?
Weaknesses?

There are so many. There is so much color. Chicano literature is
such a diverse experience. *We have among us professors, aca-*
demics, convicts, workers, people of all classes and all walks of
life. We have people playing with surrealism, people playing
with realism, some that are still romantics, people developing
new areas such as magical realism. People in all fields of literature. Without question, one of the strengths is the diversity, its
capacity to embrace so many levels, so many forms, so many
themes, and they are all ours. You don't even have to mention
the word Chicano. If your writing reflects your true experience
and the experience of your people, it is Chicano literature. And I
don't mean only your external reality. The internal reality is just
as valid. Internal reality is more universal than external reality,
which is fixed by time and space, while internal reality is not.
Internal reality is infinitely open, infinitely universal.

One of the roots which nurtures and makes our literature
flower is the great diversity. Now, this diversity can be veri-
fied or analyzed if one examines the time-space in which the
thoughts, letters, sentiments, and intuitions of our writers func-
tion. The point-moment in which every one of our authors
moves, all of the characters of the universe which he or she per-
ceives, that is what gives us the diversity. That is what gives us
the strength. It is one of the principal qualities. All of the au-
thors paint a reality, approach a unity, a definition of that
which guides us, that which motivates us to paint the visions
which we experience. Now, recognizing this diversity, one of its
definite weaknesses can be the focusing on one of the time-
spaces that one of the authors elaborates, and saying that this,
over all others, is the one that represents what is Chicano literature or the one that best expresses it. To some degree that has
happened, as we were able to experience at the Floricanto in
Austin, 1975. *There are some among us who think that one*
should say, "This is the greatest." That is one of its disadvan-
tages, not recognizing the great diversity that constitutes us, not
recognizing the great expressive and interpretive capacity that it
nurtures. We have to be cognizant and sensitive to the fact that
among us there are many point-moments, many time-spaces,
many points of view, many levels of technical skill, of mastering
the craft or art of writing. *And right now one cannot say* this is

it, what I am doing is what everybody else should be doing. *Naturally, everyone affirms his own creation and says that it is the best, this is the clearest that I can paint. But one should be willing to listen to the rest, and in that way grow, because only in that way, through writing, through self-criticism, through collective criticism, through the attention that we pay one another, will we arrive at defining, through the work, what it's about, what it is that distinguishes Chicano literature.* What it is that makes our literature a literature that can have a name, that can stand on its own as a literature in the world, such as Greek literature, or Nahuatl literature, or any other literature that receives a national nomenclature. *Ours, too, is a national literature, and will have to reflect all the levels that our nation implies, all that IS our people.*

What are the milestones so far in Chicano literature?

We can begin with José Antonio Villarreal's Pocho. *In doing that we will be speaking about a milestone in Chicano litera*ture since 1848 that was published by a major publishing house. Now, that is not to say that there were not other Chicano and Chicana novelists, *storytellers,* poets, critics prior to 1959. *What happens is that before a Chicano had not come to publish at the massive level at which North American publishers can operate, given the capital that they work with.* I think lots of research is in order in this area. We need to take the time to investigate if we're going to talk about the history. *We'll do it through popular media.* Let's look up the newspapers that we've been producing since 1848 in Texas, in *New Mexico, in Arizona, and also in California; but it's the border region that started first. Let's look at literature from the resistance; let's look at the manner in which our ancestors defined themselves through their visions, from their stories, from their legends. It hasn't been done and it should be. In the modern period we can begin with* Pocho. *In* 1967 *there are various books. We have Rodolfo Corky Gonzales, with his* I Am Joaquín, *a classic, let's say, in our contemporary tradition. We can proceed with the work developed by Quinto Sol and its anthology,* El Espejo. *The Teatro Campesino starts getting into the picture, and then it's literature in motion with their own theatrical works. Quinto Sol comes out with its first prize, . . . y no se lo tragó la tierra, Tomás Rivera in the Chicano short story. Estampas del valle comes out, and, brother, you know! Rolando Hinojosa-Smith, what force, brother!*

I think for me to comment at this point on the important milestones—well I know so many *brothers* and *sisters with whom we've been working these last years, since '67.* People that have discovered *the power of the word, the destructive as well as the* healing power, *and who have transformed that energy into an autochthonous and legitimate one, ours through the novel, poetry.* I could talk about where we've been and what we've been trying to do, but *the work is the one that speaks.* To identify one, two, three, or four would be limiting. I really have not done it. I would be bullshitting. *I would have to organize the question and take my time. I can speak about authors; for example, I really love brother Montoya's work. I think that among us he's one of the Fathers. Among the poets he is among the best. He lets his heart spill over and it's very clear. He uses a simple, popular language and identifies with the people through his work because he reflects it. He has many levels, not just historical time-space. He has a personal psychological timespace that is very rich. The same is true of his mythological level. I love Anaya's work because of its mythological levels. It has an internal personal reality, of the child, that is deeply explored. Then there is the historical situation, the social influences on the life of a child in New Mexico, with very little political reality, if you prefer, or even less economic. All of this transcends the mythological levels that are founded through faith and logic, and the battle between these two and intuition and will. Anaya's work is tremendous. Tomás Rivera, well, he has a very delicious novel. I haven't had the pleasure of meeting Tino Villanueva, but I've met his work and it surges forward. There are many sisters who've also come out. Lin Romero with a little work that's called* Rostros de Amerindia *which will be coming out of San Diego soon. Without a doubt, sister Tafoya from San Antonio is also good. Unexpected surprises. There are many. Sincerely, it's better if I guard my comments for a more serious study, because here it would be quite informal.*

What is the future of Chicano literature: distinctiveness, or the de-emphasis of the distinctive characteristics?

Well, we have many things that distinguish us, and that distinction is nascent and flowering. It's a process of development that we find ourselves in. Right now it's sprouting. What distinguishes us from other literatures in the world is a developing energy. *What distinguishes us is the diversity, the many lan-*

guages, the different levels. The very language that we use, that speaks without borders. That's one of the things we have to look at closely. What is the future of Chicano literature? *I would say that it has to do with creating a revolution within the literature as much as the literature itself should awaken the desire for liberty in the people. And within the literature we have to develop, create perceptions, we have to amplify our perceptions of the time-space in which we live. We have to reach a description of reality which paints it as it is. Reality is multidimensional. The personality of persons is multidimensional. We exist simultaneously in more than one time-space. We exist. We have our being, we believe in ourselves. We create and build in more than one time and one space. More than one point-moment. Simultaneously there is more than one point-moment in our consciousness and in our being, in what we produce. And it concerns itself, then, with creating these different levels, which in the process have to be, have to receive* some kind of nomenclature, as our Latin American brothers and sisters have approached *what they call* "magical realism," synthesis of that which in the past was held to be magical, metaphysical, and abstract, and that which is held to be real and pragmatic. *They mix it and they call it* "magical realism." *I don't know what kind of nomenclature we are going to develop.* That is more the work of critics than of writers themselves. *But one thing that I'm pretty certain of* is that we have an opportunity here, and we would be fools to throw it away. That opportunity is to continue to work and work very hard. *Write with desire.* This cultivation is going to reap a good crop. *The historical time-space in which we live is going to focus on this terrenal belly-button of consciousness between Hispanic America and Anglo-Saxon North America. Amerindia is going to bloom.* That's inevitable. We can either join *this serpent which moves history* deliberately and willfully, or we can be swept like a leaf in the wind if we leave it up to chance. But it will come to pass. *The empire falls.* The strength with which *this empire can strangle and maintain the control in Central and Latin America and Africa and Asia is loosening,* is ripping at the seams, bleeding internally. *That is how we can cultivate a tree of life which will give much flower and fruit with time, if we sing it with love.*

Who are the leaders among Chicano writers, and why?

¡Ay yayay! It seems that that is part of the argument now and this is the type of question that I'd rather not answer. I don't know. I don't think Chicano writers want to be considered in relationship to each other as leaders and followers. I think a better construction of reality in terms of relationship would be brethren-in-struggle. *Cultural guerillas, brothers and sisters who use the expressive techniques* and route them in our cultural development and the development of our consciousness as a historical people, rather than who leads and who follows. When we get into that kind of perspective I can see why some of our brothers and sisters get into the trip of *"I am the baddest." And that's not what it's about. I mean, for me, a description of the time-space of a brother or a sister is as valid as the description of another. Now, there are differences, sure, but if there weren't, it would be boring. So I'd rather not get into who are the leaders in that sense.*

What really should be criticized is the work, and the work should not be judged in terms of who is the best, or who is the leader, who carries the vanguard. Let's examine the work, and the effectiveness of that work, the capacity of that work to reflect the historical time-space, personal and mythological, of our people. Let's examine its capacity for self-criticism, to criticize our own society, our own movement and revolutionary development, as well as criticizing the structures, the dogmas, which rigidify and dominate the world today. Domination exists, and it has to be criticized. Let us judge the work as to how it touches the heart of our people, and how it cures the wounds which colonization has produced, how to heal the wounds so that they stop bleeding, to rejuvenate ourselves, not afflict ourselves, to restore faith in ourselves and affirm our capacity to build a new world, right? To self-create. We have to examine the work of each one, and all of us, and see what kind of fruit will be harvested, having examined the words which have been cultivated.

Selected Bibliography

Abelardo. *See* Delgado, Abelardo Lalo.

Acosta, Oscar Zeta. *The Autobiography of a Brown Buffalo.* San Francisco: Straight Arrow Books, 1972.

————. *The Revolt of the Cockroach People.* San Francisco: Straight Arrow Books, 1973.

Alurista. *Dawn. El Grito* 7, no. 4 (June–August 1974): 55–84.

————. *Floricanto en Aztlán.* Los Angeles: Chicano Studies Center of UCLA, 1971.

————. *Nationchild Plumaroja.* San Diego: Toltecas en Aztlán Publications, 1972.

————. *Timespace Huracán.* Albuquerque: Pajarito Publications, 1976.

————, ed. *Festival de Flor y Canto: An Anthology of Chicano Literature.* Los Angeles: University of Southern California Press, 1976.

Anaya, Rudolfo A. *Bless Me, Ultima.* Berkeley: Quinto Sol Publications, 1972.

————. *Heart of Aztlán.* Berkeley: Editorial Justa, 1976.

————. *Tortuga.* Berkeley: Editorial Justa, 1979.

Arias, Ron. *The Road to Tamazunchale.* Reno: West Coast Poetry Review, 1975.

Armas, José, ed. *Mestizo.* Albuquerque: Pajarito Publications, 1978.

Barrio, Raymond. *The Plum Plum Pickers.* Sunnyvale, Calif.: Ventura Press, 1969.

Brito, Aristeo. *El diablo en Texas.* Tucson: Editorial Peregrinos, 1976.

Bruce-Novoa. *Inocencia perversa/Perverse Innocence.* Phoenix: Baleen Press, 1977.

Candelaria, Nash. *Memories of the Alhambra.* San José: Cibola Press, 1977.

Cárdenas, Margarita Cota. *Noches despertando inconsciencias.* Tucson: Scorpion Press, 1975.

Carrillo, Leonardo, et al. *Canto al pueblo.* San Antonio: Penca Books, 1978.

De Hoyos, Angela. *Arise, Chicano, and Other Poems.* Bloomington: Backstage Books, 1975.

————. *Chicano Poems for the Barrio.* Bloomington, Ind.: Backstage Books, 1975.